GENERAL SCOTT

AND

HIS STAFF:

LANDING OF THE TROOPS AT VERA CRUZ.

GENERAL SCOTT.

GENERAL SCOTT

AND

HIS STAFF:

COMPRISING

MEMOIRS OF GENERALS

SCOTT, TWIGGS, SMITH, QUITMAN, SHIELDS, PILLOW, LANE, CADWALADER, PATTERSON AND PIERCE;

COLONELS CHILDS, RILEY, HARNEY, AND BUTLER,

AND

OTHER DISTINGUISHED OFFICERS ATTACHED TO GENERAL SCOTT'S ARMY;

TOGETHER WITH

NOTICES OF GENERAL KEARNY, COLONEL DONIPHAN, COLONEL FREMONT, AND OTHER OFFICERS DISTINGUISHED IN THE CONQUEST OF CALIFORNIA AND NEW MEXICO.

INTERSPERSED WITH

NUMEROUS ANECDOTES OF THE MEXICAN WAR,

AND

PERSONAL ADVENTURES OF THE OFFICERS.

COMPILED FROM PUBLIC DOCUMENTS AND PRIVATE CORRESPONDENCE.

~~~~~~~~~~

WITH

ACCURATE PORTRAITS, AND OTHER BEAUTIFUL ILLUSTRATIONS.

BOOKS FOR LIBRARIES PRESS
FREEPORT, NEW YORK

First Published 1848
Reprinted 1970

STANDARD BOOK NUMBER:
8369-5235-9

LIBRARY OF CONGRESS CATALOG CARD NUMBER:
77-109626

PRINTED IN THE UNITED STATES OF AMERICA

PREFACE.

~~~~~~~~

THE present war with Mexico has developed, in a very extraordinary manner, the military resources of this country. It has made the world acquainted with many facts and principles which are worthy of especial attention to every one who feels an interest in our national history, and a desire that the national honour shall always be maintained. It has demonstrated that a people devoted to the arts of peace, and possessing free political institutions, can easily vanquish a military people, governed by military despots. It has shown that fresh volunteers, under the command of intelligent and able officers, can take fortified cities and castles, garrisoned by double the number of the assailants; and gain victories, in pitched battles, over disciplined armies five times as numerous as themselves. These are interesting facts; and particularly interesting to Americans, as they evidently involve the principle, that political freedom is the chief element of military success.

All this has been accomplished by a small army, with a staff of officers never surpassed in valour and ability. To afford the public sketches of the personal history of these officers, and to give details of their service in this war, is the purpose of the present work. It is compiled from authentic materials, consisting of public documents and private correspondence and memoirs, derived in many instances from family connections of the officers. The author has endeavoured to give in every instance the truth without respect to persons, and he hopes that in this he has been as successful as the nature of the undertaking would permit.

Philadelphia, Jan. 1, 1848.

CONTENTS.

MAJOR-GENERAL SCOTT, Commander-in-Chief of the American Army ....Page 11
MAJOR-GENERAL PILLOW............................ 78
MAJOR-GENERAL QUITMAN 85
BRIGADIER-GENERAL TWIGGS........................ 106
GENERAL SMITH 117
BRIGADIER-GENERAL SHIELDS 125
BRIGADIER-GENERAL LANE 129
BRIGADIER-GENERAL CADWALADER 136
BRIGADIER-GENERAL PIERCE......................... 140
MAJOR-GENERAL PATTERSON........................ 145
COLONEL HARNEY 149
COLONEL CHILDS 155
GENERAL CUSHING.................................... 159
COLONEL RILEY 160
COLONEL BUTLER..................................... 161
MAJOR VINTON 164
CAPTAIN THORNTON 171
GENERAL KEARNY 174
COLONEL DONIPHAN.................................. 181
LIEUTENANT-COLONEL FREMONT 204
BRIGADIER-GENERAL JONES.......................... 215
LIEUTENANT CHRISTOPHER CARSON................ 219

1*

MAJOR-GENERAL SCOTT,

COMMANDER-IN-CHIEF OF THE AMERICAN ARMY.

MAJOR-GENERAL WINFIELD SCOTT is a native of Virginia, born near Petersburg, June 13th, 1786. The accounts of his early life are few and meagre. He passed through the Richmond High-School, and afterwards studied law at William and Mary College. His military career began in 1807, on the reception of news concerning the Chesapeake, when he became a volunteer member of the Petersburg troop of horse. On the 3d of May, 1808, he was commissioned as captain of light artillery, and has remained in the army ever since. When the war of 1812 commenced, he had already advanced to the rank of lieutenant-colonel.

At the battle of Queenstown Heights, Scott gave assurance of his future military usefulness. After behaving in the most gallant manner, his command of three hundred men became separated from the main body, and were attacked by thirteen hundred British and Indians. He defended himself for a long while, but was at length taken prisoner, and carried with his troops to Quebec. While here, he challenged the respect of the British officers, by his independent and soldier-like bearing. His rescue of the Irish prisoners is well known; and many other anecdotes are related of him during this confinement. In a little while he was exchanged and sent to Boston.

In the following year, Scott was engaged in a still more glorious affair at Fort Grey. In the passage of the river, before taking this place, he led the van and rushed up the steep Canadian bank amid a shower of balls, and drove the British into the woods. At the fort, he tore down the flag with his own hands, and afterward pur-sued the enemy until evening.

The summer passed without any attack from the British, and, burning for active operations, Scott was permitted by General Wilkinson to resign the command of Fort George, which he then held, to General McClure, and join the main army at Sackett's Harbour; marching to the mouth of the Genesee river, where the commander-in-chief promised that transports should meet him. In this, however, Scott was disappointed, and he was compelled to advance over roads almost impassable along the whole distance from Niagara to the St. Lawrence. Leaving his column near Utica, under the command of Major Hindman, Scott hastened forward himself, reached the St. Lawrence at Ogdensburg on the 6th November, in time to take part in the descent, and was appointed to command the advance guard; and owing to his being in advance, had no part in the indecisive battle of Chrystler's Field, or the events which took place in the rear. He did, however, encounter and overcome severe resistance at the Hoophole creek, near Cornwall, where he routed a nearly equal British force under Colonel Dennis—making many prisoners, and pursuing the fugitives till night; and also at Fort Matilda, erected to guard the narrowest part of the river. He took the fort, its commander, and many of his men. But with victory within his grasp — for there was no force between Scott and Montreal which could have arrested his march six hours, and no garrison in Montreal that could have obstructed his entry — he, as well as the nation, was doomed to disappointment, by the incompetency and the quarrels of two of its generals — Wilkinson and Wade Hampton: Wilkinson ordering a retreat because Hampton would not join him with his detachment, and Hampton refusing to join, because, as he alleged, provisions were insufficient; the campaign closed in disaster. But it was brilliantly redeemed by that of the following year.

On the 9th of March, 1814, Colonel Scott was promoted to the rank of brigadier, and immediately joined General Brown, then in full march from French Mills to the Niagara frontier. Brown, who was an able but self-taught commander, perceiving the need of instruction and discipline, left the camp expressly for the purpose of giving the command to General Scott, and enabling him to carry out a system of instruction and discipline with the troops as they assembled at Buffalo. For more than three months this duty was assiduously and most successfully discharged by General Scott.

Now it was that the knowledge of the art of war, which he had so sedulously acquired during his year of suspension, came into play. He personally drilled and instructed all the officers, and then in turn superintended them as they instructed the soldiers. By assiduous labour, he succeeded, at the end of three months, in presenting in the field an army skilful in manœuvres, and confident alike in their officers and in themselves. When all was ready for action, General Brown resumed the command. The army was crossed over to Canada in two brigades, Scott's and Ripley's, the former below, the latter above Fort Erie, which almost immediately surrendered, and then marched to attack the main British army, lying behind the Chippewa river, under the command of General Riall. On the morning of the 4th of July—auspicious day!—Scott's brigade, several hours in advance, fell in with the 100th regiment, British, commanded by the Marquis of Tweedale, and kept up a running fight with it till it was driven across the Chippewa. Scott encamped for the night behind Street's creek, about two miles from the British camp, behind the Chippewa, with a level plain extending between, skirted on the east by the Niagara river, on the west by woods.

On the 5th—a bright, hot day—the morning began with skirmishing in the woods, between the New York volunteers, under General Porter, and the British irregulars; and it was not till four o'clock in the afternoon, and just as Scott, despairing of bringing on an action that day, was drawing out his brigade on the plain for drill, that General Brown, who had been reconnoitring on the left flank, and perceived that the main body of the British army was moving forward, rode up to General Scott, and said, "The enemy is advancing; you will have a fight:" and without giving any order, such was his reliance upon Scott, proceeded to the rear to bring up Ripley's brigade. Scott immediately prepared for action; and there, on the plain of Chippewa, with his own brigade only, consisting of the 9th, 11th, and 25th regiments of infantry, with a detachment of the 22d, Towson's company of artillery, and Porter's volunteers—in all, nineteen hundred men—encountered, routed, and pursued a superior force of some of the best regiments of the British service—the Royal Scots, the 8th and 100th regiments, a detachment of the 19th dragoons, another of the Royal Artillery, and some Canadian militia—in all, twenty-one hundred men. Here it was that the

2   B

discipline so laboriously taught by Scott, in the camp of instruction, told; and this it was that enabled him, as at a turning point of the battle he did, in a voice rising above the roar of artillery, to say to McNeil's battalion of the 11th infantry :—"The enemy say that we are good at long shot, but cannot stand the cold iron. I call upon the Eleventh instantly to give the lie to the slander. Charge !" And they did charge ; and, aided by Leavenworth's battalion, they quickly put the enemy to rout, before the 21st, of Ripley's brigade, which was hastening to take part in the battle, or any portion of that brigade, could get up.

Justly, indeed, did General Brown, in his official report of the battle, say : "Brigadier-General Scott is entitled to the highest praise our country can bestow : to him, more than to any other man, am I indebted for the victory of the 5th of July." The fight was fierce and bloody in an unwonted degree, the killed on both sides amounting to eight hundred and thirty, out of about four thousand engaged—more than one in five. This action—which was chiefly valuable for the good effect it produced upon the feelings of the nation, by proving that in the open field, and hand to hand, our troops were equal at least, and in this instance had proved themselves superior to the best troops of England —was followed in just three weeks by another, yet more decisive of the courage and discipline of the American army—that at Lundy's Lane. General Riall, unknown to General Brown, had been largely reinforced by General Drummond from below ; and when, on the morning of the 26th of July, General Scott in advance, as usual, was on a march to attack General Riall's forces, he suddenly came upon the British troops, which, reinforced that very day by Drummond, were themselves bent on attack. Scott had with him but four small battalions, commanded, respectively, by Brady, Jessup, Leavenworth, and McNeil ; and Towson's artillery, with Captain Harris's detachment of regular and irregular cavalry —the whole column not exceeding thirteen hundred men. With this small force, Scott found himself in presence of a superior body. His position was critical, but it was precisely one of those where promptness and decision of action must supply the want of battalions. Despatching officers to the rear to apprise General Brown that the whole British army were before him, General Scott at once engaged the enemy, who all the while believed they had to do with the whole of General Brown's army, not at all expecting that a mere detachment of it would venture upon the apparently desperate course of encountering such greatly superior numbers as the British knew they had in the field.

The battle began about half an hour before sunset, within the spray, almost, of the everlasting Falls of Niagara, and beneath the halo of its irradiated bow of promise and of hope.` It is recorded as a fact, that the head of our advancing column was actually encircled by this beautiful bow, and all took courage from the omen. The battle raged with unequal fortune and desperate valour, till far into the night. When Miller made his famous and decisive charge upon the battery of the British, which was the key of their position, darkness covered the earth; and Scott, who knew the localities, piloted Miller on his way, till the fire from the battery revealed its position completely. Scott then resumed the attack in front, while Miller gallantly stormed and carried the battery, and held it against repeated charges from the oft-rallied, but as oft-dispersed, British troops. Twice, mean time, had Scott charged through the British lines—two horses had been killed under him—he was wounded in the side—and about eleven o'clock at night, on foot and yet fighting, he was finally disabled by a shot, which shattered the left shoulder, and he was borne away about midnight from the battle; his commander, General Brown, having been previously, in like manner, carried away wounded from the field.

The honours of the battle belonged to the American arms, although, from the want of horses, they could not carry off the British cannon, captured with so much gallantry by Miller. But the American troops retired to Chippewa, and thence to Fort Erie, where they were soon besieged by General Drummond. Scott was absent, suffering under his wounds; but the spirit and the discipline with which his efforts and his example had inspired the army, failed not, though he was no longer with them; and after being beleaguered near fifty days, General Brown, who had sufficiently recovered to resume the command, made a sortie, on the 17th of September, in which he defeated the troops in the trenches, captured and destroyed their works, and so effectually overthrew all that it had cost long weeks to accomplish, that the British commander, General Drummond, withdrew his troops, and soon after the American army went into winter quarters at Buffalo.

This was virtually, in this region, the end of the war; for peace was negotiated at Ghent at the close of 1814, and was ratified early the ensuing spring.

Scott, who had been carried to Buffalo, where he was most kindly and cordially received and watched over, as soon as he could bear the motion, was borne in a litter from place to place by the citizens themselves, who would not commit to mercenary hands the care and comfort of a gallant soldier, still disabled by his wounds, until he reached the house of his old friend Nicholas, at Geneva. But his great desire was to reach Philadelphia, in order to avail himself of the eminent skill of Doctors Physick and Chapman; for the possibility of being so crippled, for life, as to be incapable of further service to his country, was to Scott an intolerable thought, and hence he sought the best surgical aid. He, therefore, by slow progress, reached Philadelphia—everywhere welcomed and honoured on his route as the suffering representative of the army on the Niagara, which had won imperishable laurels for the country and itself.

At Princeton, where he happened to arrive on the day of the annual commencement, the faculty, students, and citizens all insisted on his taking part in the ceremonial; and pale, emaciated, and weak as he was, that he should be present during a part, at least, of the public performances. He was fain to comply; and when, at the close of an oration " on the public duties of a good citizen, in peace and in war," the youthful and graceful orator turned to Scott, and made him the personification of the civic and heroic virtues which had just been inculcated, the edifice rang with applause, woman's gentle voice mingling in with the harsher tones of the other sex. The faculty conferred on him the degree of A. M., which his early training and literary pursuits, not less than his public services, rendered wholly appropriate. On approaching Philadelphia, he found the governor of the state, Snyder, at the head of a division of militia, with which he had marched out to receive him.

Baltimore being still menaced by the British, General Scott, at the earnest request of the citizens, consented, wounded as he was, and incapable of exertion, to assume the command of the district; and in such command the tidings of peace found him. After declining the post of Secretary at War, proffered to him by President Madison, and aiding in the painful and delicate task of reducing the army to a peace establishment, he was sent by the government to

Europe, both for the restoration of his health and professional improvement. He was, moreover, commissioned to ascertain the views and designs of different courts and prominent public men respecting the revolutionary struggle then commenced in the Spanish American colonies, and especially those of England, respecting the island of Cuba—all at that time subjects of solicitude at Washington. How he acquitted himself of these commissions may be inferred from the fact that, by order of President Madison, a special letter of thanks was written to him by the Secretary of State. After two years spent in Europe, where he associated with the most distinguished men in all the walks of life, attended courses of public lectures, and visited and inspected the great fortresses and naval establishments, Scott returned to the United States, and was assigned to the command of the seaboard, making New York his head-quarters; and there, for twenty years, except with occasional absences on duty in the west, he remained. The gratitude of the country for his war services was testified in various shapes. Congress voted him a gold medal, and passed resolutions of thanks, in which he was not only complimented for his skill and gallantry at Chippewa and Niagara, but *for his uniform good conduct throughout the war*—a compliment paid by Congress to no other officer. The gold medal was presented by President Monroe. Virginia and New York each voted a sword to him; which, for Virginia, was presented by Governor Pleasants; for New York, by Governor Tompkins. He was also elected an honorary member of the Cincinnati, and numerous states named new counties after him.

In the long interval of comparative inaction which followed the close of the war, Scott's services were availed of by the general government—first, in that most painful task of reducing the army to a peace establishment, which necessarily imposed upon the general the responsibility of deciding between the merits and fitness of many gallant men, who had stood with him unflinching on the red fields of battle. But in the discharge of this, as of every other duty to his country, Scott acted with a single eye to its honour and welfare. Neither the relations of general friendship, nor the influences of various sorts, brought to bear from without, were suffered to warp his firm mind. He was there for his country, and in consonance with what he thought its clear interests, was his course throughout. The next important benefit rendered, and which, perhaps, was not

2* B 2

the least of all the many he was capable of rendering, was to translate from the French, prepare, digest, and adapt to our service, a complete system of military tactics. In the execution of this trust, his previous military studies gave him great facilities and advantages; and the system thus introduced, carried into effect by those jewels of the nation, the West Point cadets, has recently proved itself at Palo Alto and Fort Brown, Resaca de la Palma, and Monterey.

The frankness of his nature, and his high sense of subordination, and ever-present and active respect for the spirit as well as letter of the Constitution of his country, involved him, about the year 1817, in an unpleasant controversy, first with General Jackson, and second, as a consequence of the first, with De Witt Clinton. The particulars of the controversy have passed from memory, and it is not our purpose to revive them. In the lifetime, before the Presidency of General Jackson, a very complete and soldierly reconciliation took place between General Scott and himself. But, we may add, in the way of caution and reprobation, that the whole difficulty arose from the unjustifiable and ungentlemanly repetition of some observations made at a private dinner-table by General Scott.

Another controversy arose between General Scott and General Gaines, on the subject of *brevet* rank, on occasion of the appointment of General Macomb to the command of the army, after the death of General Brown. The government did not sustain the views taken by General Scott of the rights of brevet rank, and this officer, in consequence, tendered the resignation of his commission, not from any mere personal feelings, but because he thought that in his person a great military principle was violated. Happily, General Jackson (then become president) would not act upon the proffered resignation; and in order to allow time for reflection, and at the same time to prevent any damage to the service from an open collision on points of duty between General Scott and his official superior, a furlough of one year was sent to him.   Scott took advantage of the furlough to revisit Europe; and on his return, under the earnest advice of his friends, and, as is believed, with the unanimous approval of his brother officers, Scott withdrew his resignation, and reported himself for duty.

The Secretary of War, Major Eaton, in acknowledging General Scott's letter, frankly and honourably says:

"It affords the department much satisfaction to perceive the conclusion at which you have arrived as to your *brevet* rights. None will do you the injustice to suppose that the opinions declared by you on the subject are not the result of reflection and conviction; but since the constituted authorities of the government have, with the best feelings entertained, come to conclusions adverse to your own, no other opinions were cherished, or were hoped for, but that on your return to the United States you would adopt the course your letter indicates, and with good feelings resume those duties of which your country has so long had the benefit."

The general was ordered in conclusion to report himself at once for duty to General Macomb. He was assigned anew to the eastern department, and there remained till called by the Black Hawk war in 1832, to assume command.

It was in this capacity that Scott had the opportunity of showing himself a "hero of humanity," as he had before shown himself a "hero in the battle-field." The Asiatic cholera in this year first reached this continent, and, sweeping with rapid but irregular strides from point to point, it manifested itself most fatally on board the fleet of steamboats on Lake Erie, in which General Scott, with a corps of about one thousand regulars, embarked for Chicago. They left Buffalo in the beginning of July. On the 8th, the cholera declared itself on board the steamboat in which General Scott and staff, and two hundred and twenty men were embarked, and in less than six days one officer and fifty-one men died, and eighty were put on shore sick at Chicago. It was amid the gloom and the terror of this attack from a disease, known only by its fatal approaches, that General Scott displayed those attributes of moral courage, of genuine philanthropy, which would weigh so much more in the scale of national gratitude, than the exercise of physical courage—that quality common to our race in the battle-field. From cot to cot of the sick soldiers, their general daily went, soothing the last moments of the dying, sustaining and cheering those who hoped to survive, and for all, disarming the pestilence of that formidable character of contagion which seemed to render its attack inevitable, and almost synonymous with death, by showing in his own person that he feared it not. Of the numbers whom his heroic self-confidence and generous example, in such circumstances, saved from death, by dissipating their apprehensions, no estimate has ever been made; but such deeds and such devotion are not unmarked by the eye of Providence, and cannot be without their reward.

Of the nine hundred and fifty men that left Buffalo, not more than four hundred survived for active service. On leaving Chicago, with this diminished command, Scott proceeded as rapidly as possible to the Mississippi, and there joined General Atkinson at Prairie du Chien, who, in the battle of the Badaxe, had already scattered the forces of Black Hawk.

In spite of all the precaution adopted by Scott and Atkinson, the cholera was communicated anew to the army assembled at Rock Island, and great were its ravages. Here, again, as on board the steamboat, when the malady first appeared, Scott's self-sacrificing care and solicitude for his men were unceasing.

It was late in September before the dread disease was extirpated from the camp, and then commenced the negotiations with the Sacs and Foxes; this was concluded by Scott with consummate skill, and resulted in the cession, for a valuable consideration, of the fine region which now constitutes the state of Iowa. Another treaty was made on the same terms by him with the Winnebagoes, by which they ceded some five million acres of land east of the Mississippi and between the Illinois and Wisconsin, now constituting a valuable portion of the territory of Wisconsin. In reference, as well to his successful negotiations, as to his humane conduct under the calamity of pestilence, the then Secretary of War, General Cass, wrote thus to General Scott:

"Allow me to congratulate you upon the fortunate consummation of your arduous duties, and to express my entire approbation of the whole course of your proceedings, during a series of difficulties requiring higher moral courage than the operations of an active campaign under ordinary circumstances."

Scarcely had Scott reached home and his family in New York, when he was detailed by President Jackson to a new, important, and most delicate duty, that of maintaining at home the supremacy of the United States against South Carolina nullification. He immediately proceeded to Washington, and there, in personal interviews with the president and the cabinet, becoming fully possessed of their views, and having expressed to them his own, he was invested with very ample discretionary power to meet the perilous crisis. In no scene of his life, perhaps, has General Scott exhibited more thorough patriotism—more entire devotion to the laws and constitution of his country—more anxious, and skilfully-conducted efforts to arrest that direst of calamities, civil war—more self-command—more tact and talent—than while stationed at Fort Moultrie, in Charleston Harbour, and face to face, as it were, with nullification in arms. A single drop of blood shed at that moment might have deluged the nation in blood — and yet the laws of the United States, made in conformity with the constitution, Scott was sworn and commissioned to uphold, defend, and enforce : the point of difficulty was to avert the bloodshed, and yet maintain the laws ; and he came off entirely successful in both—under circumstances that history will do justice to, as those who remember the fearful apprehensions of that day did at the time, and still do.

His next field of public service was in Florida, where the Seminoles — in possession of the everglades, and having taken our troops at unawares—owing to the want of adequate preparation by the administration, although timely warned of the danger by the gallant Clinch — seemed for a time to set the whole efforts of our country at defiance.

On the 20th January, 1836, General Scott was ordered to the command of the troops in Florida, and he displayed his habitual promptitude in obeying the order. He was apprised of the will of the president at four o'clock in the afternoon, and asked when he could set forth. "This night," was the reply. But a day's delay was required to draw up the requisite instructions, and he left Washington on the 21st.

We enter not here into an examination of the steps taken and the plans devised by General Scott, to bring to a rapid and sure termination these disastrous and discreditable hostilities, nor into the manner or the motives of his unmilitary recall, and of the subsequent investigation of his conduct by a court of inquiry ; these are among the historic archives of the nation. Our only concern here with them is to say, that this court unanimously approved his conduct—pronounced the plan of his Seminole campaign "well devised," and added that it "was prosecuted with energy, steadiness, and ability." With regard to the Creek war, which at the same time fell upon his hands, the court found "that the plan of campaign adopted by Major-General Scott was well calculated to lead to successful results ; and that it was prosecuted by him, as far as practicable, with zeal and ability, until he was recalled from the command."

Mr. Van Buren, who had now become president, approved the finding of the court, and the nation at large ratified the verdict. Public dinners were tendered to General Scott by the citizens of New York, of Richmond, and of other places, all of which, however, he declined; and was in the discharge of the ordinary duties of his station, when the patriot troubles broke out in 1837 on the Canada frontier. For two years these troubles agitated our country, and seriously menaced its peace. To no man in so great a degree as to General Scott is it indebted for the preservation of that peace. His honour and patriotism, his approved military service, his reputation and his bearing as a soldier, gave great effect to his frank and friendly expostulations with the deluded American citizens, who supposed they were acting patriotically in taking part with the Canadian revolters; and by kindness and reason, combined with much skill and assiduity in discovering and tracing the ramifications of the patriot lodges, he was enabled to prevent any outbreak that might compromise our country with Great Britain. His return from the Niagara frontier was greeted with compliments at Albany and elsewhere, and all felt that a great national good had been accomplished by this gallant soldier.

In 1838, another difficult and painful service was confided to General Scott—that of removing the Cherokees from the homes of their fathers, to the region beyond the Mississippi. Here he was as successful as in all previous public service: tempering humanity with power, and operating more by moral influence than force, he effected this most trying object in a manner that secured the gratitude of those whom he was, acting for his country, obliged to wrong. It was this service, connected with his subsequent pacific arrangement of the north-eastern boundary difficulties, that drew from the lamented Channing—that apostle of human rights—this fine tribute:

"To this distinguished man belongs the rare honour of uniting with military energy and daring the spirit of a philanthropist. His exploits in the field, which placed him in the first rank of our soldiers, have been obscured by the purer and more lasting glory of a pacificator, and of a friend of mankind. In the whole history of the intercourse of civilized with barbarous or half-civilized communities, we doubt whether a brighter page can be found than that which records his agency in the removal of the Cherokees. As far as the wrongs done to this race can be atoned for, General Scott has made the expiation.

"In his recent mission to the disturbed borders of our country, he has succeeded, not so much by policy as by the nobleness and generosity of his character, by moral influences, by the earnest con viction with which he has enforced upon all with whom he has had to do, the obligations of patriotism, justice, humanity, and religion. It would not be easy to find among us a man who has won a purer fame, and I am happy to offer this tribute, because I would do some- thing — no matter how little—to hasten the time when the spirit of Christian humanity shall be accounted an essential attribute, and the brightest ornament to a public man."

This is justly said, and most justly applied.

In 1839, Scott was again deputed by the government to keep the peace, and, soldier as he is, to use all his great influence to prevent the occurrence of war. The dispute respecting the contested boun- dary on the north-eastern frontier had become alarming — Massa- chusetts and Maine on one side, and New Brunswick on the other, had in some degree taken the matter into their own hands, and hostile bands stood facing each other; a single indiscretion among them might have precipitated war beyond the possibility of its being averted. Happily, a friendship formed on the field of battle, in years long past, between General Scott and General Sir John Har- vey, the governor of New Brunswick, contributed to smooth the difficulties between the two nations. General Scott having over- come the first great obstacles in soothing the irritated feelings of the American borderers, made overtures to Sir John Harvey for the mutual withdrawal of troops from the disputed territory; and Sir John frankly acceded to them, saying in his letter of the 23d March, 1839, to General Scott, "My reliance upon *you*, my dear general, has led me to give my willing assent to the proposition which you have made yourself the very acceptable means of conveying to me."

The menacing position of affairs was now effectually changed into feelings of reciprocal forbearance, and Daniel Webster finally accom plished, by the treaty at Washington, the good work so satisfactorily commenced by the pacificator, Scott.

Soon after the commencement of actual hostilities between the United States and Mexico, Scott requested of government permission to join General Taylor with a large army, and push forward for the enemy's capital. This was denied him, and he remained at Washington until November. Receiving orders to proceed to the seat of war, he embarked from New York, and reached the mouth of the Rio Grande January 1st, 1847. After mustering an army of nearly twelve thousand men, part of them from General Taylor's force, he proceeded against the city and castle of Vera Cruz, the first object of the campaign. The following graphic description of the landing of the troops and siege of the city, is from the pen of an eye-witness :—

"On the fifth day of March, 1847, while the American squadron was lying at Anton Lizardo, a norther sprang up, and commenced blowing with great violence. The ships rolled and pitched, and tugged at their anchors, as if striving to tear them from their hold, while the sea was white with foam. About noon, General Scott's fleet of transports, destined for the reduction of Vera Cruz, came like a great white cloud bearing down before the storm. The whole eastern horizon looked like a wall of canvass. Vessel after vessel came flying in under reduced sail, until the usually quiet harbour was crowded with them. A perfect wilderness of spars and rigging met the eye at every turn ; and for five days, all was bustle, activity and excitement. Officers of the two services were visiting about from ship to ship; drums were beating, bands of music playing, and every thing told of an approaching conflict.

"On the 10th, the army were conveyed in huge surf-boats from the transports to the different ships of war, which immediately got under way for Vera Cruz. During the passage down to the city, I was in the fore-top of the United States' sloop-of-war 'Albany,' from which place I had a good view of all that occurred. It was a 'sight to see !' The tall ships of war sailing leisurely along under their top-sails, their decks thronged in every part with dense masses of troops, whose bright muskets and bayonets were flashing in the sunbeams ; the gingling of spurs and sabres ; the bands of music playing ; the hum of the multitude rising up like the murmur of the distant ocean ; the small steamers plying about, their decks crowded with anxious spectators ; the long lines of surf-boats towing astern of the ships, ready to disembark the troops ; all these tended to render the scene one of the deepest interest.

"About three o'clock, P. M., the armada arrived abreast of the

little desert island of Sacrificio, where the time-worn walls and battlements of Vera Cruz, and the old grim castle of San Juan d'Ulloa,
with their ponderous cannon, tier upon tier, basking in the yellow
rays of the sun, burst upon our view. It was a most beautiful, nay,
a *sublime* sight, that embarkation. I still retained my position in
the fore-top, and was watching every movement with the most
anxious interest; for it was thought by many that the enemy would
oppose the landing of our troops. About four o'clock, the huge
surf-boats, each capable of conveying one hundred men, were hauled to the gang-ways of the different men-of-war, and quickly laden
with their 'warlike fraughtage;' formed in a single line, nearly a
mile in length; and at a given signal, commenced slowly moving
toward the Mexican shore. It was a grand spectacle! On, on
went the long range of boats, loaded down to the gunwales with
brave men, the rays of the slowly-departing sun resting upon their
uniforms and bristling bayonets, and wrapping the far inland and
fantastic mountains of Mexico in robes of gold. On they went;
the measured stroke of the countless oars mingling with the hoarse
dull roar of the trampling surf upon the sandy beach, and the shriek
of the myriads of sea-birds soaring high in air, until the boats struck
the shore, and quick as thought our army began to land. At this
instant, the American flag was planted, and unrolling its folds, floated proudly out upon the evening breeze; the crews of the men-of-
war made the welkin ring with their fierce cheering; and a dozen
bands of music, at the same time, and as if actuated by one impulse,
struck up

'T is the star-spangled banner! O, long may it wave,
O'er the land of the free, and the home of the brave!'

"Early the next morning, the old grim castle of San Juan d'Ulloa
commenced trying the range of its heavy guns, throwing Paixhan
shells at the army, and continued it at intervals for a week; but
with the exception of an occasional skirmish with a party of the
enemy's lancers, they had all the fun to themselves. In the mean
time our forces went quietly on with their preparations, stationing
their pickets, planting their heavy mortars, landing their horses,
provisions and munitions of war, constantly annoyed with a ceast-
less fire from the Mexican batteries, which our troops were as yet
too busy to return.

3   c

"On the 24th, Lieutenant Oliver Hazard Perry, with a zeal worthy of his illustrious father, 'the hero of Lake Erie,' dismounted one of the waist guns of the 'Albany,' a sixty-eight-pounder, procured a number of volunteers who would willingly have charged up to the muzzles of the Mexican cannon with such a leader, and taking about forty rounds of Paixhan shells, proceeded on shore, where, after dragging his gun through the sand for three miles, he arrived at a small fortification, which the engineers had constructed of sand-bags for him, and there planted his engine of destruction, in a situation which commanded the whole city of Vera Cruz. Roused by such a gallant example, guns from each of the other ships of the squadron were disembarked, and conveyed to the breast-work, which was as yet concealed from the eyes of the Mexicans, by being in the rear of an almost impervious *chapparal*, and in a short time a most formidable fortress was completed, which was styled the Naval Battery.

"At this period, General Scott, having quietly made all his arrangements, while a constant shower of shot and shell were thrown at his army by the enemy, sent a flag of truce, with a summons for the immediate surrender of the city of Vera Cruz, and the castle of San Juan d'Ulloa, and with a full understanding that unless his demand was immediately complied with, an attack would follow. As a matter of course, the Mexicans, expecting an assault, for which they were well prepared, and not a bombardment, returned an indignant refusal, and were told that at four o'clock, P. M., they should hear farther from us. In the mean time, the chapparal had been cut away, disclosing the Naval Battery to the gaze of the astonished Mexicans, and the mortars and heavy artillery, which had been planted upon the hills overlooking the city, and were ready to vomit forth their fires of death. Every person was now waiting with trembling anxiety the commencement of the fray.

"About four o'clock, P. M., while the crews of the squadron were all at supper, a sudden and tremendous roar of artillery on shore proclaimed that the battle had begun. The tea-things were left to 'take care of themselves,' and pellmell tumbled sick and well up the ladders to the spar-deck. I followed with the human tide, and soon found myself in the fore-top of the 'Albany,' and looking around me, a sublime but terrific sight my elevated perch presented to the view. Some two hundred sail of vessels were lying immediately around us, their tops, cross-trees, yards, shrouds — every thing where a foot-hold could be obtained — crowded with human beings, clustered like swarming bees in mid-summer on the trees, all intently watching the battle. I turned my eyes on shore. JONA-THAN had at last awakened from his slumber, and had set to work in earnest. Bomb-shells were flying like hail-stones into Vera Cruz from every quarter; sulphurous flashes, clouds of smoke, and the dull boom of the heavy guns arose from the walls of the city in return, while ever and anon a red sheet of flame would leap from the great brass mortars on the ramparts of the grim castle, followed by a report, which fairly made the earth tremble. The large ships of the squadron could not approach near enough to the shore to participate in the attack upon the city, without exposing them to the fire of the castle; but all the gun-boats, small steamers, and every thing that *could* be brought to bear upon the enemy, were sent in and commenced blazing away; a steady stream of fire, like the red glare of a volcano! This state of things continued until sunset, when the small vessels were called off; but the mortars kept throwing shells into the devoted town the live-long night. I was watching them until after midnight, and it was one of the most striking displays that I ever beheld.

"A huge black cloud of smoke hung like a pall over the American army, completely concealing it from view; the Mexicans had ceased firing, in order to prevent our troops from directing their guns by the flashes from the walls; but the bombardiers had obtained the exact range before dark, and kept thundering away, every shell falling directly into the doomed city. Suddenly, a vivid, lightning-like flash would gleam for an instant upon the black pall of smoke hanging over our lines, and then as the roar of the great mortar came borne to our ears, the ponderous shell would be seen to dart upward like a meteor, and after describing a semi-circle in the air, descend with a loud crash upon the house-tops, or into the resounding streets of the fated city. Then, after a brief but awful moment of suspense, a lurid glare, illuminating for an instant the white domes and grim fortresses of Vera Cruz, falling into ruins with the shock, and the echoing crash that came borne to our ears, told that the shell had exploded, and executed its terrible mission!

"Throughout the whole night these fearful missiles were travelling into the city in one continued stream; but the enemy did not return the fire. At day-light, however, the Mexicans again opened their batteries upon our army, with the most determined bravery.

"About eight o'clock, A. M., the gallant Perry and his brave associates, having finished the mounting of their guns, and completed all their arrangements, opened with a tremendous roar the Naval Battery upon the west side of the city, and were immediately answered from four distinct batteries of the enemy. The firm earth trembled beneath the discharge of these ponderous guns, and the shot flew like hail into the town, and were returned with interest by the Mexicans. Their heavy guns were served with wonderful precision; and almost every shot struck the little fort, burst open the sand-bags of which it was constructed, and covered our brave officers and men with a cloud of dust. Many shot and shell were thrown directly through the embrasures; and to use the expressions of one of our old tars who had been in several engagements, 'the red-skins handled their long thirty-two's as if they had been rifles!' Several of our men and one officer had fallen, but the remainder of the brave fellows kept blazing away; while the forts and ramparts of the city began to crumble to the earth. This state of things continued until the twenty-seventh; the army throwing a constant shower of bombs into the city, and the Naval Battery, (manned daily by fresh officers and men,) beating down the fortifications, and destroying every thing within its range, when a flag of truce was sent out with an offer, which was immediately accepted, of an unconditional surrender of the city of Vera Cruz and the castle of San Juan d'Ulloa."

Before the siege commenced, General Scott had sent printed passports to the different consuls, and also requested a surrender of the city, in order to preserve the lives of the non-combatants. These were disregarded at the time; but when the siege was in full operation, he received a communication from the consuls, requesting that the women and children might be permitted to pass out. His answer we give in his own words:—

"I enclose a copy of a memorial received last night, signed by the consuls of Great Britain, France, Spain, and Prussia, within Vera Cruz, asking me to grant a truce to enable the neutrals, together with Mexican women and children, to withdraw from the scene of havoc about them. I shall reply, the moment that an opportunity may be taken, to say—1. That a truce can only be granted on the application of Governor Morales, with a view to surrender. 2. That in sending safeguards to the different consuls, beginning as far back as the 13th inst., I distinctly admonished them—particularly the French and Spanish consuls—and of course, through the two, the other consuls, of the dangers that have followed. 3. That although at that date I had already refused to allow any person whatsoever to pass the line of investment either way, yet the blockade had been left open to the consuls and other neutrals to pass out to their respective ships of war up to the 22d instant; and 4th:

"I shall enclose to the memorialists a copy of my summons to the governor, to show that I had fully considered the impending hardships and distresses of the place, including those of women and children, before one gun had been fired in that direction. The intercourse between the neutral ships of war and the city was stopped at the last-mentioned date by Commodore Perry, with my concurrence, which I placed on the ground that the intercourse could not fail to give to the enemy moral aid and comfort."

The following were the terms of surrender, finally agreed upon by Generals Worth and Pillow, and Colonel Totten, on the part of the Americans, and Villannuera, Herrera, and Robles, on the part of the Mexicans !

" 1. The whole garrison, or garrisons, to be surrendered to the arms of the United States, as prisoners of war, the 29th instant, at ten o'clock, A. M. ; the garrisons to be permitted to march out with all the honours of war, and to lay down their arms to such officers as may be appointed by the general-in-chief of the United States' armies, and at a point to be agreed upon by the commissioners.

" 2. Mexican officers shall preserve their arms and private effects, including horses and horse-furniture, and to be allowed, regular and irregular officers, as also the rank and file, five days to retire to their respective homes, on parole, as hereinafter prescribed.

" 3. Coincident with the surrender, as stipulated in article 1, the Mexican flags of the various forts and stations shall be struck, saluted by their own batteries ; and, immediately thereafter, Forts Santiago and Conception, and the castle of San Juan de Ulloa, oc cupied by the forces of the United States.

" 4. The rank and file of the regular portion of the prisoners to be disposed of after surrender and parole, as their general-in-chief

3 *   c 2

may desire, and the irregular to be permitted to return to their homes. The officers, in respect to all arms and descriptions of force, giving the usual parole, that the said rank and file, as well as themselves, shall not serve again until duly exchanged.

"5. All the *material* of war, and all public property of every description found in the city, the castle of San Juan de Ulloa, and their dependencies, to belong to the United States ; but the armament of the same (not injured or destroyed in the further prosecution of the actual war) may be considered as liable to be restored to Mexico by a definite treaty of peace.

"6. The sick and wounded Mexicans to be allowed to remain in the city, with such medical officers and attendants, and officers of the army as may be necessary to their care and treatment.

"7. Absolute protection is solemnly guarantied to persons in the city, and property, and it is clearly understood that no private building or property is to be taken or used by the forces of the United States, without previous arrangement with the owners, and for a fair equivalent.

"8. Absolute freedom of religious worship and ceremonies is solemnly guarantied."

General Scott remained about two weeks at Vera Cruz, and then set out for the capital. On the 17th of April he arrived at the pass of Sierra Gordo, where General Santa Anna was entrenched with eleven thousand men. On the same day Scott issued the following celebrated order :—

"The enemy's whole line of entrenchments and batteries will be attacked in front, and at the same time turned, early in the day to-morrow—probably before ten o'clock, A. M.

"The second (Twiggs's) division of regulars is already advanced within easy turning distance towards the enemy's left. That division has orders to move forward before daylight to-morrow, and take up position across the National Road to the enemy's rear, so as to cut off a retreat towards Jalapa. It may be reinforced to-day, if unexpectedly attacked in force, by regiments one or two, taken from Shields's brigade of volunteers. If not, the two volunteer regiments will march for that purpose at daylight to-morrow morning, under Brigadier-General Shields, who will report to Brigadier-General Twiggs on getting up with him, or the general-in-chief, if he be in advance.

"The remaining regiment of that volunteer brigade will receive instructions in the course of this day.

"The first division of regulars (Worth's) will follow the movement against the enemy's left at sunrise to-morrow morning.

"As already arranged, Brigadier-General Pillow's brigade will march at six o'clock to-morrow morning along the route he has carefully reconnoitred, and stand ready as soon as he hears the report of arms on our right—sooner, if circumstances should favour him—to pierce the enemy's line of batteries at such point—the nearer the river the better—as he may select. Once in the rear of that line, he will turn to the right or left, or both, and attack the batteries in reverse, or if abandoned, he will pursue the enemy with vigour until further orders.

"Wall's field-battery and the cavalry will be held in reserve on the National Road, a little out of view and range of the enemy's batteries. They will take up that position at nine o'clock in the morning.

"The enemy's batteries being carried or abandoned, all our divisions and corps will pursue with vigour.

"This pursuit may be continued many miles, until stopped by darkness, or fortified positions towards Jalapa. Consequently, the body of the army will not return to this encampment, but be followed to-morrow afternoon, or early the next morning, by the baggage trains for the several corps. For this purpose, the feebler officers and men of each corps will be left to guard its camp and effects, and to load up the latter in the wagons of the corps.

"As soon as it shall be known that the enemy's works have been carried, or that the general pursuit has been commenced, one wagon for each regiment, and one for the cavalry, will follow the movement, to receive, under the directions of medical officers, the wounded, who will be brought back to this place for treatment in the general hospital.

"The surgeon-general will organize this important service and designate that hospital, as well as the medical officers to be left at that place.

"Every man who marches out to attack or pursue the enemy will take the usual allowance of ammunition, and subsistence for at least two days."

This document is famous for its exact delineation of every move-

ment of the battle, with one single exception, the day before the
action really took place. This is shown by the annexed report,
written after the engagement :—

"The plan of attack, sketched in General Orders, No. 111, here-
with, was finely executed by this gallant army, before two o'clock,
P. M., yesterday. We are quite embarrassed with the results of
victory — prisoners of war, heavy ordnance, field batteries, small
arms, and accoutrements. About three thousand men laid down
their arms with the usual proportion of field and company officers,
besides five generals, several of them of great distinction. Pinson,
Jarerro, La Vega, Noriega, and Obando. A sixth general, Vasquez,
was killed in defending the battery (tower) in the rear of the whole
Mexican army, the capture of which gave us those glorious results.

"Our loss, though comparatively small in numbers, has been serious. Brigadier-General Shields, a commander of activity, zeal,
and talent, is, I fear, if not dead, mortally wounded. He is some
five miles from me at the moment. The field of operations covered
many miles, broken by mountains and deep chasms, and I have not
a report, as yet, from any division or brigade. Twiggs's division,
followed by Shields's (now Colonel Baker's) brigade, are now at, or
near Jalapa, and Worth's division is en route thither, all pursuing,
with good results, as I learn, that part of the Mexican army — perhaps six or seven thousand men, who fled before our right had carried
the tower, and gained the Jalapa road. Pillow's brigade, alone, is
near me, at this depôt of wounded, sick, and prisoners ; and I have
time only to give from him the names of 1st Lieutenant F. B. Nel-
son, and 2d C. G. Gill, both of the 2d Tennessee foot (Haskell's
regiment) among the killed, and in the brigade one hundred and six,
of all ranks, killed or wounded. Among the latter the gallant brigadier-general himself has a smart wound in the arm, but not disabled, and Major R. Farqueson, 2d Tennessee ; Captain H. F.
Murray, 2d Lieutenant G. T. Sutherland, 1st Lieutenant W. P.
Hale, (adjutant,) all of the same regiment, severely ; and 1st Lieutenant W. Yearwood, mortally wounded. And I know, from personal observation on the ground, that 1st Lieutenant Ewell, of the
rifles, if not now dead, was mortally wounded, in entering, sword
in hand, the entrenchments around the captured tower. Second
Lieutenant Derby, topographical engineers, I also saw, at the same

BATTLE OF SIERRA GORDO.

place, severely wounded; and Captain Patten, 2d United States' infantry, lost his right hand.

"Major Sumner, 2d United States' dragoons, was slightly wounded the day before, and Captain Johnston, topographical engineers—now lieutenant-colonel of infantry—was very severely wounded some days earlier, while reconnoitring.

"I must not omit to add that Captain Mason and 2d Lieutenant Davis, both of the rifles, were among the very severely wounded in storming the same tower. I estimate our total loss, in killed and wounded, may be about two hundred and fifty, and that of the enemy three hundred and fifty. In the pursuit towards Jalapa, (twenty-five miles hence,) I learn we have added much to the enemy's loss in prisoners, killed, and wounded. In fact, I suppose his retreating army to be nearly disorganized, and hence my haste to follow, in an hour or two, to profit by events.

"In this hurried and imperfect report, I must not omit to say that Brigadier-General Twiggs, in passing the mountain range beyond Cerro Gordo, crowned with the tower, detached from his division, as I suggested before, a strong force to carry that height, which commanded the Jalapa road at the foot, and could not fail, if carried, to cut off the whole, or any part of the enemy's forces from a retreat in any direction. A portion of the 1st artillery, under the often-distinguished Brevet Colonel Childs, the 3d infantry, under Captain Alexander, the 7th infantry, under Lieutenant-Colonel Plymton, and the rifles, under Major Loring, all under the temporary command of Colonel Harney, 2d dragoons, during the confinement to his bed of Brevet Brigadier-General P. F. Smith, composed that detachment. The style of execution, which I had the pleasure to witness, was most brilliant and decisive. The brigade ascended the long and difficult slope of Sierra Gordo, without shelter, and under the tremendous fire of artillery and musketry, with the utmost steadiness, reached the breastworks, drove the enemy from them, planted the colours of the 1st artillery, 3d and 7th infantry — the enemy's flag still flying — and, after some minutes of sharp firing, finished the conquest with the bayonet.

"It is a most pleasing duty to say that the highest praise is due to Harney, Childs, Plymton, Loring, Alexander, their gallant officers and men, for this brilliant service, independent of the great results which soon followed.

" Worth's division of regulars coming up at this time, he detached Brevet Lieutenant-Colonel C. F. Smith, with his light battalion, to support the assault, but not in time. The general, reaching the tower a few minutes before me, and observing a white flag displayed from the nearest portion of the enemy towards the batteries below, sent out Colonels Harney and Childs to hold a parley. The surrender followed in an hour or two.

" Major-General Patterson left a sick bed to share in the dangers and fatigues of the day ; and after the surrender, went forward to command the advanced forces towards Jalapa.

" Brigadier-General Pillow and his brigade twice assaulted with great daring the enemy's line of batteries on our left ; and though without success, they contributed much to distract and dismay their immediate opponents.

" President Santa Anna, with Generals Canalizo and Almonte, and some six or eight thousand men, escaped towards Jalapa just before Sierra Gordo was carried, and before Twiggs' division reached the National Road above.

" I have determined to parole the prisoners—officers and men— as I have not the means of feeding them here, beyond to-day, and cannot afford to detach a heavy body of horse and foot, with wagons, to accompany them to Vera Cruz. Our baggage train, though increasing, is not yet half large enough to give an assured progress to this army. Besides, a greater number of prisoners would, probably, escape from the escort in the long and deep sandy road, without subsistence — ten to one — that we shall find again, out of the same body of men, in the ranks opposed to us. Not one of the Vera Cruz prisoners is believed to have been in the lines of Sierra Gordo. Some six of the officers, highest in rank, refuse to give their paroles, except to go to Vera Cruz, and thence, perhaps, to the United States.

" The small arms and their accoutrements, being of no value to our army here or at home, I have ordered them to be destroyed, for we have not the means of transporting them. I am also somewhat embarrassed with the —— pieces of artillery—all bronze—which we have captured. It will take a brigade, and half the mules of this army to transport them fifty miles. A field battery I shall take for service with the army ; but the heavy metal must be collected, and

JALAPA.

left here for the present. We have our own siege-train and the proper carriages with us.

"Being much occupied with the prisoners, and all the details of a forward movement, besides looking to the supplies which are to follow from Vera Cruz, I have time to add no more — intending to be at Jalapa early to-morrow. We shall not, probably, again meet with serious opposition this side of Perote — certainly not, unless delayed by the want of means of transportation.

"I invite attention to the accompanying letter to President Santa Anna, taken in his carriage yesterday; also to his proclamation, issued on hearing that we had captured Vera Cruz, &c., in which he says :—'If the enemy advance one step more, the national independence will be buried in the abyss of the past.' We have taken that step.

"One of the principal motives for paroling the prisoners of war is, to diminish the resistances of other garrisons in our march."

After the capture of Puebla by General Worth, [May 15th,] the army remained there until the 7th of August, when it commenced its march for the Mexican capital. An excellent description of this march, and of the great battles consequent upon it, is given by a participator.

"We left Puebla on the morning of the 7th, and entered upon a beautiful rolling country of great fertility, supplying with its gardens the inhabitants of Puebla with food, and surrounded by lofty mountains, some of which were covered with snow. Our road was gradually ascending, and so good that on looking back from the head of the column our train could be seen for miles in rear, dotting with its snow-white tops the maguey-covered plain. On our left was Popocatapetl and Iscatafetl, the snow on their not distant tops rendering the air quite chilly. General Scott did not leave with us, but came on the next day with Captain Kearny's dragoons.

"The second day's march was like the first, gradually ascending, passing through defiles, narrow passes, and over deep chasms, where a more determined enemy might have seriously annoyed us by merely making use of the obstacles Nature everywhere presented. Thick woods of the finest forest-trees were abundant, and the rugged nature of the country would readily carry one back to the northern parts of New England, or the passes of the 'Notch.' Here and there beautiful little lakes were interspersed in the deep valleys, and the clearness and coldness of their waters were almost incredible.

" The third day we were to encounter the much-vaunted pass of ' *Rio Frio*,' and also the passage of the mountain which was to lead us to the El Dorado of our hopes, the great plain of Mexico. Our march was to be long and difficult, and three o'clock saw us under way, with heart and hopes full of the prospect before us. The dreaded defile is reached and passed. The mountains which skirt the road on the left here close upon it for about a mile, over-hanging and enfilading it completely, and affording with their crests most excellent coverings for an enemy's marksmen. The newly-cut trees and long range of breastworks thrown up on the crest, showed us that preparations had been made, while numerous para-pets with embrasures in the logs, taught us what might have been done. But no men were there; the muskets and cannon were gone. Valencia, with six thousand Mexicans, was full a day's march ahead, making for Mexico with a speed which betrayed home-sickness. Rio Frio was found to be a little stream pouring down from the Snow mountain, of icy coldness and crystal purity. After a slight pause for refreshment, we commenced our ascent of the ridge which separates the plains of Puebla and Mexico, the former of which it had hitherto skirted. For several long miles we toiled up the hill, only recompensed for our labour by what we hoped to attain at last. When all were pretty nearly worn out, a sudden turn in the road brought to our view a sight which none can ever forget. The whole vast plain of Mexico was before us. The cold-ness of the air, which was most sensibly felt at this great height, our fatigue and danger were forgotten, and our eyes were the only sense that thought of enjoyment. Mexico, with its lofty steeples and its chequered domes, its bright reality, and its former fame, its modern splendour and its ancient magnificence, was before us; while around on every side its thousand lakes seemed like silver stars on a velvet mantle.

" We encamped that night at the base of the mountain, with the enemy's scouts on every side of us. The next day we reached *Ayotla*, only fifteen miles from Mexico by the National Road, which we had hitherto been following. Here we halted until Generals Quitman, Pillow, and Worth, with their divisions, should come up. We were separated from the city by the marshes which surround

Lake Tezcuco, and by the lake itself. The road is a causeway running through the marsh, and is commanded by a steep and lofty hill called *El Pinnol*. This hill completely enfilades and commands the National Road, and had been fortified and repaired with the greatest care by Santa Anna. One side was inaccessible by nature ; the rest had been made so by art. Batteries, in all mounting fifty guns of different calibres, had been placed on its sides, and a deep ditch, twenty-four feet wide and ten deep, filled with water, had been cut, connecting the parts already surrounded by marshes. On this side Santa Anna had twenty-five thousand men against our force of a little over nine thousand, all told.

"On the 22d we made a reconnoissance of the work, which was pronounced *impracticable*, as the lives of five thousand men would be lost before the ditch could be crossed. We continued our search, and found another road, which went round on the left, but when within five miles of the city were halted by coming suddenly upon five strong batteries on the hill which commanded this road, at a place called *Mexicalcingo*. We soon countermarched, and then saw our danger. With one regiment, and three companies of cavalry, in all about four hundred men, we saw that *El Pinnol* lay directly between us and our camp, distant full fifteen miles. Every eye was fixed on the hill, with the expectation of an approaching column which should drive us back into a Mexican prison, while we stepped off with the speed and endurance of four hundred Captain Barclays ! At about midnight we arrived safely at camp, and General Scott did us the honour of calling it 'the boldest reconnoissance of the war.' General Worth was encamped about five miles off—that is, in a straight line — across the *Lake Chalco*, at a place of the same name, but about ten miles by the road. The Mexicans had a foundry in the mountains, at which we were getting some shells made, and on returning from which Lieutenant Schuyler Hamilton was badly wounded.

" By means of his scouts, General Worth had found a path round the left of Lake Chalco, which led us to the western gate of the city, and which, up to that time, had not been fortified. On the 14th, the other divisions commenced their march, while we brought up the train and the rear. In the morning, the train was sent in advance, while Smith's brigade acted as rear-guard. It was composed of the rifles, 1st artillery, and the 3d infantry, with Taylor's

4   D 2

battery. As the rear-guard, marching slowly along, reached with the train, word came to General Twiggs that a force of about five thousand men were trying to cross the road between them and the train in order to cut it off. We were then passing through a small village which, by a curious coincidence, was called *Buena Vista*. On our left were large fields of half-grown barley, through which was seen advancing in splendid order the enemy's column. It was the most splendid sight I had ever seen. The yellow cloaks, red caps and jackets of the lancers, and the bright blue and white uniforms of the infantry, were most beautifully contrasted with the green of the barley-field. Our line of battle was soon formed, and we deployed through the grain to turn their left and cut them off from the mountains. A few shots, however, from the battery, soon showed them that they were observed; and, countermarching in haste, they left their dead on the field. Thus ended our fight of Buena Vista. That night we staid at Chalco. The next day we made a long and toilsome march over a horrible road, through which, with the utmost difficulty, we dragged our wagons by the assistance of both men and mules. The next was nearly the same, except that the road was, if possible, worse than before, as the Mexicans had blocked it up with large stones, rolled down from the neighbouring hills. This night we encamped at a most beautiful olive grove, of immense size, and accommodating at once both divisions. In the town, as well as in Chalco, there are still standing the churches of the Indians, where the fire-worshippers assembled before Cortez had introduced a new religion. They are large and sombre edifices, differing but little from the churches of this country, and, being near the city, are said to have been formerly resorted to by the ancient kings.

" The next day we arrived in sight of the rest of the army, and heard the guns with which Worth was breaching the walls of San Antonio. That night the news of the death of Captain Thornton, of the 2d dragoons, reached us. He was a brave officer and a thorough gentleman, but was always unfortunate in his military career.

" On the morning of the 19th, we left the little village where we had heard this sad news, and took the road to *San Juan*, about seven miles to the west, and only about ten miles from the city. When we arrived here we heard the sound of General Worth's guns, who was said to have attacked *San Augustine*, a village three miles nearer the capital, where Santa Anna was said to be with twenty thousand men. When we arrived at San Juan, the men were told to sling their blankets across their shoulders, put their knapsacks into their wagons, and to put two days' bread and beef in their haversacks. When this order came, all knew that the time had come. The officers arranged their effects, put on their old coats, and filled their haversacks and flasks. Soon we were ready for any thing but a thrashing. We here heard the position of the enemy, which was nearly as follows: Santa Anna, with twenty thousand men, was at *San Augustine;* Valencia, with ten thousand, was at a hill called *Contreros,* which commanded another road parallel to the San Augustine road, but which led into it between the city and Santa Anna. Now, by cutting a road across, if we could whip Valencia, we could follow the road up, and thus get in between Santa Anna and Mexico, and whip him too. General Worth (supported by General Quitman) was to keep Santa Anna in check, while Twiggs (backed by Pillow) was to try and astonish Valencia, which you will see he did very effectually. Pillow, with some of the ten regiments, was to cut the road.

"We left San Juan about one o'clock, not particularly desiring a fight so late in the day, but still not shunning it in case we could have a respectable chance. About two P. M., as we had crawled to the top of a hill, whither we had been ourselves pulling Magruder's battery and the mountain howitzers, we suddenly espied Valencia fortified on a hill about two hundred yards off, and strongly reinforced by a column which had just come out of the city. We laid down close to avoid drawing their fire, while the battery moved past at a full gallop. Just then, General Smith's manly voice rung out, '*Forward the rifles — to support the battery.*' On they went till we got about eight hundred yards from the work, when the enemy opened upon them with his long guns, which were afterwards found to be sixteen and eight-inch howitzers. The ground was the worst possible for artillery, covered with rocks large and small, prickly-pear and cactus, intersected by ditches filled with water and lined with maguey-plant, itself imperviable to cavalry, and with patches of corn which concealed the enemy's skirmishers, while it impeded our own passage. The artillery advanced but slowly under a most tremendous fire, which greatly injured it before it could be got in range, and the thickness of the undergrowth caused the skirmishers thrown forward to lose their relative position, as well as the column. About four, the battery got in position under a most murderous fire of grape, canister, and round-shot. Here the superiority of the enemy's pieces rendered our fire nugatory. We could get but *three* pieces in battery, while they had *twenty-seven*, all of them three times the calibre of ours. For two hours our troops stood the storm of iron and lead they hailed upon them unmoved. At every discharge they laid flat down to avoid the storm, and then sprung up to serve the guns. At the end of that time, two of the guns were dismounted, and we badly hurt : thirteen of the horses were killed and disabled, and fifteen of the cannoniers killed and wounded. The regiment was then recalled. The lancers had been repelled in three successive charges. The 3d infantry and 1st artillery had also engaged and successfully repelled the enemy's skirmishers without losing either officers or men. The greatest loss had been at the batteries. Officers looked gloomy for the first day's fight, but the brigade was formed, and General Smith in person took command. All felt revived, and followed him with a yell, as, creeping low to avoid the grape, (which was coming very fast,) we made a circuit in rear of the batteries ; and, passing off to the right, we were soon lost to view in the chapparal and cactus.

" Passing over the path that we scrambled through, behold us at almost six o'clock in the evening, tired, hungry, and sorrowful, emerging from the chaparral and crossing the road between it and Valencia. Here we found Cadwalader and his brigade already formed, and discovered Riley's brigade skirmishing in rear of the enemy's works. Valencia was ignorant of our approach, and we were as yet safe. In front of us was Valencia, strongly entrenched on a hill-side and surrounded by a regular field-work, concealed from us by an orchard in our rear. Mendoza, with a column of six thousand, was in the road, but thinking us to be friends. On our right was a large range of hills whose continued crest was parallel to the road, and in which were formed in line of battle five thousand of the best Mexican cavalry. On our left we were separated from our own forces by an almost impassable wilderness, and it was now twilight. Even Smith looked round for help. Suddenly a thousand *vivas* came across the hill-side like the yells of prairie wolves in the dead of night, and the squadrons on our right formed for charging. Smith is himself again ! " Face to the rear !" " Wait till you see their red caps, and then give it to them!" Furiously they came on a few yards, then changed their minds, and, disgusted at our cool reception, retired to their couches.

On the edge of the road, between us and Valencia, a Mexican hamlet spread out, with its mud huts, large orchards, deep-cut roads, and a strong church; and through the centre of this hamlet ran a path parallel to the main road, but concealed from it; it is nearly a mile long. In this road Smith's and Riley's brigade bivouacked. Shields, who came up in the night, lay in the orchard, while Cadwalader was nearest the enemy's works. As we were within range of their batteries, which could enfilade the road in which we lay, we built a stone breastwork at either end to conceal ourselves from their view and grape. There we were, completely surrounded by the enemy, cut off from our communications, ignorant of the ground, without artillery, weary, dispirited, and dejected. We were a disheartened set. With Santa Anna and Salas's promise of " no quarter," a force of four to one against us, and one half defeated already, no succour from Puebla, and no news from General Scott, all seemed dark. Suddenly the words came whispered along, "*we storm at midnight.*" Now we are ourselves again! But what a horrible night! There we lay, too tired to eat, too wet to sleep, in the middle of that muddy road, officers and men side by side, with a heavy rain pouring down upon us, the officers without blankets or overcoats, (they had lost them in coming across,) and the men worn out with fatigue. About midnight the rain was so heavy that the streams in the road flooded us, and there we stood crowded together, drenched and benumbed, waiting till daylight.

At half-past three the welcome word "*fall in*" was passed down, and we commenced our march. The enemy's works were on a hill-side, behind which rose other and slightly higher hills, separated by deep ravines and gullies, and intersected by streams. The whole face of the country was of stiff clay, which rendered it almost impossible to advance. We formed our line about a quarter of a mile from the enemy's works, Riley's brigade on our right. At about four we started, winding through a thick orchard which effectually concealed us, even had it not been dark, debouching into a deep ravine which ran within about five hundred yards of the work, and which carried us directly in rear and out of sight of their batteries. At dawn of day we reached our place after incredible exer-

4 *

tions, and got ready for our charge. The men threw off their wet blankets and looked to their pieces, while the officers got ready for a rush, and the first smile that lit up our faces for twelve hours boded but little good for the Mexicans. On the right, and opposite the right of their work, was Riley's brigade of the 2d and 1st infantry and 4th artillery, next the rifles, then the 1st artillery and 3d infantry. In rear of our left was Cadwalader's brigade, as a support, with Shields's brigade in rear as a reserve—the whole division under command of General Smith, in the absence of General Twiggs. They had a smooth place to rush down on the enemy's work, with the brow of the hill to keep under until the word was given.

"At last, just at daylight, General Smith slowly walking up, asked if all was ready. A look answered him. ' *Men forward!*' And we *did* 'forward.' Springing up at once, Riley's brigade opened, when the crack of a hundred rifles startled the Mexicans from their astonishment, and they opened their fire. Useless fire! for we were so close that they overshot us, and, before they could turn their pieces on us we were on them. Then such cheers arose as you never heard. The men rushed forward like demons, yelling and firing the while. The carnage was frightful, and, though they fired sharply, it was of no use. The earthen parapet was cleared in an instant, and the blows of the stocks could be plainly heard mingled with the yells and groans around. Just before the charge was made, a large body of lancers came winding up the road looking most splendidly in their brilliant uniforms. They never got to the work, but turned and fled. In an instant all was one mass of confusion, each trying to be foremost in the flight. The road was literally blocked up, and, while many perished by their own guns, it was almost impossible to fire on the mass from the danger of killing our own men. Some fled up the ravine on the left, or on the right, and many of these were slain by turning their own guns on them. Towards the city the rifles and 2d infantry led off the pursuit. Seeing that a large crowd of the fugitives were jammed up in a pass in the road, some of our men ran through the cornfield, and by thus heading them off and firing down upon them, about thirty men took over five hundred prisoners, nearly a hundred of them officers. After disarming the prisoners, as the pursuit had ceased, we went back to the fort, where we found our troops in full possession, and the rout complete.

"We found that the enemy's position was much stronger than we had supposed, and their artillery much larger and more abundant. Our own loss was small, which may be accounted for by their perfect surprise at our charge, as to them we appeared as if rising out of the earth, so unperceived was our approach. Our loss was one officer killed, Captain Hanson of the 7th infantry, and Lieutenant Van Buren of the rifles shot through the leg, and about fifty men killed and wounded. Their force consisted of eight thousand men, under Valencia, with a reserve, which had not yet arrived, under Santa Anna. Their loss, as since ascertained, was as follows: Killed and buried since the fight, seven hundred and fifty; wounded, one thousand, and fifteen hundred prisoners, exclusive of officers, including four generals—Salas, Mendoza, Garcia, and Guadalupe—in addition to dozens of colonels, majors, captains, &c. We captured in all on the hill twenty-two pieces of cannon, including five eight-inch howitzers, two long eighteens, three long sixteens, and several of twelve and eight inches, and also the two identical six-pounders captured by the Mexicans at Buena Vista, taken from Captain Washington's battery of the 4th artillery. The first officer who saw them happened to be the officer of the 4th, selected by General Scott to command the new battery of that regiment, Captain Drum. In addition were taken immense quantities of ammunition and muskets; in fact, the way was strewed with muskets, escopets, lances, and flags for miles. Large quantities of horses and mules were also captured, though large numbers were killed.

"Thus ended the glorious battle of Contreros, in which two thousand men, under General P. F. Smith, completely routed and destroyed an army of eight thousand men, under General Valencia, with Santa Anna and a force of twenty thousand men, within five miles. Their army was so completely routed that not fifteen hundred men rejoined Santa Anna and participated in the second battle. Most people would have thought that a pretty good day's work. Not so. We had only saved ourselves, not conquered Mexico, and men's work was before us yet.

"At eight A. M. we formed again, and General Twiggs having taken command, we started on the road to Mexico. We had hardly marched a mile before we were sharply fired upon from both sides of the road, and our right was deployed to drive the enemy in. We soon found that we had caught up with the retreating party, from the very brisk firing in front, and we drove them through the little town of San Angelo, where they had been halting in force. About half a mile from this town we entered the suburbs of another called San Katherina, when a large party in the church-yard fired on the head of the column, and the balls came right among us. Our men kept rushing on their rear and cutting them down, until a discharge of grape-shot from a large piece in front drove them back to the column. In this short space of time five men were killed, ten taken prisoners, and a small colour captured, which was carried the rest of the day.

"Meanwhile General Worth had made a demonstration on San Antonio, where the enemy was fortified in a strong hacienda; but they retired on his approach to Churubusco, where the works were deemed impregnable. They consisted of a fortified hacienda, which was surrounded by a high and thick wall on all sides. Inside the wall was a stone building, the roof of which was flat and higher than the walls. Above all this was a stone church, still higher than the rest, and having a large steeple. The wall was pierced with loop-holes, and so arranged that there were two tiers of men firing at the same time. They thus had four different ranges of men firing at once, and four ranks were formed on each range, and placed at such a height that they could not only overlook all the surrounding country, but at the same time they had a plunging fire upon us. Outside the hacienda, and completely commanding the avenues of approach, was a field-work extending around two sides of the fort, and protected by a deep wet ditch, and armed with seven large pieces. This hacienda is at the commencement of the causeway leading to the western gate of the city, and had to be passed before getting on the road. About three hundred yards in rear of this work another field-work had been built where a cross-road meets the causeway, at a point where it crosses a river, thus forming a bridge head, or *tête de pont*. This was also very strong, and armed with three large pieces of cannon. The works were surrounded on every side by large corn-fields, which were filled with the enemy's skirmishers, so that it was difficult to make a reconnoissance. It was therefore decided to make the attack immediately, as they were full of men, and extended for nearly a mile on the road to the city, completely covering the causeway. The attack commenced about one, P. M. General Twiggs's division attacked on the side

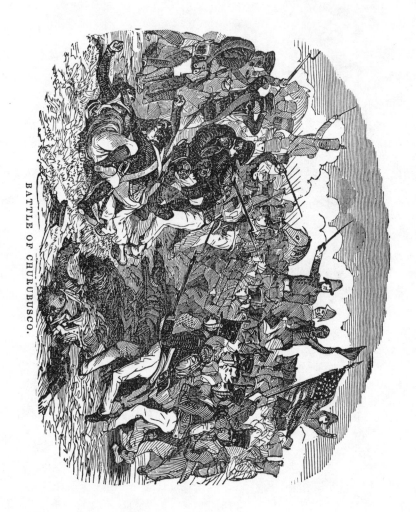

BATTLE OF CHURUBUSCO.

towards which they approached the fort; that is, opposite the city. General Worth's attacked the bridge head, which he took in about an hour and a half; while Generals Pillow and Quitman were on the extreme left, between the causeway and Twiggs's division. The rifles were on the left and in rear of the work, intrusted by General Scott with the task of charging it in case General Pierce gave way. The firing was most tremendous—in fact, one continued roll while the combat lasted. The enemy, from their elevated station, could readily see our men, who were unable to get a clear view from their position. Three of the pieces were manned by 'the Deserters,' a body of about one hundred, who had deserted from the ranks of our army during the war. They were enrolled in two companies, commanded by a deserter, and were better uniformed and disciplined than the rest of the army. These men fought most desperately, and are said not only to have shot down several of our officers whom they knew, but to have pulled down the white flag of surrender no less than three times.

"The battle raged most furiously for about three hours, when, both sides having lost a great many, the enemy began to give way. As soon as they commenced retreating, Kearny's squadron passed through the *tête de pont*, and, charging through the retreating column, pursued them to the very gate of the city. When our men got within about five hundred yards of the gate, they were opened upon with grape and canister, and several officers wounded. Amongst the number was Captain Kearny, 1st dragoons, who lost his left arm above the elbow. Lieutenant Graham, of New York, received a severe flesh-wound in his left arm. Captain McReynolds, ditto. Our loss in this second battle was large. We lost in killed seven officers : Captains Capron, Burke, 1st artillery ; Lieutenants Irons, Johnston, Hoffman, Captain Anderson, Lieutenant Easely, 2d infantry ; Captain Hanson, 7th infantry. Lieutenant Irons died on the 28th. Colonel Butler, of South Carolina, and about thirty officers wounded, exclusive of the volunteers. The official returns give our loss in killed and wounded at one thousand one hundred and fifty, besides officers. The Mexican loss is five hundred killed in the second battle, one thousand wounded, and eleven hundred prisoners, exclusive of officers. Three more generals were taken, among them General Rincon and Anaya, the provisional President; also, ten pieces of cannon and an immense amount of ammunition and stores. Santa Anna, in his report, states his loss in killed, wounded, and missing at twelve thousand. He has only eighteen thousand left out of thirty thousand, which he gives as his force on the 20th in both actions.

"Thus ended the battle of Churubusco, one of the most furious and deadly, for its length, of any of the war. For reasons which he deemed conclusive, General Scott did not enter the city that night, but encamped on the battle-field, about four miles from the western gate of the city. The next day a flag of truce came out, and propositions were made which resulted in an armistice.

"Meanwhile, the army is encamped in the villages around the city, recruiting from their fatigue and nursing the sick and wounded. There are but few sick, and the wounded are getting along comfortably in their hospitals.

The New Orleans Delta has the following remarks on these battles :

"Never have there been exhibited in one day so many individual instances of heroic courage, indomitable valour, and determination in overcoming great and apparently insurmountable obstacles. From one end of the army to the other there prevailed but one feeling and one resolve, and that was victory or death. Our officers set noble examples to their men, which were imitated with as much cool determination as they were set. There was no faltering, no holding back, and there is no corps or command but acquitted itself with honour to themselves and credit to the country. The regulars added new laurels to those already acquired, and the volunteers have given a repetition of the noble bearing of their countrymen on the bloody field of Buena Vista. South Carolina chivalry and the sons of the Empire State have inscribed their names on the roll of fame, and will return home bright ornaments to the states from whence they came.

"The Mexicans also fought as they never fought before ; they strongly resisted us at every point, and contested every inch with the strongest determination and even to desperation. They knew that their capital and their all depended upon the issue, and with this knowledge and thus prompted, they threw themselves into the breach as no person ever expected they would—and one of the best evidences of this is the number of killed and wounded on both sides.

"General Scott, at the head of our army during the engagement, received a slight wound in the leg, and, what is very remarkable, no person whatever except himself was aware of it until after the battle was over. A great deal has been said and written in reference to the ability of General Scott as a military man, but those who have not seen him in command and under fire, cannot form any just conception of his abilities. His cool consideration of every thing around him — his quick perception — his firm resolves and immediate execution—equal if they do not surpass those of any of the great generals whose deeds have been made so conspicuous in history."

After the works at Churubusco had been carried by storm, the dragoons, under their valiant leader, Colonel Harney, were ordered forward to pursue the retreating foe ; and onward they went, like winged messengers of death, their bright sabres glittering in the sunbeams, amidst the huzzas of the light troops, flushed with the victory over the fort. The horses seemed to partake of the enthusiasm of their riders, and dashed forward with supernatural strength, and in this spirit and state of feeling they overtook the flying army, and continued to cut them down to the very gates of the city.

Ayotla is twenty miles from Mexico, on the main road from Vera Cruz to that capital. About midway between Ayotla and Mexico are the strong fortifications of Penon ; and others at another pass called Mexicalcingo. Mexicalcingo lies to the southward of the Vera Cruz road, at the head of Lake Xochimilco. It is about six miles S. S. E. from Mexico, while Penon is about nine miles E. S. E. The town of Chalco is situated on the eastern border of the lake of the same name, three or four miles south of the Vera Cruz road. The Venta de Chalco, or village of Chalco, is immediately on said road, two or three miles south-east of Ayotla. The route of the army from that point ran along the northern and then the western border of Lake Chalco, between which and Lake Xochimilco on the west there is only half a mile of land. The road around the town passes entirely to the southward of Lake Chalco.

Contreros, where the first battle was fought, is a fortified position between San Augustin and San Angel. Churubusco, the scene of the second great conflict, is about two miles north of San Angel, and perhaps four south of Mexico.

On the evening of the 20th, General Scott offered a cessation of hostilities to the Mexican authorities, in order to afford an opportunity to negotiate a treaty of peace. This was accepted. Commis-

E 2

sioners were appointed by Santa Anna to confer with those from the American army, named by General Scott. The following terms of a preparatory armistice were concluded by these gentlemen :—

"ART. 1. Hostilities shall instantly and absolutely cease between the armies of the United States of America and the United Mexican States, within thirty leagues of the capital of the latter states, to allow time to the commissioners appointed by the United States and the commissioners to be appointed by the Mexican republic to negotiate.

"2. The armistice shall continue as long as the commissioners of the two governments may be engaged on negotiations, or until the commander of either of the said armies shall give formal notice to the other of the cessation of the armistice, and for forty-eight hours after such notice.

"3. In the mean time neither army shall, within thirty leagues of the city of Mexico, commence any new fortification or military work of offence or defence, or do anything to enlarge or strengthen any existing work or fortification of that character within the said limits.

"4. Neither army shall be reinforced within the same. Any reinforcements in troops or munitions of war, other than subsistence now approaching either army, shall be stopped at the distance of twenty-eight leagues from the city of Mexico.

"5. Neither army or any detachment from it, shall advance beyond the line it at present occupies.

"6. Neither army, nor any detachment or individual of either, shall pass the neutral limits established by the last article, except under a flag of truce bearing the correspondence between the two armies, or on the business authorized by the next article, and individuals of either army who may chance to straggle within the neutral limits shall, by the opposite party, be kindly warned off or sent back to their own armies under flags of truce.

"7. The American army shall not by violence obstruct the passage, from the open country into the city of Mexico, of the ordinary supplies of food necessary to the consumption of its inhabitants or the Mexican army within the city; nor shall the Mexican authorities, civil or military, do any act to obstruct the passage of supplies from the city or the country needed by the American army.

"8. All American prisoners of war remaining in the hands of the

Mexican army, and not heretofore exchanged, shall immediately, or as soon as practicable, be restored to the American army, against a like number, having regard to rank, of Mexican prisoners captured by the American army.

"9. All American citizens who were established in the city of Mexico prior to the existing war, and who have since been expelled from that city, shall be allowed to return to their respective business or families therein, without delay or molestation.

"10. The better to enable the belligerent armies to execute these articles, and to favour the great object of peace, it is further agreed between the parties, that any courier with despatches that either army shall desire to send along the line from the city of Mexico or its vicinity, to and from Vera Cruz, shall receive a safe conduct from the commander of the opposing army.

"11. The administration of justice between Mexicans, according to the general and state constitutions and laws, by the local authorities of the towns and places occupied by the American forces, shall not be obstructed in any manner.

"12. Persons and property shall be respected in the towns and places occupied by the American forces. No person shall be molested in the exercise of his profession; nor shall the services of any one be required without his consent. In all cases where services are voluntarily rendered a just price shall be paid, and trade remain unmolested.

"13. Those wounded prisoners who may desire to remove to some more convenient place, for the purpose of being cured of their wounds, shall be allowed to do so without molestation, they still remaining prisoners.

"14. The Mexican medical officers who may wish to attend the wounded shall have the privilege of doing so if their services be required.

"15. For the more perfect execution of this agreement, two commissioners shall be appointed, one by each party, who in case of disagreement shall appoint a third.

"16. This convention shall have no force or effect unless approved by their Excellencies, the commanders respectively of the two armies, within twenty-four hours, reckoning from the 6th hour of the 23d day of August, 1847."

These articles were signed by Generals Quitman, P. F. Smith,

5

and Franklin Pierce, on the part of the Americans; and Ignacio de Maria y Villamil and Benito Quijano on that of the Mexicans. Afterwards the following notes were appended:—

"Considered, approved, and ratified, with the express *understanding* that the word '*supplies*,' as used the second time, without qualification in the seventh article of this military convention—American copy—shall be taken to mean (as in both the British and American armies) arms, munitions, clothing, equipments, subsistence (for men,) forage, and in general, all the wants of an army. That word 'supplies' in the Mexican copy, is erroneously translated 'viveres' instead of 'recursos.'"

This was signed by General Scott. Santa Anna replied as follows:—

"Ratified, suppressing the ninth article, and explaining the fourth, to the effect that the temporary peace of this armistice shall be observed in the capital, and twenty-eight leagues around it; and agreeing that the word *supplies* shall be translated *recursos;* and that it comprehends every thing which the army may need, except arms and ammunitions."

This qualification was accepted and ratified by the American general.

Hopes were now entertained by General Scott and the friends of peace in both nations, that the long-protracted struggle was about to be amicably adjusted. These, however, were disappointed. Mr. Trist, the American envoy, demanded the cession of California and the territory between the Nueces and Rio Grande rivers, while the Mexicans refused to yield any portion of Texas. The negotiations accordingly closed.

On the 6th of September, General Scott accused Santa Anna of violating the armistice, by constructing fortifications within the capital. The Mexican general replied by laying a similar charge to the Americans, and affirming his willingness to recommence hostilities immediately. The subsequent operations are given in General Scott's report, which we annex, omitting the details of General Worth's operations, which have already been given.

"Negotiations were actively continued with, as was understood some prospect of a successful result up to the 2d instant, when our commissioner handed in his *ultimatum* (on boundaries), and the negotiators adjourned to meet again on the 6th.

" Some infractions of the truce, in respect to our supplies from the city, were earlier committed, followed by apologies, on the part of the enemy. Those vexations I was willing to put down to the imbecility of the government, and waived pointed demands of reparation while any hope remained of a satisfactory termination of the war. But on the 5th, and more fully on the 6th, I learned that as soon as the *ultimatum* had been considered in a grand council of ministers and others, President Santa Anna, on the 4th or 5th, without giving me the slightest notice, actively recommenced strengthening the military defences of the city, in gross violation of the 3d article of the armistice.

" On that information, which has since received the fullest verification, I addressed to him my note of the 6th. His reply, dated the same day, received the next morning, was absolutely and notoriously false, both in recrimination and explanation.   *   *   *   *

" Being delayed by the terms of the armistice more than two weeks, we had now, late on the 7th, to begin to reconnoitre the different approaches to the city, within our reach, before I could lay down any definitive plan of attack.

" The same afternoon, a large body of the enemy was discovered hovering about the Molinos del Rey, within a mile and a third of this village, (Tacubaya,) where I am quartered with the general staff and Worth's division.

" It might have been supposed that an attack upon us was intended ; but knowing the great value to the enemy of those mills, (Molinos del Rey,) containing a cannon-foundry, with a large deposit of powder in Casa Mata near them ; and having heard, two days before, that many church-bells had been sent out to be cast into guns —the enemy's movement was easily understood, and I resolved at once to drive him early the next morning, to seize the powder, and to destroy the foundry.

" Another motive for this decision — leaving the general plan of attack upon the city for full reconnoissances—was, that we knew our recent captures had left the enemy not a fourth of the guns necessary to arm, all at the same time, the strong works of each of the eight city gates ; and we could not cut the communication between the foundry and the capital without first taking the formidable castle on the heights of Chapultepec, which overlooked both and stood between.

"For this difficult operation we were not entirely ready, and moreover we might altogether neglect the castle, if, as we then hoped, our reconnoissances should prove that the distant southern approaches to the city were more eligible than this south-western approach.

"Hence the decision promptly taken, the execution of which was assigned to Brevet Major-General Worth, whose division was reinforced with Cadwalader's brigade of Pillow's division, three squadrons of dragoons under Major Sumner, and some heavy guns of the siege train under Captain Huger of the ordnance, and Captain Drum of the 4th artillery—two officers of the highest merit.

* * * * * * * *

"The enemy having several times reinforced his line, and the action soon becoming much more general than I had expected, I called up, from the distance of three miles, first Major-General Pillow, with his remaining brigade, (Pierce's,) and next Riley's brigade, of Twiggs' division — leaving his other brigade (Smith's) in observation at San Angel. Those corps approached with zeal and rapidity; but the battle was won just as Brigadier-General Pierce reached the ground, and had interposed his corps between Garland's brigade (Worth's division) and the retreating enemy."

Like General Taylor, after the capture of Monterey, the commander-in-chief was destined to experience considerable opposition, respecting his offer of the armistice. In reference to this opposition, the New Orleans Delta has the following pertinent remarks:—

"The sophist who lectured Hannibal on the art of war doubtless considered himself a supremely wise man, and the conqueror of Scipio but an indifferent general. The race to which he belonged has not passed away, but flourishes in these latter days in all the vigour and bloom of its youth. The present war has furnished ample employment to these military philosophers, and has enabled them at the same time to display the extent of their knowledge and bless mankind with a sun-flood of information. Among the subjects to which they have recently directed their powerful intellects, and upon which they have expended columns of acute disquisition and pathetic declamation, none has afforded a fairer field for their peculiar powers than the armistice granted by General Scott after the battles of Contreros and Churubusco. It is needless to say that in the opinion of these sages the general was totally in the wrong; his conduct was not only foolish, but, in view of the consequences which they ascribe to it, criminal. To him they impute the delay in capturing the city, the failure of the negotiations, and the subsequent loss of life in the combats that ensued from the 8th to the 14th of September. Bowing, as we do, with becoming deference to opinions so carefully formed, and so fearlessly promulgated, we yet beg leave to suggest, that before General Scott is finally condemned, it would be as well to wait for further information ; and, before he is even arraigned at the bar of public opinion for an alleged offence, it would be no more than fair to examine closely the information which we already possess.

"In the advance upon Mexico, the 'first line of defence' of the city, consisting of the strong posts of El Penon and Mexicalcingo, was avoided by a detour to the left, around the head of Lake Chalco. This movement began on the 15th of August, and, owing to the broken nature of the country and the necessity of cutting a road for many miles, it was a work of great toil and hardship. It was, however, accomplished in two days, and on the 18th our troops were in a position to act against Contreros and Churubusco, forming with the secondary works in their neighbourhood 'the second line of defence.' On the 19th, the movement was made against Contreros. Of the prolonged and difficult operations of that day, through dense chapparal, along rocky and precipitous paths, and amid constant combat and peril, it is not necessary to speak, for all will recollect the truthful descriptions which we have already published. To this day of toil and danger succeeded one of the most dismal nights experienced in that climate. The storm is described as terrific. The soldiers might perchance have snatched a morsel of food, but a moment's sleep was impossible. Under these circumstances, Contreros was captured and Valencia's force dispersed early in the morning, and the battle of Churubusco closed, and the second line of defence was carried after the most desperate and bloody engagement of the war at five o'clock in the afternoon. Now the first question that arises is, could General Scott have entered Mexico on the night of the 20th ? His soldiers had been watching, marching, fasting, and fighting for more than thirty-six hours ; over a thousand of his small force were killed or disabled, and the heights of Chapultepec and the line of the *garitas* were still before him, capable, as was afterwards shown, of making a strong defence. How easy soever

5 *

the achievement may seem to an editor in his closet, we apprehend that it was a labour not to be undertaken by a general in the field. The Mexican army which defended Churubusco, though defeated, was not destroyed ; it retreated towards the third and strongest line of defence, and was, or could easily have been, rallied behind its batteries. For General Scott to have attempted to enter Mexico on the night of the 20th of August, it appears to us would have been an act of desperation which nothing could have justified but the exceedingly improbable result of success. Had he undertaken it and failed, the warriors of the quill would have been the first to discover and expose the madness of the act. They would have inquired why he could not have waited until morning; why, with half-famished and exhausted troops, with the wounded calling for assistance, the dead unburied, and the living scarce able to drag one leg after the other, he had marched against strong works and a densely populated city, when one night's rest would have quadrupled the efficiency of his force ? And the voice of censure would have been as general as it would probably have been deserved.

" The conclusion has thus been forced upon us, that General Scott was obliged to pause for breath after the continued operations of the 19th and 20th, which terminated in the terrible slaughter of Churubusco.

" But that same evening he received a flag of truce from the enemy, asking for an armistice and proposing peace. Representations were at the same time made to him by those connected with the British Embassy, that there was every probability that negotiations would terminate favourably and honourably to all parties. The American commander was placed in a position of great delicacy and responsibility. It was his ardent desire to terminate the war, spare the lives of his soldiers, and avoid the infliction of unnecessary injury, even upon the foe. He had good reason to believe that by granting the armistice all these objects would be attained ; and he did grant it, making it terminable in forty-eight hours. What would have been said of him had he refused ? He must, in that case, either have taken the city or failed in the attempt. If the former, we would have been precisely in the condition in which we are at present, and General Scott would have been accused of sacrificing the lives of his countrymen, and unnecessarily prolonging the war, to promote his own ambitious aims, and gratify the pernicious vanity of claiming the conqueror's rank with Cortez. Not one in fifty of those who have now discovered that all negotiation with Mexico was an idle farce, but would have been certain that, had the Mexican proposition been entertained, we should have had an honourable and permanent peace. But in the hazards of war General Scott might have been repulsed on the morning of the 21st, and then imagination can scarcely depict the execrations which would have been poured upon his head. Whatever he might have done, it will thus be seen, he would have exposed himself to animadversion and misconstruction; to the idle comments of the unthinking, and the malicious remarks of the envious. For our own part, we are willing to believe that General Scott acted as every hero and patriot would have done, placed in his position, and burdened with his responsibilities; at any rate, we must see something stronger than has yet appeared against him, to suspect that he acted with want of judgment or want of zeal."

The following remarks upon the merits of the negotiations, and their final result, will also be read with interest:—

"The abortive negotiations which preceded the renewal of the war, are in a high degree instructive, as indicating more conclusively than any other evidence could do, the intentions and confidence of the respective parties. On the side of the United States it was proposed that the boundary-line of the two republics should run up the middle of the Rio Grande, strike off westward on reaching the limits of New Mexico, take the course of the Gila and the lower Colorado, and so through the mouth of the latter river down the middle of the Californian Gulf, into the Pacific. In other words, this would bring the south-western boundary-line of the United States about ten degrees further south, would deprive Mexico of all Upper and Lower California, as well as of the districts on the Rio Grande, and would leave her with the Gila for her northern boundary, but just above the present frontier of Sonora, which marks her settled territories. Enormous as was this claim, it was not the point upon which the negotiations broke off, for the Americans phrased their requirements considerately, and offered a liberal price for the cession they desired. Santa Anna, it is true, was for reserving a certain portion of California, for Mexican expansion, and he suggested the 37th in place of the 32d parallel, as the boundary of the two countries. Yet it is hardly disguised that on the point of cession and sale in this

F

quarter, the Mexican commissioners were amenable to the reasons which Mr. Polk brought, by millions, against them, and the tranfer might have been completed but for a comparatively insignificant slice of debateable land. The old Texan boundary-line was again brought under discussion, the one party insisting on the Rio Grande, and the other, as in honour bound, upon the Nueces; and this little difference proved incapable of adjustment between parties who had just been judiciously chaffering about ten degrees of territory! It is thus clear, that from the great object which has been so unhappily sought by a war, the Americans are now only separated by an obstacle which that very war has raised. We have before expressed our persuasion that, looking at the natural destinies and necessities of men and states, *the vast province of New California would much more reasonably fall to the lot of an expansive and enterprising people, who might reclaim its wastes and colonize its shores, than remain the nominal and desolate appanage of a stationary or retrogading race, which could never have either the motives or the means to improve its advantages for commerce, or explore the resources of its soil.*"

At the risk of some subsequent repetition we insert the admirable report of General Scott, concerning his operations after the battle of Molino del Rey. Its details are more circumstantial and satisfactory than any account that has yet appeared :—

" At the end of another series of arduous and brilliant operations, of more than forty-eight hours' continuance, this glorious army hoisted, on the morning of the 14th, the colours of the United States on the walls of this palace.

" The victory of the 8th, at the Molinos del Rey, was followed by daring reconnoissances on the part of our distinguished engineers— Captain Lee, Lieutenants Beauregard, Stevens, and Tower—Major Smith, senior, being sick, and Captain Mason, third in rank, wounded. Their operations were directed principally to the south — towards the gates of the Piedad, San Angel, (Nino Perdido,) San Antonio, and the Paseo de la Viga.

" This city stands on a slight swell of ground, near the centre of an irregular basin, and is girdled with a ditch in its greater extent— a navigable canal of great breadth and depth—very difficult to bridge in the presence of an enemy, and serving at once for drainage, custom-house purposes, and military defence ; leaving eight entrances or gates, over arches — each of which we found defended by a system of strong works, that seemed to require nothing but some men and guns to be impregnable.

" Outside and within the cross-fires of those gates, we found to the south other obstacles but little less formidable. All the approaches near the city are over elevated causeways, cut in many places (to oppose us) and flanked, on both sides, by ditches, also of unusual dimensions. The numerous cross-roads are flanked, in like manner, having bridges at the intersections, recently broken. The meadows thus checkered, are, moreover, in many spots, under water or marshy ; for, it will be remembered, we were in the midst of the wet season, though with less rain than usual, and we could not wait for the fall of the neighbouring lakes and the consequent drainage of the wet grounds at the edge of the city—the lowest in the whole basin.

" After a close personal survey of the southern gates, covered by Pillow's division and Riley's brigade of Twiggs' — with four times our numbers concentrated in our immediate front—I determined, on the 11th, to avoid that net-work of obstacles, and to seek, by a sudden inversion, to the south-west and west, less unfavourable approaches.

" To economize the lives of our gallant officers and men, as well as to insure success, it became indispensable that this resolution should be long masked from the enemy ; and, again, that the new movement, when discovered, should be mistaken for a feint, and the old as indicating our true and ultimate point of attack.

" Accordingly, on the spot, the 11th, I ordered Quitman's division from Coyoacan, to join Pillow *by daylight*, before the southern gates, and then that the two major-generals, with their divisions, should, *by night*, proceed (two miles) to join me at Tacubaya, where I was quartered with Worth's division. Twiggs, with Riley's brigade, and Captains Taylor's and Steptoe's field-batteries — the latter of twelve-pounders — was left in front of those gates, to manœuvre, to threaten, or to make false attacks, in order to occupy and deceive the enemy. Twiggs' other brigade (Smith's) was left at supporting distance, in the rear, at San Angel, till the morning of the 13th, and also to support our general depôt at Miscoac. The stratagem against the south was admirably executed throughout the 12th and down to the afternoon of the 13th, when it was too late for the enemy to recover from the effects of his delusion.

" The first step in the new movement was to carry Chapultepec, a natural and isolated mound of great elevation, strongly fortified at its base, on its acclivities and heights. Besides a numerous garrison, there was the military college of the republic, with a large number of sub-lieutenants and other students. Those works were within direct gun-shot of the village of Tacubaya; and, until carried, we could not approach the city on the west, without making a circuit too wide and too hazardous.

" In the course of the same night, (that of the 11th,) heavy batteries, within easy ranges, were established. No. 1, on our right, under the command of Captain Drum, 4th artillery, (relieved late next day, for some hours, by Lieutenant Andrews of the 3d,) and No. 2, commanded by Lieutenant Hagner, ordnance—both supported by Quitman's division. Nos. 3 and 4, on the opposite side, supported by Pillow's division, were commanded, the former by Captain Brooks and Lieutenant S. S. Anderson, 2d artillery, alternately, and the latter by Lieutenant Stone, ordnance. The batteries were traced by Captain Huger and Captain Lee, engineers, and constructed by them, with the able assistance of the young officers of those corps and the artillery.

" To prepare for an assault, it was foreseen that the play of the batteries might run into the second day; but recent captures had not only trebled our siege pieces, but also our ammunition; and we knew that we should greatly augment both, by carrying the place. I was, therefore, in no haste in ordering an assault before the works were well crippled by our missiles.

" The bombardment and cannonade, under the direction of Captain Huger, were commenced early in the morning of the 12th. Before nightfall, which necessarily stopped our batteries, we had perceived that a good impression had been made on the castle and its outworks, and that a large body of the enemy had remained outside, towards the city, from an early hour, to avoid our fire, and to be at hand on its cessation, in order to reinforce the garrison against an assault. The same outside force was discovered the next morning, after our batteries had re-opened upon the castle, by which we again reduced its garrison to the *minimum* needed for the guns.

" Pillow and Quitman had been in position since early in the night of the 11th. Major-General Worth was now ordered to hold his division in reserve, near the foundry, to support Pillow; and

Brigadier-General Smith, of Twiggs' division, had just arrived with his brigade from Piedad, (two miles,) to support Quitman. Twiggs' guns, before the southern gates, again reminded us, as the day before, that he, with Riley's brigade and Taylor's and Steptoe's batteries, was in activity, threatening the southern gates, and there holding a great part of the Mexican army on the defensive.

"Worth's division furnished Pillow's attack with an assaulting party of some two hundred and fifty volunteer officers and men, under Captain McKenzie, of the 2d artillery; and Twiggs' division supplied a similar one, commanded by Captain Casey, 2d infantry, to Quitman. Each of those little columns was furnished with scaling ladders.

"The signal I had appointed for the attack was the momentary cessation of fire on the part of our heavy batteries. About eight o'clock on the morning of the 13th, judging that the time had arrived, by the effect of the missiles we had thrown, I sent an aid-de-camp to Pillow, and another to Quitman, with notice that the concerted signal was about to be given. Both columns now advanced with an alacrity that gave assurance of prompt success. The batteries, seizing opportunities, threw shot and shells upon the enemy over the heads of our men, with good effect, particularly at every attempt to reinforce the works from without to meet our assault.

"Major-General Pillow's approach on the west side lay through an open grove, filled with sharp-shooters, who were speedily dislodged; when, being up with the front of the attack, and emerging into open space, at the foot of a rocky acclivity, that gallant leader was struck down by an agonizing wound. The immediate command devolved on Brigadier-General Cadwalader, in the absence of the senior brigadier (Pierce) of the same division — an invalid since the events of August 19th. On a previous call of Pillow, Worth had just sent him a reinforcement—Colonel Clarke's brigade.

"The broken acclivity was still to be ascended, and a strong redoubt, midway, to be carried before reaching the castle on the heights. The advance of our brave men, led by brave officers, though necessarily slow, was unwavering, over rocks, chasms, and mines, and under the hottest fire of cannon and musketry. The redoubt now yielded to resistless valour, and the shouts that followed announced to the castle the fate that impended. The enemy were steadily driven from shelter to shelter. The retreat allowed not time to fire a single mine, without the certainty of blowing up friend and foe. Those who at a distance attempted to apply matches to the long trains, were shot down by our men. There was death below as well as above ground. At length the ditch and wall of the main work were reached; the scaling ladders were brought up and planted by the storming parties; some of the daring spirits first in the assault were cast down — killed or wounded; but a lodgment was soon made; streams of heroes followed; all opposition was overcome, and several of our regimental colours flung out from the upper walls, amidst long-continued shouts and cheers, which sent dismay into the capital. No scene could have been more animating or glorious.

"Major-General Quitman, nobly supported by Brigadier-Generals Shields and Smith, [P. F.] his other officers and men, was up with the part assigned him. Simultaneously with the movement on the west, he had gallantly approached the south-east of the same works over a causeway with cuts and batteries, and defended by an army strongly posted outside, to the east of the works. Those formidable obstacles Quitman had to face, with but little shelter for his troops or space for manœuvring. Deep ditches, flanking the causeway, made it difficult to cross on either side into the adjoining meadows, and these again were intersected by other ditches. Smith and his brigade had been early thrown out to make a sweep to the right, in order to present a front against the enemy's line, (outside,) and to turn two intervening batteries, near the foot of Chapultepec. This movement was also intended to support Quitman's storming parties, both on the causeway. The first of these, furnished by Twiggs' division, was commanded in succession by Captain Casey, 2d infantry, and Captain Paul, 7th infantry, after Casey had been severely wounded; and the second, originally under the gallant Major Twiggs, marine corps, killed, and then Captain Miller, 2d Pennsylvania volunteers. The storming party, now commanded by Captain Paul, seconded by Captain Roberts of the rifles, Lieutenant Stewart, and others of the same regiment, Smith's brigade, carried the two batteries in the road, took some guns, with many prisoners, and drove the enemy posted behind in support. The New York and the South Carolina volunteers, (Shields' brigade,) and the 2d Pennsylvania volunteers, all on the left of Quitman's line, together with portions of his storming parties, crossed the mea-

FORTRESS OF CHAPULTEPEC.

dows in front, under a heavy fire, and entered the outer enclosure of Chapultepec just in time to join in the final assault from the west.

"Besides Major-Generals Pillow and Quitman, Brigadier-Generals Shields, Smith and Cadwalader, the following are the officers and corps most distinguished in those brilliant operations: The voltigeur regiment, in two detachments, commanded respectively, by Colonel Andrews and Lieutenant-Colonel Johnstone — the latter mostly in the lead, accompanied by Major Caldwell, Captains Barnard and Biddle, of the same regiment—the former the first to plant a regimental colour, and the latter among the first in the assault; — the storming party of Worth's division, under Captain McKenzie, 2d artillery, with Lieutenant Seldon, 8th infantry, early on the ladder and badly wounded; Lieutenant Armistead, 6th infantry, the first to leap into the ditch to plant a ladder; Lieutenants Rodgers of the 4th, and J. P. Smith of the 5th infantry — both mortally wounded—the 9th infantry, under Colonel Ransom, who was killed while gallantly leading that regiment; the 15th infantry under Lieutenant-Colonel Howard and Major Woods, with Captain Chase, whose company gallantly carried the redoubt, midway up the acclivity; Colonel Clarke's brigade, (Worth's division,) consisting of the 5th, 8th, and part of the 6th regiments of infantry, commanded respectively by Captain Chapman, Major Montgomery, and Lieutenant Edward Johnson—the latter specially noticed, with Lieutenants Longstreet, (badly wounded — advancing — colours in hand,) Picket, and Merchant—the last three of the 8th infantry; portions of the United States' marines, New York, South Carolina, and 2d Pennsylvania volunteers, which, delayed with their division (Quitman's) by the hot engagement below, arrived just in time to participate in the assault of the heights—particularly a detachment under Lieutenant Reid, New York volunteers, consisting of a company of the same, with one of marines; and another detachment, a portion of the storming party, (Twiggs' division, serving with Quitman,) under Lieutenant Steel, 2d infantry — after the fall of Lieutenant Gantt, 7th infantry.

"In this connection, it is but just to recall the decisive effect of the heavy batteries, Nos. 1, 2, 3, and 4, commanded by those excellent officers—Captain Drum, 4th artillery, assisted by Lieutenants Benjamin and Porter of his own company; Captain Brooks and Lieu-

6

tenant Anderson, 2d artillery, assisted by Lieutenant Russell, 4th infantry, a volunteer; Lieutenants Hagner and Stone, of the ordnance, and Lieutenant Andrews, 3d artillery—the whole superintended by Captain Huger, chief of ordnance with this army — an officer distinguished by every kind of merit. The mountain howitzer battery under Lieutenant Reno, of the ordnance, deserves also to be particularly mentioned. Attached to the voltigeurs, it followed the movements of that regiment, and again won applause.

"In adding to the list of individuals of conspicuous merit, I must limit myself to a few of the many names which might be enumerated : Captain Hooker, assistant adjutant-general, who won special applause, successively, in the staff of Pillow and Cadwalader ; Lieutenant Lovell, 4th artillery, (wounded,) chief of Quitman's staff; Captain Page, assistant adjutant-general, (wounded,) and Lieutenant Hammond, 3d artillery, both of Shields' staff, and Lieutenant Van Dorn, (7th infantry,) aid-de-camp to Brigadier-General Smith.

"Those operations all occurred on the west, south-east, and heights of Chapultepec. To the north, and at the base of the mound, inaccessible on that side, the 11th infantry, under Lieutenant Colonel Herbert, the 14th under Colonel Trousdale, and Captain Magruder's field battery, 1st artillery—one section advanced under Lieutenant Jackson—all of Pillow's division—had, at the same time, some spirited affairs against superior numbers, driving the enemy from a battery on the road, and capturing a gun. In these, the officers and corps named gained merited praise. Colonel Trousdale, the commander, though twice wounded, continued on duty until the heights were carried.

"Early on the morning of the 13th, I repeated the orders of the night before to Major-General Worth, to be, with his division, at hand, to support the movement of Major-General Pillow from our left. The latter seems soon to have called for that entire division, standing, momentarily, in reserve, and Worth sent him Colonel Clarke's brigade. The call, if not unnecessary, was, at least, from the circumstances, unknown to me at the time ; for, soon observing that the very large body of the enemy in the road in front of Major-General Quitman's right, was receiving reinforcements from the city—less than a mile and a half to the east—I sent instructions to Worth, on our opposite flank, to turn Chapultepec with his division, and to proceed cautiously, by the road at its northern base, in order, if not met by very superior numbers, to threaten or to attack, in rear, that body of the enemy. The movement, it was also believed, could not fail to distract and to intimidate the enemy generally.

"Worth promptly advanced with his remaining brigade—Colonel Garland's—Lieutenant-Colonel C. F. Smith's light battalion, Lieutenant-Colonel Duncan's field-battery—all of his division—and three squadrons of dragoons under Major Sumner, which I had just ordered up to join in the movement.

"Having turned the forest on the west, and arriving opposite to the north centre of Chapultepec, Worth came up with the troops in the road, under Colonel Trousdale, and aided by a flank movement of a part of Garland's brigade, in taking the one-gun breastwork, then under the fire of Lieutenant Jackson's section of Captain Magruder's field battery. Continuing to advance, this division passed Chapultepec, attacking the right of the enemy's line, resting on that road, about the moment of the general retreat, consequent upon the capture of the formidable castle and its outworks.

"Arriving some minutes later, and mounting to the top of the castle, the whole field to the east lay plainly under my view.

"There are two routes from Chapultepec to the capital, the one on the right entering the same gate, Belen, with the road from the south via Piedad; and the other obliquing to the left, to intersect the great western or San Cosme road, in a suburb outside the gate of San Cosme.

"Each of these routes (an elevated causeway) presents a double roadway, on the sides of an aqueduct of strong masonry and great height, resting on open arches and massive pillars, which together afford fine points both for attack and defence. The sideways of both aqueducts are, moreover, defended by many strong breastworks, at the gates, and before reaching them. As we had expected, we found the four tracks unusually dry and solid for the season.

"Worth and Quitman were prompt in pursuing the retreating enemy — the former by the San Cosme aqueduct, and the latter along that of Belen. Each had now advanced some hundred yards.

"Deeming it all-important to profit by our successes, and the consequent dismay of the enemy, which could not be otherwise than general, I hastened to despatch from Chapultepec — first Clarke's brigade, and then Cadwalader's, to the support of Worth, and gave orders that the necessary heavy guns should follow. Pierce's brigade was, at the same time, sent to Quitman, and, in the course of the afternoon, I caused some additional siege pieces to be added to his train. Then, after designating the 15th infantry, under Lieutenant-Colonel Howard—Morgan, the colonel, had been disabled by a wound at Churubusco — as the garrison of Chapultepec, and giving directions for the care of the prisoners of war, the captured ordnance and ordnance stores, I proceeded to join the advance of Worth ; within the suburb, and beyond the turn at the junction of the aqueduct with the great highway from the west to the gate of San Cosme.

" At this junction of roads we first passed one of those formidable systems of city defences spoken of above, and it had not a gun !—a strong proof — 1. That the enemy had expected us to fail in the attack upon Chapultepec, even if we meant any thing more than a feint ; 2. That, in either case, we designed, in his belief, to return and double our forces against the southern gates — a delusion kept up by the active demonstrations of Twiggs and the forces posted on that side ; and 3. That advancing rapidly from the reduction of Chapultepec, the enemy had not time to shift guns — our previous captures had left him, comparatively, but few — from the southern gates.

" Within those disgarnished works I found our troops engaged in a street-fight against the enemy, posted in gardens, at windows and on house-tops—all flat, with parapets. Worth ordered forward the mountain howitzers of Cadwalader's brigade, preceded by skirmishers and pioneers, with pick-axes and crow-bars, to force windows and doors, or to burrow through walls. The assailants were soon in an equality of position fatal to the enemy. By eight o'clock in the evening, Worth had carried two batteries in this suburb. According to my instructions, he here posted guards and sentinels, and placed his troops under shelter for the night. There was but one more obstacle — the San Cosme gate (custom-house) between him and the great square in front of the cathedral and palace—the heart of the city ; and that barrier, it was known, could not, by daylight, resist our siege guns thirty minutes.

"I had gone back to the foot of Chapultepec, the point from which the two aqueducts begin to diverge, some hours earlier, in order to be near that new depot, and in easy communication with Quitman and Twiggs as well as with Worth.

" From this point I ordered all detachments and stragglers to their respective corps, then in advance ; sent to Quitman additional siege guns, ammunition, entrenching tools; directed Twiggs' remaining brigade (Riley's) from Piedad, to support Worth, and Captain Steptoe's field battery, also at Piedad, to rejoin Quitman's division.

" I had been, from the first, well aware that the western, or San Cosme, was the less difficult route to the centre and conquest of the capital ; and therefore intended that Quitman should only manœuvre and threaten the Belen or southwestern gate, in order to favour the main attack by Worth—knowing that the strong defences at the Belen were directly under the guns of the much stronger fortress, called the Citadel, just within. Both of these defences of the enemy were also within easy supporting distances from the San Angel (or Nino Perdido) and San Antonio gates. Hence the greater support, in numbers, given to Worth's movement as the *main* attack.

" Those views I repeatedly, in the course of the day, communicated to Major-General Quitman ; but, being in hot pursuit—gallant himself, and ably supported by Brigadier-Generals Shields and Smith—Shields badly wounded before Chapultepec, and refusing to retire—as well as by all the officers and men of the column—Quitman continued to press forward, under flank and direct fires—carried an intermediate battery of two guns, and then the gate, before two o'clock in the afternoon, but not without proportionate loss, increased by his steady maintenance of that position.

" Here, of the heavy battery—4th artillery—Captain Drum and Lieutenant Benjamin were mortally wounded, and Lieutenant Porter, its third in rank, slightly. The loss of those two most distinguished officers the army will long mourn. Lieutenants J. B. Moragne and William Canty, of the South Carolina volunteers, also of high merit, fell on the same occasion — besides many of our bravest non-commissioned officers and men—particularly in Captain Drum's veteran company. I cannot, in this place, give names or numbers, but full returns of the killed and wounded of all corps in their recent operations, will accompany this report.

" Quitman, within the city—adding several new defences to the position he had won, and sheltering his corps as well as practicable

6 *   G

—now awaited the return of daylight under the guns of the formidable citadel, yet to be subdued.

"At about four o'clock next morning, (September 14,) a deputation of the *ayuntamiento* (city council) waited upon me to report
that the federal government and the army of Mexico had fled from
the capital some three hours before, and to demand terms of capitulation in favour of the church, the citizens, and the municipal authorities. I promptly replied that I would sign no capitulation ;
that the city had been virtually in our possession from the time of
the lodgements effected by Worth and Quitman the day before ;
that I regretted the silent escape of the Mexican army ; that I should
levy a moderate contribution, for special purposes ; and that the
American army should come under no terms, not self-imposed—
such only as its own honour, the dignity of the United States, and
the spirit of the age, should, in my opinion, imperiously demand
and impose.

*   *   *   *   *   *   *   *   *   *   *   *

"At the termination of the interview with the city deputation, I
communicated, about daylight, orders to Worth and Quitman to advance slowly and cautiously (to guard against treachery) towards
the heart of the city, and to occupy its stronger and more commanding points. Quitman proceeded to the great plaza or square, planted
guards, and hoisted the colours of the United States on the national
palace—containing the halls of Congress and executive departments
of federal Mexico. In this grateful service, Quitman might have
been anticipated by Worth, but for my express orders, halting the
latter at the head of the Alemeda, (a green park,) within three
squares of that goal of general ambition. The capital, however,
was not taken by any one or two corps, but by the talent, the science,
the gallantry, the prowess of this entire army. In the glorious conquest, all had contributed—early and powerfully—the killed, the
wounded, and the fit for duty—at Vera Cruz, Sierra Gordo, Contreros, San Antonio, Churubusco, (three battles,) the Molinos del
Rey, and Chapultepec—as much as those who fought at the gates
of Belen and San Cosme.

"Soon after we had entered, and were in the act of occupying
the city, a fire was opened on us from the flat roofs of the houses, from
windows and corners of streets, by some two thousand convicts,
liberated the night before by the flying government—joined by per-

haps as many Mexican soldiers, who had disbanded themselves and thrown off their uniforms. This unlawful war lasted more than twenty-four hours, in spite of the exertions of the municipal authorities, and was not put down until we had lost many men, including several officers, killed or wounded, and had punished the miscreants. Their objects were, to gratify national hatred; and, in the general alarm and confusion, to plunder the wealthy inhabitants—particularly the deserted houses. But families are now generally returning; business of every kind has been resumed, and the city is already tranquil and cheerful, under the admirable conduct (with exceptions very few and trifling) of our gallant troops.

"This army has been more disgusted than surprised that, by some sinister process on the part of certain individuals at home, its numbers have been generally almost trebled in our public papers—beginning at Washington.

"Leaving, as we all feared, inadequate garrisons at Vera Cruz, Perote, and Puebla, with much larger hospitals; and being obliged, most reluctantly, from the same cause, (general paucity of numbers,) to abandon Jalapa, we marched [August 7–10] from Puebla, with only ten thousand seven hundred and thirty-eight, rank and file. This number includes the garrison of Jalapa, and the two thousand four hundred and twenty-nine men brought up by Brigadier-General Pierce, August 6.

"At Contreros, Churubusco, &c., [August 20,] we had but eight thousand four hundred and ninety-seven men engaged—after deducting the garrison of San Augustin, (our general depôt,) the intermediate sick and the dead; at the Molinos del Rey [September 8] but three brigades, with some cavalry and artillery—making in all three thousand two hundred and fifty-one men—were in the battle; in the two days [September 12 and 13] our whole operating force, after deducting, again, the recent killed, wounded, and sick, together with the garrison of Miscoac (the then general depôt) and that of Tacubaya, was but seven thousand one hundred and eighty; and, finally, after deducting the new garrison of Chapultepec, with the killed and wounded of the two days, we took possession, September 14, of this great capital, with less than six thousand men! And I re-assert, upon accumulated and unquestionable evidence, that, in not one of those conflicts, was this army opposed by fewer than three and a half times its numbers—in several of them by a still greater excess.

" I recapitulate our losses since we arrived in the basin of Mexico.

" AUGUST 19, 20.—*Killed*, 137, including 14 officers. *Wounded*, 877, including 62 officers. *Missing*, (probably killed,) 38 rank and file. Total, 1,052.

" SEPTEMBER 8.—*Killed*, 116, including 9 officers. *Wounded*, 665, including 49 officers. *Missing*, 18 rank and file. Total, 862.

" SEPTEMBER 12, 13, 14.—*Killed*, 130, including 10 officers. *Wounded*, 703, including 68 officers. *Missing*, 20 rank and file. Total, 862.

" Grand total of losses, 2,703, including 383 officers.

" On the other hand, this small force has beaten on the same occasions, in view of their capital, the whole Mexican army, of (at the beginning) thirty-odd thousand men—posted, always, in chosen positions, behind entrenchments, or more formidable defences of nature and art ; killed or wounded, of that number, more than seven thousand officers and men ; taken three thousand seven hundred and thirty prisoners, one-seventh officers, including thirteen generals, of whom three had been presidents of this republic ; captured more than twenty colours and standards, seventy-five pieces of ordnance, besides fifty-seven wall pieces, twenty thousand small arms, an immense quantity of shot, shells, powder, &c. &c.

" Of that enemy, once so formidable in numbers, appointments, artillery, &c., twenty-odd thousand have disbanded themselves in despair, leaving, as is known, not more than three fragments, the largest about two thousand five hundred—now wandering in different directions, without magazines or a military chest, and living *at free quarters* upon their own people.

" General Santa Anna, himself a fugitive, is believed to be on the point of resigning the chief magistracy, and escaping to neutral Guatemala. A new president, no doubt, will soon be declared, and the federal Congress is expected to re-assemble at Queretaro, one hundred and twenty-five miles north of this, on the Zacatecas road, some time in October. 1 have seen and given safe conduct through this city, to several of its members. The government will find itself without resources ; no army, no arsenal, no magazines, and but little revenue, internal or external. Still, such is the obstinacy, or rather infatuation, of this people, that it is very doubtful whether the new authorities will dare to sue for peace on terms which, in the recent negotiations, were made known by our Minister.   *   *   *

"In conclusion, I beg to enumerate, once more, with due commendation and thanks, the distinguished staff officers, general and personal, who, in our last operations in front of the enemy, accompanied me, and communicated orders to every point and through every danger. Lieutenant-Colonel Hitchcock, acting inspector-general; Major Turnbull and Lieutenant Hardcastle, topographical engineers; Major Kirby, chief paymaster; Captain Irwin, chief quartermaster; Captain Grayson, chief commissary; Captain H. L. Scott, in the adjutant-general's department; Lieutenant Williams, aid-de-camp; Lieutenant Lay, military secretary, and Major J. P. Gaines, Kentucky cavalry, volunteer aid-de-camp. Captain Lee, engineer, so constantly distinguished, also bore important orders from me (September 13) until he fainted from a wound and the loss of two nights' sleep at the batteries.

"Lieutenants Beauregard, Stephens, and Tower, all wounded, were employed with the divisions, and Lieutenants G. W. Smith and G. B. McClellan with the company of sappers and miners. Those five lieutenants of engineers, like their captain, won the admiration of all about them. The ordnance officers, Captain Huger, Lieutenants Hagner, Stone, and Reno, were highly effective, and distinguished at the several batteries; and I must add that Captain McKinstry, assistant quartermaster, at the close of the operations, executed several important commissions for me as a special volunteer.

"Surgeon-General Lawson, and the medical staff generally, were skilful and untiring in and out of fire in ministering to the numerous wounded."

The city of Mexico is thus described in Murray's Encyclopedia of Geography :—

"The state of Mexico comprises the valley of Mexico, a fine and splendid region, variegated by extensive lakes, and surrounded by some of the loftiest volcanic peaks of the new world. Its circumference is about two hundred miles, and it forms the very centre of the great table-land of Anahuac, elevated from six to eight thousand feet above the level of the sea. In the centre of this valley stands the city of Mexico; the ancient Mexico, or Tenochtitlan, having been built in the middle of a lake, and connected with the continent

by extensive causeways or dykes. The new Mexico is three miles
from the lake of Tezcuco, and nearly six from that of Chalco; yet
Humboldt considers it certain, from the remains of the ancient
teocalli, or temples, that it occupies the identical position of the former city, and that a great part of the waters of the valley have been
dried up. Mexico was long considered the largest city of America;
but it is now surpassed by New York, perhaps even by Rio Janeiro.
Some estimates have raised its population to two hundred thousand;
but it may, on good grounds, be fixed at from one hundred and
twenty to one hundred and forty thousand. It is beyond dispute
the most splendid. 'Mexico is undoubtedly one of the finest cities
built by Europeans in either hemisphere; with the exception of St.
Petersburgh, Berlin, and Philadelphia, and some quarters of West-
minster, there does not exist a city of the same extent which can be
compared to the capital of New Spain, for the uniform level of the
ground on which it stands, for the regularity and breadth of the
streets, and the extent of the squares and public places. The architecture is generally of a very pure style, and there are even edifices
of a very beautiful structure.' The palace of the late viceroys, the
cathedral, built in what is termed the Gothic style, several of the
convents, and some private palaces, reared upon plans furnished by
the pupils of the Academy of the Fine Arts, are of great extent and
magnificence; yet, upon the whole, it is rather the arrangement,
regularity, and general effect of the city which render it so striking.
Nothing in particular can be more enchanting than the view of the
city and the valley from the surrounding heights. The eye sweeps
over a vast extent of cultivated fields to the very base of the colossal
mountains, covered with perpetual snow. The city appears as if
washed by the waters of the lake of Tezcuco, which, surrounded by
villages and hamlets, resembles the most beautiful of the Swiss lakes;
and the rich cultivation of the vicinity forms a striking contrast with
the naked mountains. Among these rise the famous volcano Popo-
catepetl and the mountain of Iztaccihuatl, of which the first, an enormous cone, burns occasionally, throwing up smoke and ashes in
the midst of eternal snows. The police of the city is excellent; most
of the streets are handsomely paved, lighted, and cleansed. The
annual consumption in Mexico has been computed at sixteen thousand three hundred beeves; two hundred and seventy-nine thousand
sheep; fifty thousand hogs; one million six hundred thousand fowls,

including ducks and turkeys; two hundred and five thousand pigeons and partridges. The markets are remarkably well supplied with animal and vegetable productions, brought by crowds of canoes along the lake of Chalco, and the canal leading to it. These canoes are often guided by females, who at the same time are weaving cotton in their simple portable looms, or plucking fowls, and throwing the feathers into the water. Most of the flowers and roots have been raised in *chinampas*, or floating gardens, an invention peculiar to the new world. They consist of rafts formed of reeds, roots, and bushes, and covered with black saline mould, which, being irrigated by the water of the lake, becomes exceedingly fertile. It is a great disadvantage to Mexico, however, that it stands nearly on a level with the surrounding lake; which, in seasons of heavy rain, overwhelms it with destructive inundations. The construction of a *desague*, or canal, to carry off the waters of the lake of Zumpango, and of the principal river by which it is fed, has, since 1629, prevented any very desolating flood. The desague, though not conducted with skill and judgment, cost five millions of dollars, and is one of the most stupendous hydraulic works ever executed. Were it filled with water, the largest vessels of war might pass by it through the range of mountains which bound the plain of Mexico. The alarms, however, have been frequent, and cannot well cease, while the level of that lake is twenty feet above that of the great square of Mexico."

The New Orleans Picayune gives the following description of the fortifications around the Mexican capital:—

" Much as has already been said, our people even up to this time have but an imperfect idea of the immense superiority of force General Scott's little army had to contend with in the valley of Mexico. Some weeks since one of the editors of this paper, writing fron the seat of war, attempted to draw a parallel between the deeds of the early Spaniards and those of our own gallant soldiers; but at the time he did not know the full strength of the Mexican works and fortifications, all completed previous to the noted 13th September, and ready to repel the onslaughts of the comparatively insignificant band of invaders. From a statement by Captain Lee, one of the best engineers in the American or any other service, it would seem that the Mexicans had at the

Penon	- - - 20 batteries,	for	51 guns,	and	15 inf. breastworks.
Mexicalcingo	- 8 "	38 "	"	1 "	"
San Antonio	- 7 "	24 "	"	2 "	"
Churubusco	- 2 "	15 "	"	— "	"
Contreros	- 1 "	22 "	"	— "	"
Chapultepec	- 7 "	19 "	"	7 "	"
Total,	45	169		25	

"These were the outer works, admirably well situated for defence, and presenting a most formidable appearance to those who were compelled to attack them from causeways, marshes, and open plains. The works at El Molino, including the battery and the lines of infantry intrenchments and strong buildings, are not enumerated in the above. Immediately around the city of Mexico, independent of the innumerable ditches — these ditches filled with water, generally twenty-five feet wide and five feet deep, whose banks formed natural parapets — there were forty-seven additional batteries, prepared like the others for one hundred and seventy-seven guns, and with seventeen infantry breastworks. Adding these to the above, and we have on all the lines defending the approaches to the city no less than ninety-two batteries, prepared for three hundred and forty-six guns, and forty-two infantry breastworks! When it is added that to all these works—and our own engineers were forcibly struck with the admirable style in which all the batteries of the enemy were constructed—that the city of Mexico was naturally defended by canals, houses of solid and heavy masonry, mud ditches, water, &c. &c.; that all the buildings have flat roofs with solid parapets; that the convents and many other public edifices are but so many fortifications—when all these circumstances are taken into consideration, with the immense numerical superiority of the Mexicans, the achievements of the invaders will appear almost incredible.

"The science of engineering is probably as well understood by the Mexicans as by any of the European nations, as an examination of their works will at once prove, while their artillery practice is most effective; yet all availed them nothing against the bold and steady advance of the Americans. The sanguinary battle of El Molino, costly as it was to General Worth's division, was appallingly disastrous to the enemy, as there his two best infantry regiments, the

11th and 12th of the line, were utterly annihilated. From that day until the capital was entered, comparatively speaking, our army suffered but little from the musketry of the enemy, his cannon doing nearly all the execution. General Quitman's advance upon the Garita of Belen, one of the most daring deeds of the war, was through an avenue of blood caused by the grape, canister and round shot of the Mexican cannon ; while the streets of San Cosme, through which the remnant of General Worth's division was compelled to advance, was literally swept by the heavy cannon and wall pieces at the garita of the same name. The infantry firing around the base of Chapultepec was as nothing compared with the incessant tornado of bullets which rattled amid the ranks of our columns as they advanced upon Churubusco and the Molino del Rey.

"And who constructed the batteries and breastworks around the capital of Mexico? Men, women, and children, as by a common impulse, were busy night and day, and even ladies of the higher class are said to have been liberal in their toil in adding to the common defence. Works complete in every part sprung up, as if by magic ; the morning light would dawn upon some well-barricaded approach, which the night before was apparently open to the advance of armed men. From the outposts of the Americans, at any time between the 8th and 12th September, thousands and thousands of the enemy could be seen, spade and mattock in hand, strengthening old and forming new barriers, and the busy hum of labour reached our sentinels even during the still hours of the night, as fresh guns were placed in position, or new avenues of approach were closed against the invaders. Yet all would not do. The Mexicans had not the stern courage to defend the works they had constructed with such zeal and care, and one after another fell before the unflinching bravery of men who had but victory or death before them."

The Hartford Times thus speaks of General Scott's campaign in Mexico : —

"It seems to us that the merit of General Scott, in gaining the late astounding victories before Mexico, has not as yet received its fitting tribute from the public press. His political opinions must necessarily ever debar him from receiving the suffrages of the Democratic party for the chief magistracy of the Union. But this circumstance cannot prevent us from seeing that this great soldier has

7

deserved exceedingly well of the Republic, and acquired a very strong title to the fervent gratitude of his countrymen. Perhaps, indeed, to a man whose hairs are already silvered in the service of his country, the due appreciation and acknowledgment of that service may prove a more acceptable reward than the highest office that could be conferred upon him. At all events, the least that can be done is to award just honour and praise, in no stinted or niggardly measure, to those who have no other remuneration to expect for their brave deeds. The battles of Contreros and Churubusco certainly rank among the most brilliant military achievements of the age. A little band of eleven thousand audacious invaders have defeated, with immense slaughter, an army of thirty thousand troops, drawn up in a position of their own choosing, on their own soil, to defend their altars and hearths, in the very heart of their country. But it was not alone the indomitable valour of our troops which distinguished these battles. They were to an equal degree marked with all the skill, science, and foresight of a masterly strategy.

"In turning the rocky and almost impregnable passes of Penon and Mexicalcingo, fortified with terrific batteries, upon which the enemy had expended the labour of months, General Scott displayed the most consummate generalship. It was not the mere avoiding or evading these formidable posts which constituted its merit. It was, that his cool and practised eye discerned at a glance that a passage could be cut through dense forests and tangled defiles, and heaps of huge rock, where the enemy never dreamed that such an exploit was conceivable. It was a repetition of the same skilful outflanking manœuvre by which he had before spared so much valuable life at Sierra Gordo — a movement which rendered all the laborious preparations and defences of the enemy useless, and which Santa Anna himself pronounced to be masterly and worthy of Napoleon. It has been the crowning merit of Scott, that, while he has been everywhere victorious, he has also everywhere husbanded his forces. Daring and intrepid to the last degree where those qualities were called for, he has at the same time been careful never wantonly to waste the lives of his troops in unnecessary stormings or reckless assaults. Under almost any other general, his mere handful of troops would long since have melted away from repeated collisions with inert but overwhelming masses. With a humanity not less conspicuous than his bravery, Scott has always abstained from any indiscriminate slaughter even of a sanguinary and merciless foe. * * * It was a great thing to have mastered the renowned fortress of San Juan de Ulloa—a second Gibraltar—with so trifling a loss of life. The victory over Santa Anna at Sierra Gordo, in the manner as well as in the magnitude of the achievement, was a daring and masterly exploit. It was also a great thing—a sight, in fact, full of moral grandeur—when four thousand two hundred tattered and wayworn soldiers under his command entered the magnificent city of Puebla, and, with all the confidence of conquerors, stacked their arms and laid themselves down to sleep in the great square, surrounded by a hostile population of eighty thousand.

"But, last of all, and more admirable than all, has been the care with which he has nursed and kept together his little band of eleven thousand, and the almost fabulous audacity and still more incredible success with which he has pushed them, step by step, to the very heart of a civilized nation of seven millions, and to the gates of a capital of two hundred thousand souls, the renowned seat of a legendary and mythic magnificence, and the most ancient and best-built city on the continent. If modern warfare has any parallel for this great feat of arms, we know not where to look for it.

"The successive triumphs of Vera Cruz, of Sierra Gordo, of Puebla, and of Mexico, undimmed as they have hitherto been by a single reverse, have unquestionably raised the reputation of the commander to a very great height, and placed it, to say the least, fully on a level with that of the greatest generals of his time. Nor is there any denying that those victories have been of such an order that, while they elevate the successful leader, they also, to at least an equal degree, exalt the character and extend the renown of his country. Hence we cannot bring ourselves to make any apology for what appears to us a just notice of General Scott, on the score of his being a Whig. A sense of gratitude for his distinguished services in this war would not permit us to say less. The fame of a victorious general cannot justly be held to belong to any party. It is the property of the whole nation."

The Baltimore American of October 22d, says:—

"The records of the gallant achievements of our troops in Mexico add new lustre to the martial history of the Republic. From the landing at Vera Cruz, to the entrance of our army into the city of Mexico, a series of brilliant exploits has marked every step of their

H

way. If the retreat of Xenophon, with ten thousand men, from the heart of an enemy's country, is regarded with admiration, and mentioned in history as one of those extraordinary things which genius and enterprise can accomplish when favoured by fortune, what must be said of the advance of an army little exceeding ten thousand into the valley of Mexico, into the capital of the enemy's country, three hundred miles from the coast, storming its way as it marched, defeating armies far exceeding it in numbers, and entrenched in strong fortifications, and holding its position victoriously in a city of one hundred and eighty thousand inhabitants, in the midst of a dense and hostile population around ?

" The army which has done this is composed, too, in part of volunteer soldiers who have seen service for the first time—of men who hurried from the peaceful avocations of life to encounter the perils and hardships of war, with no preparation, no habitual discipline, expecting to receive their first lessons in military affairs upon the field of battle. Noble scholars indeed have they proved themselves to be! The soldiers of one campaign, they are veterans already, able to cope with the veterans of any service.

" The masterly generalship of the commander-in-chief has exhibited the most admirable combinations of discretion and daring throughout this whole career of bold invasion, of determined perseverance and heroic achievements. The laurels of Chippewa, which crowned the youthful brow of Scott, are renewed and freshened by those plucked from the battle-fields of Mexico. Long may they flourish in the brightness of their verdure !

" The forbearance of General Scott when he entered the city of Mexico, as testified to by the letters of resident foreigners who had witnessed the sacking of European cities when entered by an excited and victorious soldiery, is a characteristic of the most exalted kind, reflecting unspeakable honour upon the commander who ordered, and upon the troops that obeyed such directions of forbearance at such a moment. The evidence is direct, that no houses were molested, except those from which shots were fired upon our men.

" The country has reason to be proud indeed of this brave little army, of its eminent general, of its noble and accomplished officers. Worthily have they sustained the American name ; gloriously have they exalted its martial renown in the eyes of the world. It is now for the country to sustain them, to strengthen that gallant band, to uphold them in that distant and hostile land upon which they have enstamped the impress of American valour, and displayed victory on the folds of the national flag."

Such has been the career of Major-General Scott up to the present time. Beginning his military course at Chippewa, he attained, during the late war, a renown for bravery, skill, and generalship, as flattering as it was singular; and his recent unparalleled campaign in Mexico has confirmed all former opinion of his merits, proven his efficiency in planning and executing a series of protracted operations, and placed him before the world as one of the ablest generals of his age.

7*

MAJOR-GENERAL PILLOW.

MAJOR-GENERAL GIDEON J. PILLOW, although well-tried in the glorious campaign under Scott, has but recently entered the army. His commission bears date April 13th, 1847, but he assisted in the bombardment of Vera Cruz. He was born in Tennessee, and entered the army from that state.

At Vera Cruz, Pillow was employed in extending the American line, in order completely to invest the city. He frequently encountered parties of the enemy, with whom he had some slight skirmishes, in one of which several of his men were wounded. He took an active part in the siege, and was one of the commissioners to negotiate the capitulation.

At Sierra Gordo, Pillow attacked a fort to the left of the main work, in which was a large Mexican force under General La Vega. He had carefully reconnoitred this station, and led his troops to the assault in the face of a galling fire. La Vega, however, defended himself with an obstinacy worthy of the fame he had acquired on the Rio Grande, and the Americans were obliged to fall back. A second attempt was attended with similar results. While chagrined with this unavoidable repulse, Pillow was gratified to learn that he had held the Mexicans long enough employed to prevent their succouring Santa Anna's forces, whose capture had, consequently, been much accelerated. On perceiving that the battle was lost, General La Vega surrendered.

General Pillow has borne his full share in the recent operations before the capital. His services in the first series of operations are related in the following extracts from his own report:

"In compliance with the order of the general-in-chief, I moved with my division, consisting of the 9th, 11th, 12th, 14th and 15th

(78)

GENERAL PILLOW.

Page 78.

infantry, the voltigeur regiment, the field battery of Captain Magruder, and the howitzer battery under Lieutenant Callender, early on the morning of the 19th instant, and opened the road over the mountain on the route indicated by Captain Lee, of the engineer corps, assisted by Lieutenants Beauregard, Stephens, Tower, Smith, McClelland, and Foster. Brigadier-General Twiggs, with his division, reported to me for duty, under instructions from the general-in-chief, whilst my own division was moving over the mountain.

"Perceiving that the enemy was in large force on the opposite side of the valley, with heavy batteries of artillery commanding the only road through a vast plain of broken volcanic stone and lava, rent into deep chasms and fissures, effectually preventing any advance except under his direct fire, I resolved to give him battle. For this purpose, I ordered General Twiggs to advance with his finely-disciplined division, and with one brigade to assault the enemy's works in front, and with the other to turn his left flank, and assail it in reverse. Captain Magruder's fine field battery and Lieutenant Callender's howitzer battery (both of which constitute part of my division) were placed at the disposal of Brigadier-General Twiggs.

"This officer, in executing my order of attack, directed Brevet Brigadier-General Smith to move with his brigade upon the enemy's front, whilst Colonel Riley, with his, was ordered to turn his left, and assail him in rear. To sustain these movements, Brigadier-General Cadwalader was ordered to advance with his brigade and support Colonel Riley, and Brigadier-General Pierce, with his command, to support the column moving upon the enemy's front, under Brigadier-General Smith. This last command was soon closely engaged with the enemy, as were also the batteries of Captain Magruder and Lieutenant Callender.

"Colonel Riley's command, having now crossed the vast, broken-up plain of lava, passing the village on the right, and whilst in the act of turning the enemy's left, was confronted by several thousand lancers, who advanced to the charge, when a well-directed fire from the brigade twice compelled them to fall back in disorder, under cover of their artillery. About this time Brigadier-General Cadwalader's command had also crossed the plain, when some five or six thousand troops of the enemy were observed moving rapidly from the direction of the capital to the field of action. Colonel

Morgan, with his large and fine regiment, which I had caused to be detached from the rear of Pierce's brigade, was now ordered to the support of Cadwalader, by direction of the general-in chief, who had now arrived upon the field.

" The general, having discovered this large force moving upon his right flank and to the rear, with decided military tact and promptitude threw back his right wing and confronted the enemy, with the intention to give him battle, notwithstanding his overwhelming force.

" This portion of the enemy's force moved steadily forward until a conflict seemed inevitable, when Colonel Morgan's regiment, having reached this part of the field, presented a front so formidable as to induce the enemy to change his purpose, and draw off to the right and rear of his former position.

" During all this time, the battle raged fiercely between the other portions of the two armies, with a constant and destructive fire of artillery. Magruder's battery, from its prominent position, was much disabled by the heavy shot of the enemy, as were also Callender's howitzers. A part of the enemy's artillery had been turned upon Riley's command, whilst actively engaged with large bodies of lancers; but even these combined attacks could only delay the purpose of the gallant old veteran and his noble brigade.

" The battle all this day was conducted under my immediate orders, and within my view; a short time before sunset, having previously engaged in the fight all the forces at my disposal, myself and staff started to cross the plain, to join in the terrible struggle on the immediate field of action.

" The battle being won before the advancing brigades of Worth's and Quitman's divisions were in sight, both were ordered back to their late positions — Worth, to attack San Antonio, in front, with his whole force, as soon as approached in the rear by Pillow's and Twiggs' divisions—moving from Contreros, through San Angel and Coyoacan. By carrying San Antonio, we knew that we should open another—a shorter and better road to the capital—for our siege and other trains.

" On my way thither, I was joined by Brigadier-General Twiggs and staff; but the darkness of the night, rendered still more obscure by a heavy rain, caused us to miss our way through the broken-up lava, and to wander to the close neighbourhood of the works of the enemy ; and it was not until the shrill blasts of his bugles apprized us of our position, that we became satisfied we could not reach, during the night, our destination. We then returned, and reported to the general-in-chief.

" During the night, Brigadier-General Smith disposed the forces present, to renew the action at daylight, and complete the original order of attack. Before dark, however, the enemy had placed two pieces of artillery on a height nearly west of Cadwalader's position, which had opened with several discharges upon his forces. Brigadier-General Smith, just before daylight, moved a portion of the forces up the ravine to the rear of the enemy's position, so as to be within easy turning distance of his left flank—leaving Colonel Ransom with the 9th and 12th infantry to make a strong diversion in front. The day being sufficiently advanced, the order was given by Brigadier-General Smith for the general assault; when, General Smith's command upon the left, and Colonel Riley with his brigade upon the right, supported by General Cadwalader, with his command, moved up with the utmost gallantry, under the furious fire from the enemy's batteries, which were immediately carried ; a large number of prisoners were taken, including four generals, with twenty-three out of the twenty-eight pieces of artillery, and a large amount of ammunition and public property.

" The retreating enemy was compelled to pass through a severe fire, both from the assaulting forces and Cadwalader's brigade, as well as Shields' command, who had remained at the position occupied by the former general the previous night, with the purpose of covering the movement upon the battery. The forces of the enemy engaged at this place, including the reinforcements of the preceding evening, constituted a force of about sixteen thousand men, five thousand of whom were cavalry ; the whole were under the immediate command of General Santa Anna in person, assisted by Generals Valencia, Salas, Blanco, Mendoza, Garcia and others ; the last four mentioned were taken prisoners.

" Our forces, consisting of my division, Generals Twiggs' and Shields' commands, amounted to about four thousand five hundred men. The loss of the enemy, as nearly as I can ascertain, was between fifteen hundred and two thousand men killed and wounded, and eight hundred prisoners, including the four generals previously

mentioned, four colonels, thirty captains, and many officers of infe-
rior grades.   *   *   *   *   *   *   *   *

"Having myself crossed the plain and reached this bloody theatre
as the last scene of the conflict was closing, as soon as suitable dispositions were made to secure the fruits of the victory, I resolved upon
pursuing the discomfited enemy, in which I found that Brigadier-
Generals Twiggs and Smith had already anticipated me by having
commenced the movement. At the same time, I apprized the general-in-chief of my advance, requesting his authority to proceed
with all the forces still under my command, sweeping around the
valley, attack the strong works of San Antonio in rear; and requested the co-operation of General Worth's division, by an assault
upon that work in front; which the general-in-chief readily granted
and directed accordingly—having, as I learn, upon being advised of
the victory, previously given the order. I had moved rapidly forward in execution of this purpose, until I reached the town Coyoacan,
where the command was halted to await the arrival of the general-
in-chief, who I was informed was close at hand. Upon his arrival,
the important fact was ascertained, that the enemy's forces at San
Antonio having perceived that the great battery had been lost, and
the total defeat and rout of their forces at Contreros, by which their
rear was opened to assault, had abandoned the work at San Antonio,
and fallen back upon their strong entrenchments in rear at Churubusco.

"Upon the receipt of this information, the general-in-chief immediately ordered Brigadier-General Twiggs's division to move forward
and attack the work on the enemy's right, and directed me to move
with Cadwalader's brigade, and assault the tête du pont on its left.
Moving rapidly in execution of this order, I had great difficulty in
passing the command over some marshy fields, and wide and deep
ditches, filled with mud and water. I was compelled to dismount
in order to cross these obstacles, which were gallantly overcome by
the troops, when the whole force gained the main causeway; at
which place I met General Worth, with the advance of his division,
moving upon the same work. It was then proposed that our united
divisions should move on to the assault of the strong tête du pont,
which, with its heavy artillery, enfiladed the causeway. This being
determined upon, the troops of the two divisions moved rapidly to
attack the work on its left flank, and, notwithstanding the deadly fire

of grape and round-shot from the work, which swept the roadway with furious violence, on and onward these gallant and noble troops moved with impetuous valour, and terrible and long was the bloody conflict. But the result could not be doubted. At length the loud and enthusiastic cheer of the Anglo-Saxon soldier told that all was well, and the American colours moved in triumph over the bloody scene." General Pillow, as we have seen, was concerned in the storming of Chapultepec. On the 14th, he entered with the army into the Mexican capital.*

---

* The General's father, Gideon Pillow, was born in Rockingham County, N. C., September 24th, 1774. He was the second son of John and Ursula Johnson Pillow, who, in 1789, removed from North Carolina to Davidson County, Ten., and settled temporarily with his family at 'John Brown's,' a thin frontier station four miles south of Nashville. He was killed in the fall of 1790, leaving William and Gideon to protect six younger brothers and sisters. These young men, one or both of them, went upon almost every excursion sent from Davidson County against the savages from 1789 to 1794. In the latter year the Indians discontinued their annoyances. Both fought bravely at Nickojack. William was colonel of a regiment under General Jackson in the late Creek war, and was shot through the body at Talladega, whilst pursuing the enemy. He now resides on his farm in Maury County. Gideon was a farmer and landdealer, but died from home (Madison Co., Ten.), February 26th, 1830, leaving three sons and three daughters.

The General was born June 10th, 1806, in Williamson County, Ten. He graduated (Oct., 1827) at the University of Nashville, and studied law at Columbia, under Judge Kennedy. Admitted to the bar in October, 1829, he became distinguished, and acquired extensive practice. As an advocate he was forcible and eloquent, prompt in action, and indomitable in perseverance. General Pillow was a member of the National Democratic Convention, held in Baltimore in 1844, but has never filled any other public station, preferring the enjoyment of his ample fortune in the domestic circle to the cares of politics. On the 24th of March, 1831, he married Miss Mary E. Martin, by whom he has seven children; and about the same time was appointed by General Carroll Inspector-General of the State militia. General Pillow is a member of the Presbyterian church. Even on the battle-field, the Bible is constantly found in his tent, and its pages are perused as often as camp duties will permit.

MAJOR-GENERAL QUITMAN.

MAJOR-GENERAL JOHN A. QUITMAN, like his fellow officer, Pillow, has but recently entered upon active service. He served as a volunteer at Monterey, and was appointed to the regular army, April 14th, 1847, from Mississippi, although New York is his native state.

The following detailed report is a complete description of the services of his brigade at Monterey :—

"Being ordered, on the morning of the 22d, to relieve Colonel Garland's command, which had, during the preceding night, occupied the redoubt and fortifications taken on the 21st, my command marched from their encampment about nine o'clock in the morning. Colonel Campbell, of the Tennessee regiment, being indisposed from the fatigue and exposure of the preceding day, the command of his regiment devolved on Lieutenant-Colonel Anderson. Both regiments were much reduced by the casualties of the twenty-first, and the necessary details for the care of the wounded. The march necessarily exposed the brigade for a short distance to a severe fire of artillery from the works still in possession of the enemy on this side of the city, and from the cross-fire of the citadel. We were not allowed to reach our post without some loss. Private Dubois, of Captain Crump's company of Mississippi riflemen, was killed, and two men of the same company wounded, before entering the works. The redoubt and adjacent works being occupied by my brigade, and Lieutenant Ridgely's battery, a portion of the troops were engaged, under the direction of Lieutenant J. M. Scarritt, of engineers, in strengthening our position on the side next to town.

"At intervals during the whole day, until nine o'clock at night, the enemy kept up from their fortifications, and from the citadel, discharges of shell, round shot, and grape. It was in the forenoon of this day, that, by the aid of our glasses, we were presented with

(84)

a full view of the storming of the Bishop's palace by troops under General Worth on the heights beyond the city. The shout by which our brave volunteers greeted the display of the American flag on the palace, was returned by the enemy from their works near us by a tremendous fire of round shot and grape upon us without effect. During the day, plans of assault on the adjacent Mexican works were considered of, but in the evening my attention was drawn to a line of about fifteen hundred Mexican infantry at some distance in rear of their works. The presence of this force, amounting to nearly three times our effective numbers, and which appeared to be posted for the protection of the works, induced me to give up all idea of forcing the works without reinforcements. During the night several reconnoissances were made with details of Captain Whitfield's company, in the direction of the redoubt 'El Diablo.' Frequent signals between the different posts of the enemy during the night kept us on the alert; and at the first dawn of day on the 23d, it was discovered that the enemy had abandoned, or were abandoning, the strong works nearest to us. Colonel Davis, with a portion of his command, supported by Lieutenant-Colonel Anderson, with two companies of the Tennessee regiment, was ordered to take possession of the works. This was promptly done. The enemy had withdrawn their artillery during the night, and nothing of value fell into our hands but some prisoners and ammunition. From this work, which commanded a view of the cathedral, and a portion of the great plaza of the city, we perceived another half-moon or triangular redoubt in advance of us, and on our right, which appeared to be immediately connected with heavy stone buildings and walls adjoining the block of the city. Having reported my observations to the commanding general, who had approached the field of our operations, I received permission to advance upon the defences of the city in this direction, and, if deemed practicable, to occupy them. It was sufficiently apparent that all the approaches to the city on this side were strongly fortified. Wishing to proceed with caution, under the qualified permission of the commanding general, I sent out a party of riflemen, under Lieutenant Graves, to reconnoitre, supporting them at some distance by a company of Tennessee infantry, under Captain McMurray. Some active movements of the enemy in the vicinity induced me to halt this party, and to order out Colonel Davis, with two companies of his command, and two com-

8   I

panies of Tennessee troops, to advance on these works. As the troops advanced, armed men were seen flying at their approach. Upon reaching the redoubt which had attracted our attention, we perceived that it was open, and exposed to the fire of the enemy from the stone buildings and walls in the rear. It was, therefore, necessary to select another position less exposed. Posting the two companies of infantry, in a position to defend the lodgement we had effected, I directed Colonel Davis to post his command as he might deem most advantageous for defence or active operations, intending here to await further orders or reinforcements. In reconnoitring the place, several shots were fired at Colonel Davis by the enemy, and several files of the riflemen who had advanced to the slope of a breastwork, (No. 1,) which had been thrown across the street for the defence of the city, returned the fire. A volley from the enemy succeeded. Our party having been reinforced by additions from the riflemen and infantry, a brisk firing was soon opened on both sides, the enemy from the house-tops and parapets attempting to drive us from the lodgement we had effected. A considerable body of the enemy, securely posted on the top of a large building on our left, which partially overlooked the breastwork, No. 1, continued to pour in their fire, and killed private Tyree, of company K, whose gallant conduct at the breastwork had attracted the attention of both his colonel and myself. From this commencement, in a short time the action became general. The enemy appearing to be in great force, and firing upon our troops from every position of apparent security, I despatched my aid, Lieutenant Nichols, with orders to advance the whole of my brigade which could be spared from the redoubts occupied by us. A portion of the Mississippi regiment, under Major Bradford, advanced to the support of the troops engaged, but Lieutenant-Colonel Anderson, with a part of the Tennessee regiment, was required to remain for the protection of the redoubts in our possession. With this additional force more active operations upon the city were begun. Detachments of our troops advanced, penetrating into buildings and occupying the flat roofs of houses, and by gradual approaches, driving the enemy back. They had been engaged more than an hour, when they were reinforced by a detachment of dismounted Texan rangers, commanded by General Henderson, with whose active and effectual co-operations the attack upon the city was gradually, but successfully prosecuted.

Buildings, streets, and courts were occupied by our troops without much loss, until, after being engaged for about five hours, having advanced within less than two squares of the great plaza, apprehensive that we might fall under the range of our own artillery, which had been brought up to our support, and our ammunition being nearly exhausted, active operations were ordered to cease until the effect of the batteries, which had been brought forward into one of the principal streets, could be seen.

"It being found that the barricades in the neighbourhood of the plaza were too strong to be battered down by our light artillery, the commanding general, who had taken position in the city, ordered the troops gradually and slowly to retire to the defences taken in the morning. This was done in good order, the enemy firing occasionally upon us, but not venturing to take possession of the part of the town we had occupied. Our forces had scarcely retired from their advanced position in the city, when we heard the commencement of the attack of the division under General Worth on the opposite side of the town. The force under my command had been engaged from eight o'clock in the morning to three P. M. It should be recorded, to the credit of the volunteer troops, that the greater portion of them had been without sustenance since the morning of the 22d, and exposed throughout the very inclement and rainy night of the 22d, to severe duty, without blankets or overcoats, and yet not a murmur was heard among them—their alacrity remained unabated to the last moment. The character of this affair, the troops being necessarily separated into many small parties, gave frequent occasion to the exhibition of individual courage and daring. The instances occurred so frequently, in which both officers and men distinguished themselves, that to recount those which fell under my own observation, or which were brought to my notice by officers, would extend this report to an improper length. It is my duty and pleasure to mention the fact, that the veteran, General Lamar, of Texas, joined my command as a volunteer in the commencement of the attack on the city, and by his counsel and example aided and encouraged the troops. Major E. R. Price, of Natchez, and Captain J. R. Smith, of Louisiana, both from the recently disbanded Louisiana troops, acted with distinguished bravery as volunteers in Colonel Davis's regiment."

General Quitman performed much laborious service before Vera

Cruz, but was not in the battle of Sierra Gordo. But his military fame rests principally upon the battles before the Mexican capital. In these he has wrought himself an undying reputation, which has placed him before our people as one of the ablest of their commanders. He accompanied the army in its march from Puebla toward the capital, but was not actively concerned in the battles of the 19th and 20th of August. He was one of the commissioners who negotiated the armistice, and on the recommencement of hostilities, was in continued action until the fall of the capital. His report is as follows: —

"The general-in-chief, having concluded to carry the strong fortress of Chapultepec, and through it advance upon the city, ordered me, on the 11th, to move my division, after dark, from its position at Coyoacan to Tacubaya.   *   *   *   *

"Two batteries had been erected during the night. My division being intended to support these batteries, and to advance to the attack by the direct road from Tacubaya to the fortress, was placed in position near battery No. 1, early on the morning of the 12th — detachments from its left extending to the support of battery No. 2. At seven o'clock, the guns — two sixteen-pounders and an eight-inch howitzer — were placed in battery No. 1, in position so as to rake the road, sweep the adjoining grounds, and have a direct fire upon the enemy's batteries and the fortress of Chapultepec.

"Our fire was then opened and maintained with good effect throughout the day, under the direction of that excellent and lamented officer, Captain Drum, of the 4th artillery, zealously aided by Lieutenants Benjamin and Porter, of his company. The fire was briskly returned from the castle with round shot, shells and grape. During the day, I succeeded, under cover of our batteries, in making an important reconnoissance of the grounds and works immediately at the base of the castle, a rough sketch of which was made by my aid, Lieutenant Lovel, on the ground. This disclosed to us two batteries of the enemy — one on the road in front of us, mounting four guns, and the other a flanking work of one gun, capable also of sweeping the low grounds on the left of the road, and between it and the base of the hill.

"The supporting party on this reconnoissance was commanded by the late Major Twiggs, of the marines, and sustained during the observation a brisk fire from the batteries and small arms of the enemy, who, when the party were retiring, came out of the works in large numbers; and although repeatedly checked by the fire of our troops, continued to advance as the supporting party retired, until they were dispersed, with considerable loss, by several discharges of canister from the guns of Captain Drum's battery, and a well-directed fire from the right of the 2d Pennsylvania regiment, posted on the flank of the battery for its support. Our loss in this affair was seven men wounded; but the information gained was of incalculable advantage to the operations of the succeeding day. In the evening, Captain Drum's company was relieved by Lieutenant Andrews' company, 3d artillery, by whom a steady and well-directed fire was kept up from the battery, until the fortress could no longer be seen in the darkness. During the day, my command was reinforced by a select battalion from General Twiggs' division, intended as a storming party, consisting of thirteen officers and two hundred and fifty men and non-commissioned officers and privates, chosen for this service out of the rifles, 1st and 4th regiments of artillery, and the 2d, 3d, and 7th regiments of infantry — all under the command of Captain Silas Casey, 2d infantry.

"Having received instructions from the general-in-chief to prevent, if possible, reinforcements from being thrown into Chapultepec during the night, Captain Paul of the 7th infantry, with a detachment of fifty men, was directed to establish an advanced picket on the road to Chapultepec. During the night a brisk skirmish occurred between this detachment and the advanced posts of the enemy, which resulted in driving back the enemy; but, apprehensive that this demonstration was intended to cover the passage of reinforcements into Chapultepec, I ordered Lieutenant Andrews to advance a piece of artillery and rake the road with several discharges of canister. This was promptly executed, and during the remainder of the night there were no appearances of movements in the enemy's lines. During the night, the platforms of battery No. 1 were repaired, under the direction of Lieutenant Tower, of engineers, who had reported to me for duty, and a new battery for one gun established in advance of No. 1 a short distance, by Lieutenant Hammond, of General Shields' staff.

"The protection of battery No. 2, which was completed on the morning of the 12th, under direction of Captain Huger, was in

8* I 2

trusted to Brigadier-General Shields. This battery, after the guns had been placed, opened and maintained a steady fire upon the castle, under the skilful direction of that experienced officer, Lieutenant Hagner, of ordnance.

" At dawn, on the morning of the 13th, the batteries again opened an active and effective fire upon the castle, which was returned by the enemy with spirit and some execution, disabling for a time the eighteen-pounder in battery No. 1, and killing one of the men at the guns.

" During this cannonade, active preparations were made for the assault upon the castle. Ladders, pickaxes, and crows were placed in the hands of a pioneer storming party of select men from the volunteer division, under command of Captain Reynolds of the marine corps, to accompany the storming party of one hundred and twenty men, which had been selected from all corps of the same division, and placed under the command of Major Twiggs, of the marines. Captain Drum had again relieved Lieutenant Andrews at the guns, retaining from the command of the latter Sergeant Davidson and eight men to man an eight-pounder, which it was intended to carry forward to operate on the enemy's batteries in front of us; and, to relieve the command from all danger of attack on our right flank from reinforcements which might come from the city, that well-tried and accomplished officer, Brevet Brigadier-General Smith, with his well-disciplined brigade, had reported to me for orders. He was instructed to move in reserve on the right flank of the assaulting column, protect it from skirmishers, or more serious attack in that quarter; and, if possible, on the assault, cross the aqueduct leading to the city, turn the enemy, and cut off his retreat. Those dispositions being made, the whole command, at the signal preconcerted by the general-in-chief, with enthusiasm and full of confidence advanced to the attack. At the base of the hill, constituting a part of the works of the fortress of Chapultepec, and directly across our line of advance, were the strong batteries before described, flanked on the right by some strong buildings, and by a heavy stone wall about fifteen feet high, which extended around the base of the hill towards the west. Within two hundred yards of these batteries were some dilapidated buildings, which afforded a partial cover to our advance. Between these and the wall extended a low meadow, the long grass of which concealed a number of wet ditches by which it was inter-

sected. To this point the command, partially screened, advanced
by a flank, the storming parties in front, under a heavy fire from
the fortress, the batteries, and breastworks of the enemy. The advance was here halted under the partial cover of the ruins, and upon
the arrival of the heads of the South Carolina and New York regiments, respectively, General Shields was directed to move them
obliquely to the left, across the low ground, to the wall at the base
of the hill. Encouraged by the gallant general who had led them
to victory at Churubusco, and in spite of the obstacles which they
had to encounter in wading through several deep ditches, exposed
to a severe and galling fire from the enemy, these tried regiments
promptly executed the movement, and effected a lodgement at the
wall. The same order was given to Lieutenant-Colonel Geary, and
executed by his regiment with equal alacrity and success. These
dispositions, so necessary to the final assault upon the works, were
not made without some loss. In directing the advance, Brigadier-
General Shields was severely wounded in the arm. No persuasions,
however, could induce that officer to leave his command, or quit the
field. The brave Captain Van O'Linden, of the New York regiment, was killed at the head of his company. Lieutenant-Colonel
Baxter, of the same regiment, a valuable and esteemed officer, while
gallantly leading his command, fell mortally wounded near the wall.
And Lieutenant-Colonel Geary, 2d Pennsylvania regiment, was for
a time disabled from command by a severe contusion from a spent
ball.

   " In the mean time, Brigadier-General Smith on our right was
driving back skirmishing parties of the enemy ; Lieutenant Benjamin, from battery No. 1, was pouring shot after shot into the fortress
and woods on the slope of the hill ; and Lieutenant H. J. Hunt, 2d
artillery, who had on the advance reported to me with a section of
Duncan's battery, had obtained a favourable position in our rear,
from which he threw shells and shrapnal shot into the Mexican lines
with good effect. Perceiving that all the preliminary dispositions
were made, Major Gladden, with his regiment, having passed the
wall by breaching it, the New York and Pennsylvania regiments
having entered over an abandoned battery on their left, and the battalion of marines being posted to support the storming parties, I ordered the assault at all points.

   " The storming parties, led by the gallant officers who had volunteered for this desperate service, rushed forward like a resistless tide. The Mexicans behind their batteries and breastworks stood with more than usual firmness. For a short time the contest was hand-to-hand ; swords and bayonets were crossed, and rifles clubbed. Resistance, however, was vain against the desperate valour of our brave troops. The batteries and strong works were carried, and the ascent of Chapultepec on that side laid open to an easy conquest. In these works were taken seven pieces of artillery, one thousand muskets, and five hundred and fifty prisoners — of whom one hundred were officers — among them, one general and ten colonels.

"The gallant Captain Casey having been disabled by a severe wound, directly before the batteries, the command of the storming party of regulars in the assault devolved on Captain Paul, 7th infantry, who distinguished himself for his bravery.   In like manner the command of the storming party from the volunteer division devolved on Captain James Miller, of the 2d Pennsylvania regiment, by the death of its chief, the brave and lamented Major Twiggs, of the marine corps, who fell on the first advance at the head of his command.

"Simultaneously with these movements on our right, the volunteer regiments, with equal alacrity and intrepidity, animated by a generous emulation, commenced the ascent of the hill on the south side. Surmounting every obstacle, and fighting their way, they fell in and mingled with their brave brethren in arms, who formed the advance of Major-General Pillow's column. Side by side, amid the storm of battle, the rival colours of the two commands struggled up the steep ascent, entered the fortress, and reached the buildings used as a military college, which crowned its summit. Here was a short pause ; but soon the flag of Mexico was lowered, and the stars and stripes of our country floated from the heights of Chapultepec, high above the heads of the brave men who had planted them there. The gallant New York regiment claims for their standard the honour of being the first waved from the battlements of Chapultepec. The veteran Mexican general, Bravo, with a number of officers and men, were taken prisoners in the castle. They fell into the hands of Lieutenant Charles Brower, of the New York regiment, who reported them to me. The loss of the enemy was severe, especially on the eastern side, adjoining the batteries taken. It should also be mentioned, that, at the assault upon the works, Lieutenant Frederick Steele, 2d infantry, with a portion of the storming party, advanced in front of the batteries towards the left, there scaled the outer wall through a breach near the top, made by a cannon-shot, ascended the hill directly in his front, and was among the first upon the battlements. The young and promising Lieutenant Levi Gantt, 7th infantry, was of this party. He had actively participated in almost every battle since the opening of the war, but was destined here to find a soldier's grave.

"After giving the necessary directions for the safe-keeping of the prisoners taken by my command, and ordering the several corps to form near the aqueduct, I hastily ascended the hill, for the purpose of reconnoitring the positions of the enemy in advance towards the city. I there had the pleasure of meeting Major-General Pillow, who, although seriously wounded, had been carried to the heights to enjoy the triumph in which he and his brave troops had so largely shared.

"Perceiving large bodies of the enemy at the several batteries on the direct road leading from Chapultepec to the city, by the garita or gate of Belen, my whole command, after being supplied with ammunition, was ordered to be put in readiness to march by that route. When the batteries were taken, the gallant rifle regiment, which had been deployed by General Smith on the right of his brigade, formed under the arches of the aqueduct in position to advance by the Chapultepec or Tacubaya road. As the remainder of General Smith's brigade came up from their position in reserve, that officer, with his usual foresight, caused them to level the parapets and fill the ditches which obstructed the road where the enemy's batteries had been constructed, so as to permit the passage of the heavy artillery, which was ordered up by the general-in-chief immediately upon his arrival at the batteries. In the mean time, while General Shields, with the assistance of his and my staff officers, was causing the deficient ammunition to be supplied, and the troops to be formed for the advance, Captain Drum, supported by the rifle regiment, had taken charge of one of the enemy's pieces, and was advancing towards the first battery occupied by the enemy, on the road towards the city in our front.

"The Chapultepec road is a broad avenue, flanked with deep ditches and marshy grounds on either side. Along the middle of this avenue runs the aqueduct, supported by arches of heavy masonry, through the garita or gate of Belen into the city. The rifles, supported by the South Carolina regiment, and followed by the remainder of Smith's brigade, were now advanced, from arch to arch, towards another strong battery which had been thrown across the road, about a mile from Chapultepec, having four embrasures with a redan work on the right.

"At this point, the enemy in considerable force made an obstinate resistance; but, with the aid of* the effective fire of an eight-inch howitzer, directed by the indefatigable Captain Drum, and the daring bravery of the gallant rifle regiment, it was carried by assault. The column was here reorganized for an attack upon the batteries at the garita of the city. The regiment of riflemen, intermingled with the bayonets of the South Carolina regiment, were placed in the advance—three rifles and three bayonets under each arch. They were supported by the residue of Shields' brigade, the 2d Pennsylvania regiment, and the remainder of Smith's brigade, together with a part of the 6th infantry, under Major Bonneville, who had fallen into this road. In this order, the column resolutely advanced from arch to arch of the aqueduct, under a tremendous fire of artillery and small arms from the batteries at the garita, the Paseo, and a large body of the enemy on the Piedad road to the right, extending from the left of the garita.

"Lieutenant Benjamin having brought up a sixteen-pounder, Captain Drum and his efficient subalterns were pouring a constant and destructive fire into the garita. As the enfilading fire of the enemy from the Piedad road became very annoying to the advance of the column, a few rounds of canister were thrown by our artillery in that direction, which effectually dispersed them. The whole column was now under a galling fire, but it continued to move forward steadily and firmly. The rifles, well sustained by the South Carolinians, gallantly pushed on to the attack; and at twenty minutes past one the garita was carried, and the city of Mexico entered at that point. In a few moments the whole command was compactly up—a large part of it within the garita.

"The obstinacy of the defence at the garita may be accounted for by our being opposed at that point by General Santa Anna in person, who is said to have retreated by the Paseo to the San Cosme road, there to try his fortune against General Worth.

"On our approach to the garita, a body of the enemy who were seen on a cross road threatening our left, were dispersed by a brisk fire of artillery from the direction of the San Cosme road. I take pleasure in acknowledging that this seasonable aid came from Lieutenant-Colonel Duncan's battery, which had been kindly advanced from the San Cosme road in that direction by General Worth's orders.

"Upon the taking of the garita, the riflemen and South Carolina regiment rushed forward and occupied the arches of the aqueduct, within a hundred yards of the citadel. The ammunition of our heavy guns having been expended, a captured eight-pounder was turned upon the enemy, and served with good effect until the ammunition taken with it was also expended. The piece, supported by our advance, had been run forward in front of the garita. Twice had Major Gladden, of the South Carolina regiment, furnished additional men to work the gun, when the noble and brave Captain Drum, who, with indomitable energy and iron nerve, had directed the artillery throughout this trying day, fell mortally wounded by the side of his gun. A few moments afterwards, Lieutenant Benjamin, who had displayed the same cool, decided courage, met a similar fate.

"The enemy, now perceiving that our heavy ammunition had been expended, redoubled their exertions to drive us out of the lodgement we had effected. A terrible fire of artillery and small arms was opened from the citadel, three hundred yards distant, from the batteries on the Paseo, and the buildings on our right in front. Amid this iron shower, which swept the road on both sides of the aqueduct, it was impossible to bring forward ammunition for our large guns. While awaiting the darkness to bring up our great guns and place them in battery, the enemy, under cover of their guns, attempted several sallies from the citadel and buildings on the right, but were readily repulsed by the skirmishing parties of rifles and infantry. To prevent our flank from being enfiladed by musketry from the Paseo, Captains Naylor and Loeser, 2d Pennsylvania regiment, were ordered with their companies to a low sandbag defence, about a hundred yards in that direction. They gallantly took this position, and held it in the face of a severe fire until the object was attained.

"At night the fire of the enemy ceased. Lieutenant Tower, of the engineers, who before and at the attack upon the batteries at

Chapultepec had given important aid, had been seriously wounded. It was therefore fortunate that, in the commencement of the route to the city, Lieutenant Beauregard, of engineers, joined me. I was enabled, during the day, to avail myself of his valuable services; and, although disabled for a time by a wound received during the day, he superintended, during the whole night, the erection of two batteries within the garita for our heavy guns, and a breastwork on our right for infantry, which, with his advice, I had determined to construct. Before the dawn of day, by the persevering exertions of Captains Fairchild and Taylor, of the New York regiment, who directed the working parties, the parapets were completed, and a twenty-four-pounder, and eighteen-pounder, and eight-inch howitzer placed in battery by Captain Steptoe, 3d artillery, who, to my great satisfaction, had rejoined my command in the evening. The heavy labour required to construct these formidable batteries, under the very guns of the citadel, was performed with the utmost cheerfulness by the gallant men whose strong arms and stout hearts had already been tested in two days of peril and toil.

"During the night, while at the trenches, Brigadier-General Pierce —one of whose regiments (the 9th infantry) had joined my column during the day—reported to me in person. He was instructed to place that regiment in reserve at the battery in rear, for the protection of Steptoe's light battery and the ammunition at that point. The general has my thanks for his prompt attention to these orders.

"At dawn of day on the 14th, when Captain Steptoe was preparing his heavy missiles, a white flag came from the citadel, the bearers of which invited me to take possession of this fortress, and gave me the intelligence that the city had been abandoned by Santa Anna and his army. My whole command was immediately ordered under arms. By their own request, Lieutenants Lovell and Beauregard were authorized to go to the citadel, in advance, to ascertain the truth of the information. At a signal from the ramparts, the column, General Smith's brigade in front, and the South Carolina regiment left in garrison at the garita, marched into the citadel. Having taken possession of this work, in which we found fifteen pieces of cannon mounted and as many not up, with the extensive military armaments which it contained, the 2d Pennsylvania regiment was left to garrison it. Understanding that great depredations were going on in the palace and public buildings, I moved the column in that direction in the same order, followed by Captain Steptoe's light battery, through the principal streets into the great plaza, where it was formed in front of the National Palace. Captain Roberts, of the rifle regiment, who had led the advance company of the storming party at Chapultepec, and had greatly distinguished himself during the preceding day, was detailed by me to plant the star-spangled banner of our country upon the National Palace. The flag, the first strange banner which had ever waved over that palace since the conquest of Cortez, was displayed and saluted with enthusiasm by the whole command. The palace, already crowded with Mexican thieves and robbers, was placed in charge of Lieutenant-Colonel Watson, with his battalion of marines. By his active exertions it was soon cleared and guarded from further spoliation.

" On our first arrival in the plaza, Lieutenant Beauregard was dispatched to report the facts to the general-in-chief, who was expected to enter the city by the Alameda, with the column under General Worth. About eight o'clock the general-in-chief arrived in the plaza, and was received and greeted with enthusiasm by the troops. The populace, who had begun to be turbulent immediately after our arrival in the plaza, appeared for a time to be checked ; but, in one hour afterwards, as our troops began to disperse for quarters, they were fired upon from the tops of houses and windows. This continued that day and the succeeding, until, by the timely and vigorous measures adopted by the general-in-chief, the disturbances were quelled."

Here follows a list of the officers who particularly distinguished themselves.

After the surrender of the city, General Scott immediately honoured Quitman with the appointment of military governor. His manly, dignified bearing, won the approbation of both friends and enemies, and his plan of administration is said to have been admirable.

In November, General Quitman obtained leave of absence, in order to revisit the United States. His parting on that occasion with the brave men in Mexico is thus described by an eye-witness :

" The officers of the division having assembled together, visited General Quitman in a body, when Colonel Burnett, ot New York,

9   K

on behalf of himself and brother officers, addressed him in a pertinent speech, the conclusion of which was as follows :

" ' We, as officers of your division, can only repay you upon your
sudden departure with an expression of our feelings. We shall
meet you again after the war as fellow-citizens, and our present
sentiments written upon our hearts as upon adamant, will lose nothing by the hand of time—uniting *then* with a gratified people, your
present sacrifices may be somewhat compensated by the only boon
of the patriot—the grateful acknowledgments of your country. We
shall then have deposited our standards with the authorities of our
respective states, but ever ready to rally under our victorious banners as the prestige of success, and ever ready to be directed by our
gallant general, whom we now part with as a father and a friend.'

"This speech was frequently interrupted by the company present, who expressed their approbation of the sentiments by warm
applause. When this had subsided, General Quitman replied in
substance as follows :

"He said that when he looked around him and found himself in
the presence of the gallant officers who had participated so largely
in the recent brilliant events before the city, and heard himself addressed by the senior officer of the division, yet leaning upon his
honourable crutch, in remarks so full of the elegant feeling of the
heart, he was overwhelmed with emotion, and felt himself wholly
unable to do justice to the occasion. Circumstances had rendered
it necessary as a matter of high duty that he should apply to the
proper authority for some permanent assignment to duty, where he
might be best enabled to serve his country. Had he consulted personal feeling merely, he would have been gratified to remain with
the brave associates of his cares, his perils and fortunes in war, but
he regarded it the soldier's part to seek the path where duty called
him. That path now separated him from the gallant officers and
men to whose good conduct and services he took this occasion to
say he felt himself wholly indebted for whatever reputation or
honour he might have acquired in this campaign. It was theirs,
not his. They were entitled to his regard, his esteem and his
friendship. He would bear these feelings with him wherever his
lot should be cast.

"In conclusion, he expressed his heartfelt regret at his separation
from them, and hoped that they would receive for themselves, and

bear to the gallant rank and file under their commands, his friendly
farewell.

" After General Quitman had concluded, Captain Hutton, of the
New York regiment, rose and presented Captain G. T. M. Davis
an elegant pair of silver spurs, accompanying the gift with a brief
but extremely apropos speech. Captain Davis made an appropriate
reply."

The following is a description of the festivities attending his arrival at Natchez, the place of his family residence :

" Our Quitman is at home and with us ; so excuse any high-
flown exhibition of our feelings of intense pleasure, pride, and triumph. Oh ! had you been here but yesterday morning, when that
veteran cannoneer, Captain James C. Fox, so well known in your
' city of the Delta' as one of the most accomplished of the Natchez
firemen, let off those loud-mouthed Mexican trophy-cannon, captured
at Alvarado, and presented to General Quitman with the permission
of the Secretary of the Navy, by Commodore Perry. They are
two long twelves, of a most excellent composition, originally intended for bow-chasers in the naval service. One was made in
Barcelona, old Spain, in 1768, and bears the name of El Sosto, and
the other the name of El Orion. There was a sublimity in making
these trophy-cannon announce that the hour of welcome to our victorious general had come ; and well did Fox instruct them how to
roar out a welcome to ' the free' in ' the home of the brave.'
General Quitman's mansion, called ' Monmouth,' nestles in a beautiful grove in the environs of Natchez, only about a mile from the
centre of the city. A thrill of joy, precious as love and the idolatry
of the affections could make it, must have pervaded the bosoms of
his lovely and accomplished family, as the air vibrated around their
home with the cannon-bursts, and the swell of music and the roar
of the stirred city broke upon their ears.

" Doctor Blackburn, a noble-looking and chivalrous Kentuckian,
now captain of the ' Natchez Fencibles,' was the chief marshal,
assisted by General Smith, Messrs. Andrew McCreery, S. Win-
ston, and General R. Stanton. A large and imposing procession
of military, led by the renowned ' Kendall's Brass Band, from
' Spalding's monster Circus,' now here, the masonic fraternity, survivors of the battle of New Orleans, invited guests, &c., was soon in
motion for Monmouth, where they received Major-General Quitman

and his staff; consisting of Major E. R. Price, of the 2d Mississippi rifles ; Captain Douglass Cooper, of the 1st Mississippi rifles, and Lieutenant Keiger, of the volunteers. The moment of the movement of the procession was announced by Captain R. Fitzpatrick, from a new brass piece of state artillery, named 'Quitman,' and carried in the procession. It was answered by Captain Fox, from his stationary battery on the Esplanade, who kept up a running cannon-accompaniment during the whole progress to the city. When the procession came proudly down Main street and halted opposite the City Hotel, the *coup d'œil* was most imposing — banners waved over the street, every balcony and window, and even the roofs were filled with ladies and children, while the street below, far and near, was choked with the plumed soldiery and the dense masses of citizens. The civic welcome to Quitman, amidst thunders of applause, was pronounced by the young and eloquent Martin, the district attorney for this circuit. Colonel A. L. Bingaman had been elected the orator of the day, but his unavoidable absence to New Orleans prevented his acceptance, and Martin, as well as any other orator could have done, supplied his place. Both the address and Quitman's rejoinder were extemporaneous, and thrilled the multitude with the high impulses of the occasion. How wonderful, said Martin, is it that the very city (Natchez) bearing the name of a noble fragment of the Aztec race, who, in some convulsion or other, perhaps to avoid the murderous sword of Cortez, had been expatriated from Mexico, and stood on the bluff where their proud name still remains—how remarkable was it that from the very ashes of their graves there should have risen an avenger of their wrongs, and that our Quitman, from fair Natchez, had been deputed by Providence 'to spoil the spoiler!' I do not attempt to quote his burning language. Quitman's reply was modest, and replete with gratitude to his fellow-citizens ; filled with encomiums upon those great masters in the science of war under whom he had served— Taylor and Scott — naming, with a heart full of affection, not only the officers with whom he had associated, but those who had served under his orders, and in particular the rank and file of the army ; he spoke of the immense mountain of prejudice that had been removed from the minds of the regular army entertained against the volunteer service, and trusted that the American name now stood far higher in Europe and all over the world, in consequence of the deeds performed in Mexico by both arms of the service — the regular and the voluntary.   The collation now invited our whole population — ladies, gentlemen and children — to a participation; and such a generous, hearty, abundant ' feast of the people' was rarely ever seen.   The cross-table at the head of the hall was most luxuriously spread, and was the table of welcome to General Quitman, his staff, the invited guests, and the distinguished individuals composing the committee of arrangements, the civic authorities, &c. Here the vitality of the feast, like the heart in the human body, kept alive the longest; and when the multitudinous waves of the people had a little subsided, fourteen regular toasts were drunk, including the President of the United States; the memory of Washington; Generals Scott, Taylor, Quitman, Colonel Jefferson Davis, Major Ezra R. Price, Captain Douglass H. Cooper, Lieutenants Keiger and Posey; our gallant army in Mexico; the surviving heroes of the war of 1812, and American mothers, wives and daughters.   General Felix Hoston being absent, sent in the following volunteer toast :

" *General John A. Quitman*—' Second to none !' Six hours before any other chieftain, he fought his way into the centre of Monterey ; near eight hours before any other leader, he had stormed the Garita and entered the city of Mexico ; the first to plant the Stars and the Stripes over the Halls of the Montezumas !

" Charles Reynolds, Esq., gave :

" *Natchez*—The residence of Major-General John A. Quitman, the first Anglo-Saxon governor of the ' City of the Aztecs !'

"Captain James C. Fox gave, in allusion to the fact that, a quarter of a century ago, General Quitman organized that splendid corps, the Natchez Fencibles, and was their first captain :

" *The First Captain of the Fencibles* — When the American cannon and rifle, on the afternoon of September 13th, roared at the Piedad Gate, Mexico cried out, ' Who 's dat knocking at de door ?' The answer was, John A. Quitman, a Natchez Fencible !

"There were many other striking sentiments drunk, among which were —

" *That ' Revel in the Halls of the Montezumas !'* — The dream of General Samuel Houston realized by General Quitman.

" *General Quitman's passage along the Aqueduct from Chapul-*

9 *   k 2

tepec to the Garita de Belen, and the Piedad Gate, September 13, 1847—The bridge of Lodi in American history !

" General Quitman's dinner-table response to the sentiment in his honour was most happy.   He spoke of his unexpected major-generalship without any adequate command, but was too much of an American ' to give it up so ;' had, temporarily, commanded soldiers from nearly every state in the Union—broken and wasted regiments —fragments—the odds and ends of commands—but he assured the audience that when he commanded such officers as Generals Smith and Shields, and such men as he led to Chapultepec and the Garita de Belen, they were *butt-enders*, at least !

" Among other sentiments, the ' State of Kentucky' was toasted. In response, a young and eloquent lawyer, now settled in New Orleans, Thomas H. Holt, Esq., a native of Old Kentucky, made a most eloquent and thrilling speech, which was received with tumultuous applause.   The sentiment which called him out, offered by J. A. Van Hoesen, Esq., was : —

" *Old Kentucky*—The battles in Mexico attest the valour of her sons !

" No one can conceive the enthusiasm which the eloquent Holt called up.   He concluded by relating an anecdote of Madame Quitman, the wife of the general ; said he : When the brave veteran was bursting open things at Monterey, some neighbouring ladies, thinking that Mrs. Quitman must feel in the depths of sorrow and affliction at such terrible doings, went to condole and sympathize with her—asking her if she had not dreadful feelings at the danger and exposure of her husband among those ' rude-throated engines' of death.   She confessed that she had her feelings on the occasion, among which one feeling was predominant, which was, that she ' would rather be the widow of a man who had fallen fighting the battles of his country, than the wife of a living coward !"

We cannot close this sketch of General Quitman better, than by giving extracts of a letter [October 15th, 1847] in which he gives his opinion concerning the future duty of the United States, with regard to Mexico.   However parties may disagree on this important subject, all will respect the fearlessness with which a war-worn veteran advocates the measures that he believes right.

" I wish now, instead of an epistle written in the reception-room of the successors of Cortez, I could only have you by the button for one hour; I would run over my reflections upon the future. I will not repeat what, no doubt, ere this you have been wearied of reading. How this gallant army of nine thousand men descended into this valley, broke through a line of almost impregnable batteries — in four battles defeated an enemy of thirty-five thousand, took more than one hundred guns, and four thousand prisoners, and erected the 'glorious stars and stripes' on this palace, where, since the conquest of Cortez, no stranger banner had ever waved; but I will be guilty of one egotism—I was among the first to enter the gates of the city, after an obstinate defence, and it was my good fortune that, under my personal orders, our flag was first raised on this palace. With all this you will, however, have been surfeited in these days of heroics.

"I have an opportunity to write you a line. My thoughts are full of one subject, and I proceed to it *in medias res.* The Mexican army is disbanded. The whole country, except where we govern it, is in confusion. There appears to be no prospect of the establishment of a new government. If we desire peace, there is no power, nor will there be any legitimate power with which to make peace. What, then, is to be done? I speak to you boldly, as we spoke when the Texas question arose. I say, hold on to this country. It is its destiny. It is ours. We are compelled to this policy —we cannot avoid it.

"There are but three modes of prosecuting this war. One is, to increase our force to fifty thousand men, and overrun the whole country, garrison every state capital, and take every considerable city. The second is, to withdraw our armies from the country, and take up the proposed defensive line. The third is to occupy the line, or certain points in it; and also to hold, not only the line and the ports, but this capital, preserving an open communication with the gulf. This last appears to me to be the true policy of the country. The first has the objection of being too expensive, without the prospect of any good results. It would, also, demoralize the army, as a war of details always does. The second would be equally expensive, and would protract the war indefinitely. The last appears the only practicable alternative, and it is forced upon us. If we abandon this capital, in thirty days after the army of officers and office-holders, (*empleos,*) now driven from the hive, will return and re-establish a central military government, whose bond of union would be preserved by our presence upon the frontier. They would keep alive this distant war on the frontier from choice, force us into the necessity of keeping up strong garrisons from the mouth of the Rio Grande to the Pacific; because, from the centre, they could strike a blow upon any part of the line before it could be reinforced. They would move on a semi-diameter, while our operations would be on the circumference. If, on the other hand, the twenty thousand disbanded officers, the military aristocracy of the country, should not be able to establish a government, the country would be left in a state of absolute anarchy upon our withdrawal, and would soon be wasted, plundered and depopulated. It would become derelict, and would be seized as a waif by some European power. Think you such a prize as this splendid country is, would be long without some claimant? England would be ready to throw in an army here to protect her mining interests, or to league with France to establish a monarchy. I do not exaggerate, when I say that it would become derelict! (that is, utterly forsaken.) It is already prostrated. Five, out of its seven millions of inhabitants, are beasts of burden, with as little of intellect as the asses whose burdens they share. Of the population of this city, one hundred thousand are leperos, with no social tie, no wives, no children, no homes; Santa Anna was the only man who could even for a time keep together the rotten elements of his corrupt government. Here in this capital we are in the possession of all the machinery of that miserable contrivance which was called the government; out of this capital they cannot establish another. No sensible man in this country believes it. Then it follows, that if we abandon this capital, either the official jackals return and set up the old carcase of the state, or reduced to anarchy, the country will be seized upon by some foreign power.

"On the other hand, with ten thousand men, we can hold this capital and Vera Cruz, and keep open a safe communication between the two points. Possessing the heart, there could be no sufficient force concentrated to annoy us upon the frontier line we might choose to occupy. The expense would be less to hold this point and the frontier line, than to occupy the latter, and leave this as a rallying point for the enemy. I mean to say it would require less men and less money, and would be attended with less difficulty and risk, to keep this capital and the seaports, as a part of the policy of the defensive line, than to adopt the latter exclusively. But by holding on to the seaports and the capital, and by keeping open the communication between them, a large portion of the expenses of this mode of prosecuting the war would be drawn, by very simple means, from the country.   The duties on imports into Vera Cruz, during the month of August, with the very restricted internal commerce which then existed, amounted to sixty thousand dollars.   I do not hesitate to say it will this winter amount to three times that sum per month.   If, then, we lay but half the duty on the exportation of bullion and the precious metals, existing under the Mexican government, we may readily anticipate, from these sources alone, an income of three millions of dollars per annum.

"Let foreign goods be brought to this capital under our low system of duties, and we should soon obtain a moral conquest over this country which would bring us peace—unless, indeed, it should produce so violent a friendship for our institutions and government that we would be unable to shake off our amiable neighbours—a contingency, I assure you, not unlikely to occur.   What then?   Why, the ' old hunker' will say, as he has sung since the first new state was admitted — as he said when Louisiana and Florida were purchased, and latterly when Texas was annexed, that the Union is in danger, the country will be ruined, &c. &c."   *   *   *

With a glowing account of the resources of the country, and the advantages of the commercial pass of Tehuantepec, the general boldly strikes out for the policy of holding the country in possession; and says :—

"Let us try the policy, and not be alarmed, because, in process of time, it may result in extending our federation to the isthmus."

*   *   *   *   *   *   *   *   *   *

BRIGADIER-GENERAL TWIGGS.

Brigadier-General David E. Twiggs is a native of Georgia. His father, John Twiggs, was a major-general in the Revolution, and by his valuable services obtained the title of "Saviour of Georgia." Born in Richmond county in 1790, young Twiggs grew up in the immediate sunset of the revolution, and imbibed the spirit of that glorious period in his earliest teachings. Accordingly, the study of law, which he commenced in Franklin College, and prosecuted under General Thomas Flourney, was abandoned as soon as our difficulties with England gave promise of a war. Through the exertions of his father he received a commission as captain of the 8th infantry, March 12th, 1812. He was not entrusted with a separate command during the war, but so far distinguished himself as to receive the commendations both of government and his native state.

Major Twiggs served under Generals Gaines and Jackson in the difficulties with the Spaniards and the Seminole war. At the head of two hundred and fifty men, he totally defeated a large party of Indians, under the celebrated chief Hornetlimed. In 1817, he accompanied General Jackson in his march toward St. Augustine, and was appointed to take possession of St. Marks. He was subsequently concerned in the Black Hawk war, stationed at the Augusta arsenal during the national difficulties with South Carolina, and then removed to New Orleans. His services in Florida, like those of most other officers there, were arduous but not brilliant. On the 8th of June, 1836, he was appointed colonel of the 2d dragoons.

When General Taylor approached Point Isabel in his march to the Rio Grande, he discovered it to be on fire. Colonel Twiggs was immediately despatched with two hundred and fifty men, to

(106)

GENERAL TWIGGS.

Page 106

arrest the conflagration, and succeeded in saving a few of the houses. He found the town evacuated by the authorities and military, who had fled at his approach.

The dispute between Colonels Twiggs and Worth has already been noticed. Twiggs' commission was dated June 8th, 1836, that of Worth, July 7th, 1838; but in 1842 the latter had been brevetted brigadier-general. On this circumstance he claimed precedence over Twiggs, who, however, refused to yield his authority as second in command. The matter was referred to General Taylor, who decided in favour of Twiggs.

The following extracts are from Twiggs' own account of his operations on the 8th and 9th of May:

"The enemy, at the distance of about half a mile, opened their batteries on the right, which, being immediately responded to by our two eighteen-pounders, in charge of Lieutenant Churchill, brought on the action of the 8th instant. Major Ringgold's battery was ordered to the right and front of the eighteen-pounders, at a distance of about seven hundred yards from the enemy, when the battery was opened with great effect, as was shown the next day, by the number of the enemy's dead found along his line. The infantry, in the mean time, was formed in rear of the artillery, receiving with the greatest possible coolness the enemy's fire, and only anxious for the order to rush in and participate actively in the affair.

"A regiment of the enemy's lancers was observed to move to our right, apparently to gain possession of our wagon train, a few hundred yards in rear. The 5th infantry and two pieces of Major Ringgold's artillery, under the command of Lieutenant R. Ridgely, were ordered to check this movement. Having gained ground to the right, some four or five hundred yards, the 5th was formed in square to receive a charge from the lancers, who advanced to within fifty yards, when the opposing side of the square fired into and repulsed them, having received in the mean time several irregular discharges from the enemy. The lancers re-formed, and continued their movement to get in rear of our right flank, when I ordered the 3d to move to the right and rear, around a pond of water, and prevent their progress in that direction. Seeing their movement frustrated in this point, the lancers commenced a retreat in good order, marching apparently by squadrons, when First Lieutenant R. Ridgely, of Major Ringgold's battery, assisted by Brevet Second

L

Lieutenant French, opened a fire on them, and scattered them in
all directions.   In this affair, the enemy lost some twenty-eight or
thirty men.   This portion of the right wing served in about this
position until the close of the action.   In the mean time, Major
Ringgold, with the remaining two pieces of his battery, continued
to play on the enemy with great success.   The gallant major was
mortally wounded by a cannon ball towards the close of the action,
and his horse shot under him at the same time.   The army and the
country will long deplore the loss of so brave and accomplished an
officer."

For his bravery in these battles, Twiggs was promoted to the
brevet rank of brigadier-general.   He commanded the advance at
the capture of Matamoras, and was appointed military governor of
the city.   This station he occupied until the movement of the army
toward Monterey.   Twiggs was one of the most efficient officers
concerned in the storming of Monterey.   In the street fight he especially distinguished himself; and the annexed portions of his report will show the trials endured by his command, in the eventful
"three days:"

"On the morning of the 21st instant, my division advanced toward the city.   Lieutenant-Colonel J. Garland's brigade, composed
of the 3d and 4th regiments of regular infantry, and Captain B.
Bragg's horse-artillery, Lieutenant-Colonel H. Wilson's brigade,
composed of the 1st regiment of regular infantry, and the Washington and Baltimore battalion of volunteers, were ordered to the
east and lower end of the city, to make a diversion in favour of
Brevet Brigadier-General W. J. Worth's division, which was operating against the west and upper part of the city.   It being deemed
practicable, an assault was ordered against two of the enemy's advanced works.   The regular force of my division was thrown to
the right of the two works, with orders to take possession of some
houses in the city, on the right and rear of the enemy's advanced
position, with a view of annoying him in flank and rear.   The
Washington and Baltimore battalion was ordered on the road leading
directly to the works.   Under a most galling and destructive fire
from three batteries in front and one on the right, as well as from
that of small arms from all the adjacent houses and stone walls, my
division advanced as rapidly as the ground and the stern opposition
of the enemy would admit of.   The 1st, 3d, and 4th regiments of

infantry gained the position to which they were ordered, and annoyed the enemy in flank and rear, until he was obliged to evacuate his two advanced works, which were hotly pressed by General Butler's division of volunteers, and the Washington and Baltimore battalion, under command of Lieutenant-Colonel Watson.

"The 3d and 4th advanced still further into the city, but finding the streets strongly barricaded by heavy masses of masonry, behind which batteries were placed, and the houses filled with light troops, were obliged to retire to the works first taken by the volunteers. The position of the enemy's batteries, and the arrangement of his defences, in every street and corner, rendered it necessary for the regular troops who advanced into the city to be separated, each company being led by its captain or immediate commander, and for the time acting independently. After a most manly struggle of some six hours, my men succeeded, after various repulses, in driving the enemy from each and every of his positions in the suburbs. The 3d infantry, commanded by Major W. W. Lear, and part of the 4th, all under the command of Lieutenant-Colonel J. Garland, led off towards the right, and in the direction of one of the enemy's strongest works in front of a bridge in the city. Captain B. Bragg's battery accompanied the command, under a destructive fire, which killed and disabled several of his men and horses, until directed to retire beyond the range of small arms.

*   *   *   *   *   *   *

"The number of killed and wounded in this assault, shows with what obstinacy each position was defended by the enemy, as well as the gallantry and good conduct displayed by our officers and men.

"Captain B. Bragg's battery, having suffered severely, after advancing some distance into the city, was obliged to withdraw to a point out of range of the enemy's small arms. Captain R. Ridgely, with one section of his battery, annoyed the enemy's advanced works for some time in the commencement of the assault, but was obliged to retire out of range of their batteries, that were playing on him. Having used a twelve-pounder taken from the first work, against the enemy, till the ammunition gave out, he was sent, with one section of his own battery still further in advance; but being unable to accomplish much against the enemy's heavy breastworks, returned to, and occupied with his battery, the first work taken from

10

the enemy. Captains R. Ridgely and B. Bragg, and their subalterns, W. H. Shover, G. H. Thomas, J. F. Reynolds, C. L. Kilburn, and S. G. French, deserve the highest praise for their skill and good conduct under the heaviest fire of the enemy, which, when an opportunity offered, was concentrated on them. In the advanced works referred to were taken four officers and sixteen men, prisoners of war, together with five pieces of ordnance, some ammunition and small arms. Having thrown up some slight breastworks, the 1st, 3d, and 4th infantry, and Captain R. Ridgely's battery, occupied this position until the morning of the 22d.

*   *   *   *   *   *   *   *

"On the 23d, the advance into the city was resumed—the infantry working their way from house to house, supported by Captains R. Ridgely and B. Bragg's battery, driving the enemy before them. When night closed our operations on the 23d, our men had advanced to within two squares of the centre of the city."

After the surrender of the city, Twiggs occupied it with his division, until ordered to join General Scott on the gulf coast. He assisted at the taking of Vera Cruz, and received from the commander the honour of conducting the main attack at Sierra Gordo. The annexed graphic description of the movements of his division, on the night preceding the battle, is from the pen of one of its number:—

"The day preceding the battle of Sierra Gordo was one of exceeding beauty, more so than even many of those seen beneath a tropical sun. A gentle breeze, which was wafted across the Tierra Caliente from the 'Blue Gulf,' unfolded upon the summit of the Sierra Gordo the gay ensign of the haughty Mexican, and at the same time floated the star-spangled banner in its balmy embrace over a handful of Americans who came to battle in their country's cause. Stretched along the heights behind strong fortifications, defended by frowning cannon and bristling bayonets, attired in all the gay paraphernalia of a splendid army, lay the Mexican hosts, gathered to defend their country from the 'northern barbarians,' who laid quietly encamped in the small valley of the Plan del Rio, patiently awaiting the order for battle, when they should rush forth upon that proud army and drive them in confusion from their strong holds.

"Among the latter party was myself—an humble soldier in the

cause—seated in my tent. I thought of the home I had left behind me, and the friends I had forsaken, to struggle amid strangers in a foreign land—the many chances against me in the game of life and death that is for ever going on in the midst of an army. I thought myself dreaming; but I could not lay that 'flattering unction to my soul.' It was too true — the reality was too plain. I was a soldier, and upon the eve of a battle, with many chances of being *victimized* by a Mexican bullet. Well, well, thought I, if I am killed, it shall be gloriously in defence of my country's honour; my name, among others, will be handed down to posterity, printed on the page of history, and 'enrolled upon the scroll of fame,' an example to future belligerent young gentlemen that the 'pride and pomp of glorious war,' no matter how imposing, does not counterbalance its 'circumstance' in the scale of life.

"I looked out upon the camp: my fellow-soldiers were engaged in various occupations. Some, thinking of the approaching contest, were preparing their arms and ammunition to do bloody work; others, thinking of their latter end, were writing their wills and farewell letters to their friends; others, like Sergeant Dalgetty, thinking of their *provant*, were cooking; others, thinking that they were brave, were talking in loud tones of the valorous deeds they intended to perform on the morrow; others, thinking that battles were dangerous things, were musing on the chances of going through safely; and others still, thinking of nothing at all, were whistling, singing, and *playing cards*. I was thinking of all these things, when I was suddenly startled by the sullen booming of a cannon in the direction of Sierra Gordo; then another and another; then the rapid roll of musketry and successive cracks of rifles. It was all too plain that the battle had commenced. General Twiggs had been ordered in the morning to take the position assigned his division, and protect the detail engaged in making a road for our artillery, and the enemy had attempted to drive him back. The fight raged with violence for some moments. Those ancient hills shook with the thunder of artillery—the valleys re-echoed the sound of small-arms. I thought of the many souls that took their departure from earth with each discharge—of the mangled limbs and painful looks and cries of the wounded. I had been under fire before; but somehow this seemed like getting into closer quarters than formerly. I said not a word, but, like Paddy's owl, I kept up 'a thinking.'

L 2

"Up to this time it had been the impression that our brigade would be held in reserve; hence the *nonchalance* manifested by most of the corps; but this pleasant hallucination was banished by the 'long roll,' beaten by 'old Brown,' the drum-major — a very *Paganini* on the drum. Our colonel had prevailed on General Scott to order us in the advance to support Twiggs. All thinking now ceased; he who was cleaning his musket quickly shouldered it; the letter-writer closed his mournful epistle; the cook left his supper at the mercy of the fire; the gasconading youth was silent, and hoped from the bottom of his heart that it was a false alarm; the silent thinker calmly equipped himself; the musician halted in the middle of a tune; the card-players threw down their *hands*, and, instead of *shuffling* the *papers*, thought of *shuffling* off this *mortal coil*.

"The drums beat a merry tune as the companies marched into their places. The words, 'Attention — shoulder arms!' from our adjutant, made every man a soldier; and the regiment was formed — as fine a body of men as ever took the field. Our gallant colonel drew his good sword, and, glancing proudly upon us, gave the command, 'By the right flank — right face — forward — march!' And away we went. As we reached the road, I glanced behind me upon our camp. The fires burned with lurid flickering flame; the camp-kettles, brimming full of good 'bean-soup,' sung a mournful song; our poor invalids, unable to follow us to the field of glory, gazed with tearful eyes upon their departing comrades, and mourned not so much because *they* could not go as because *we* were going. On we went at a smashing pace, and, having three miles to go, just as we were ascending the first hill between our camp and the enemy, we met Sergeant Scott, General Twiggs' orderly, coming at a forced gallop with a prisoner seated upon the crupper of his horse. Scott was a giant in comparison with the diminutive form of the Mexican, who grasped him about the waist and held on, as you have seen a dirty-faced urchin while riding behind his *daddy*, his ear glued to Scott's back, as if osculating his spine. At every bound of the horse his body flew out in a direct line from that of the sergeant's; and when he struck the horse again—oh, awful, awful, indeed, was the shock! Thus had Scott ridden with him for three miles; and I guess the Mexican did not much admire that kind of transportation. This is the way that Sergeant Scott takes prisoners. It is said that he has taken a prisoner in every fight in which his general has participated.

"Immediately after Scott, followed a wounded soldier leaning upon his comrade. Never shall I forget the look of that man; his arm had been shattered by a shot and hung powerless, while a stream of blood poured from a severed artery, flooding his whole side; yet not a look betrayed the least emotion of pain. He had sacrificed his good right arm in his country's cause, and he rejoiced in the sacrifice.

"About five o'clock, P. M., we reached the vicinity of Twiggs; as we approached his position we met many of the wounded returning from the field; and immediately in his neighbourhood we came upon the surgeons at their bloody work. To hear the groans of some, and even to witness the fortitude of others of the mangled soldiers, was truly heart-rending: there lay men in the agonies of death, and there lay lifeless bodies, which but a few moments before had moved in the full enjoyment of all their faculties, now wrapped for ever in the cold embrace of death.

"We found that the enemy had retired behind his batteries with great loss, leaving Twiggs to bivouack upon his hard-earned field. We were immediately reported to the old veteran, and directed to pile arms and await further orders, which soon came for a detail of one hundred men from each regiment (we having brigaded with the 3d Illinois and 1st New York regiments) for the purpose of placing in battery a twenty-four-pounder upon the summit of an immense hill lying between us and the Sierra Gordo. The gun was of immense weight; the hill steep and rugged; but the 'suckers' were hitched on, and up that dreadful engine went, tearing down trees and crushing huge rocks in its course.

"This work occupied a great portion of the night; and when the piece was placed in battery, the men who played *horses* had the satisfaction of reflecting that the feat they had performed excelled any thing in the annals of warfare.

"This tremendous task performed, pickets were placed, and the army sunk upon the blood-stained rocks to slumber, only to awake on the morrow in order to imbrue their hands once more in the blood of the degenerate sons of the Aztecs. Having no musket, I went in search of one, and upon the bloody battle-field I found it. It was formerly the property of a *regular;* its once bright barrel and glist-

10*

ening bayonet were dimmed with human gore. Oh, how loth was I to touch it; but self-preservation said ' take it;' and grasping it, I sought a spot clear of rocks on which to stretch my weary limbs. It was hard to find, and I made no choice, but laid myself cautiously down with my head upon a stone and my gun by my side. I tried to sleep; but sleep seemed for ever banished: as often as I closed my eyes, a bloody soldier sprang up and seemed to warn me of my fate. A thousand visions flitted across my mind. I saw war in all its hideous forms; I saw the weeping widows and orphans, and childless parents, when at the village post-office the bulletin of this battle should be read. I heard the loud hurra of the nation over the glorious victory, and saw her mourn for the loss of her sons. I saw red-mouthed cannon belching forth death and destruction upon our little army; and I saw my companions falling around me like the withered leaves of autumn."

Twiggs carried the strong work of Sierra Gordo, the key of the entire position, and after the victory pushed on with rapid marches after the fugitives. Next day he entered Jalapa, of which he took undisputed possession.

In the march toward the capital, Twiggs' troops encountered hardships more frightful than even those on the battle-field; and in turning Lake Chalco, near Penon, they were obliged to drag their cannon over rocks and ravines, and rugged lava, where horses were entirely useless. During the battles of the 19th and 20th of August, they fought and marched all day, and at night lay amid drenching rains, with tents without blankets, on bare rocks. Their bearing under these trials elicited the applause of every one, and was noticed by General Scott in terms of high commendation.

Twiggs was not concerned in the attack on Molino del Rey, although one brigade (Riley's) from his division formed the reserve of the assailing force. The following extracts show the part he took in the storming of Chapultepec :—

" Steptoe's twelve-pounder battery was placed in position during the night of the 11th, and by daylight in the morning was enabled to open on the enemy's batteries, situated at the garita in the San Antonio road; and between that and the San Angel road the firing was kept up briskly during the day on both sides, with but little loss to us, who were protected by a good temporary breastwork. On the morning of the 13th the firing was renewed with great spirit, which compelled the enemy to withdraw his guns from the garita, within the protection of the city walls.

"Smith's brigade was now ordered to proceed in the direction of Chapultepec, and support one of the columns of attack, commanded by Major-General Quitman. With the stormers from my division in front of the road, the attacking column on the left, and Smith's brigade on the right of it, the force advanced in the face of a well-directed fire from a battery at the base of Chapultepec, near a point where the aqueduct leaves it, and also from musketry sheltered by the aqueduct, and by breastworks across and on each side of the road. When within charging distance, the stormers, with the assistance of the right of Smith's brigade, which had been thrown forward toward the aqueduct, rushed on the enemy's guns, drove off or killed the cannoneers, and took possession of this strong point. Smith's brigade having advanced three companies of mounted riflemen considerably to its right, to protect the right of Quitman's division, they were found near the first battery when the stormers were about attacking, and were thus enabled to enter with the advance. The brigade pushed on and captured a second battery in the rear of the first, when several guns and many prisoners were taken; after some brisk skirmishing, the enemy was finally driven from every point on the east of the hill, and were pursued on the San Cosme road some distance by the storming party, under the command of Captain Paul, 7th infantry; this party having been overtaken by the 1st division, and their specific duties as stormers having been accomplished, were ordered to return and rejoin their respective regiments.

"Early in the action, Captain Casey, 2d infantry, who commanded the storming party from my division, was severely wounded, and obliged to retire. The command devolving upon Captain Paul, 7th infantry, Lieutenant Gantt, 7th infantry, with a portion of the party, was ordered to cross the ditch on the left of the road, and proceed further to the left of the base of Chapultepec, and, by scaling the wall, gain admittance to the body of the work. This gallant officer was shot dead at the head of his men; the command of this party devolving upon Lieutenant Steele, 2d infantry, who led his men on with intrepidity and success. * * * * * *

"Smith's brigade — the riflemen leading, supported by an eight-inch howitzer, in charge of the late and gallant Captain Drum, 4th artillery—carried a battery near the Casa Colorada, half way to the garita on the Chapultepec road. The command was here reorganized by the senior officer, Major-General Quitman, with the mounted riflemen again in the advance, supported by the South Carolina regiment — the remainder of Smith's brigade being in reserve — and charged the battery at the garita; the reserve pushing up, arrived at the battery at the same moment with the advance, and entered the city at twenty minutes past one o'clock, P. M. The brigade occupied buildings within the city during the night, and, the enemy having in the mean time abandoned the city, our forces took possession of it on the morning of the 14th. Our national colours were planted on the enemy's palace by a non-commissioned officer of the mounted rifles at seven o'clock, A. M.

"Until late in the afternoon of the 13th, Riley's brigade, with Steptoe's and Taylor's batteries, were kept in the Piedad road to watch the enemy in that quarter. It formed a junction with the 1st division on the San Cosme road early in the night of the 13th."

For the remaining operations of Twiggs' command, we refer the reader to the lives of Scott, Quitman and Pillow. Twiggs is now with the commander at the capital. Few officers can boast of more valuable service than he has rendered, and the verdict of his nation has placed him among those whom she delights to honour.

GENERAL SMITH.

Brevet Brigadier-General Persifor F. Smith has but recently entered the army, in which he now occupies so honourable a station. He is a native of Pennsylvania, although appointed from Louisiana. His first commission as colonel of mounted rifles, is dated May 27th, 1846, and he was brevetted brigadier-general in September of the same year.

Smith's first services in his new profession were brilliant and useful. He formed part of General Worth's division, and was intrusted by that officer with the storming of the forts near the Bishop's Palace. His troops marched through extensive corn-fields, over rocks and ledges, and through a branch of the San Juan river, while it was plashing and foaming with the Mexican shot. The enthusiasm with which they attacked the forts, entering them at a perfect rush, was not surpassed by any achievement of that eventful day. For his manner of conducting the attack, and his subsequent services, General Smith is mentioned by Worth among those whom it vas " his pleasing and grateful duty to present to the consideration f the general-in-chief, and through him to the government." After the capitulation, he was appointed to receive the surrender of the citadel, a ceremony which he conducted with forbearance and delicacy to the unhappy and humiliated foe.

General Smith was prevented by sickness from participating in the battle of Sierra Gordo, but at Contreros and the succeeding actions, he acted a most conspicuous part. We give extracts from his official account of these victories :—

" On the 19th instant, my brigade, with the rest of the division, marched from San Augustin to cover the division of General Pillow opening the road from San Augustin to that which runs through this place to the city, in order to turn the position of San Antonio.

Advancing about one and a half mile, we were met by the fire of the Mexican batteries opposite to us on the San Angel road. Between us was about a half mile of lava rocks, almost impassable for a single footman, then a slope down towards a ravine, on the opposite bank of which were the road and the enemy's works, on a height called Contreros. The front faced us, and the left flank swept the road below it, a turn forwards in the road bringing the work directly in the prolongation of the lower part of the road. The work had upwards of twenty large guns, was full of infantry, and large masses of cavalry and infantry were behind it and on its flanks. Magruder's battery was ordered forward to a position in front of the enemy, and partially covered by a ledge of rocks. My brigade was ordered to follow and support it, and cover the advance of the party making the road. We went forward under a very heavy fire, and took a position on the left of Magruder's battery. We found Lieutenant Callender's howitzer battery at this point. When we took this direction, Riley's brigade was sent to the right. Magruder's battery and the howitzer battery were soon disabled, and, on examining the ground, it was evident that we were advancing by the only path that crossed the broken bed of lava, and on which the enemy were prepared to receive us, having cleared away all the bushes that obstructed their view. The guns could go no further, and the infantry would, on its march down the slope, be exposed to a terrible fire, without knowing whether the crossing of the ravine below was possible. Being isolated from the division, I determined to try one of the enemy's flanks; and that on our right being preferable, as it would cut off his retreat, I determined to move in that direction. Captain Magruder was directed to open his fire as we passed his rear, to occupy the enemy, and mask our movements to the right. This he did most effectually, though suffering from a great loss, especially of officers.

"To replace this loss, Lieutenant Haskins and twenty men were detached from Major Dimick's regiment, and three companies of the 3d infantry were left to support him. With great difficulty we succeeded in crossing the rock for near a mile, and descended towards the village of Encelda, whose church was visible among the trees. As we emerged from the rocks, we saw immense numbers of troops, cavalry and infantry, approaching from Mexico, and forming on the slope on the opposite side of the village. We crossed two small streams at the bottom of deep and difficult gulleys, and found some of our troops in the village, they proving to be four regiments, chiefly of General Pillow's division, and under command of General Cadwalader, who immediately reported to me. The village lay entirely on the other side of the main road, and a small stream ran between them at the bottom of a ravine. On the road, and between it and the stream was a garden and house surrounded by a high and tolerably strong stone wall. The village was intersected by narrow lanes lying between high dikes enclosing gardens full of trees and shrubbery—the lanes affording cover, and the trees concealment for the men. At the centre stood an old stone church. I drew General Cadwalader's force up in the outer edge of the village, facing the enemy—placed the 3d infantry and rifles in column by company, left in front, on the right flank — occupied the church with Lieutenant Smith's engineer company and Captain Irwin's company of the 11th regiment—placed Major Dimick's regiment in the garden on the road, to secure that avenue and our rear.

"The enemy was now formed opposite to us in two lines — the infantry in front and cavalry in the rear—about ten thousand strong. It was now after sunset, when Colonel Riley's brigade arrived. It had crossed and gone up towards Contreros [entrenched camp] and driven off strong parties of the enemy. I now ordered an attack on the enemy's right, intending to attack in two columns—Colonel Riley's on the left, and General Cadwalader's on the right of the former—retired in echellon ; but before the troops could be disengaged from the thickets, [the officers being without horses,] it was so dark that the enemy's line could not be seen, and the order for attack was countermanded. General Cadwalader took position again in the outer edge of the village ; Riley's brigade parallel to it in a long line inside ; the rifles, under Major Loring, on his right, and the 3d infantry in the church-yard. The troops were without shelter or fire, and it rained all night. At this time Lieutenant Tower reported that he had been at the ravine towards the rear of the enemy's works at Contreros, and thought it practicable for infantry, though very difficult. We had now in front and on our left flank, eighteen thousand Mexicans, with between twenty-five and thirty guns—among the troops six or seven thousand cavalry. We were, at most, three thousand three hundred strong, and without artillery or cavalry ; and it was evident we could only maintain our

M

position, which was of the utmost importance to the commanding general, by the most prompt and energetic action. I therefore directed an attack on the works at Contreros, [the entrenched camp,] by turning their rear before day ; and Captain Lee, of the engineers, offered to return to General Scott, (a most difficult task,) and inform him of our position, and that I would march out at three o'clock, A. M., so that any diversion that he could make in our favour from that side might be prepared accordingly.

" At precisely three o'clock in the morning of the 20th, the troops commenced their march. It had rained all night, and the men had lain in the mud, without fire, and suffering from cold. It rained now, and was so dark that an object six feet off could not be seen. The men were ordered to keep within touch of each other, so that the rear could not go astray. Lieutenant Tower, of the engineers, with Lieutenant Brooks, acting assistant adjutant-general of the 2d division, now acting in my staff, had, during the night, reconnoitred the pass, to assure the practicability of the march. The path was narrow, full of rocks and mud, and so difficult was the march that it was daylight before the head of Cadwalader's brigade got out of the village, where the path descends to the ravine; and as the march was by a flank, the command was stretched out thrice its length. Having followed up the ravine to a point where it seemed possible to get at the rear of the work, the head was halted, and the rear closed up; many loads that were wet were drawn, and Riley formed two columns by divisions.

" He thus advanced further up the ravine, turning to his left, and rising over the bank, stood fronting the rear of the work, but still sheltered from its fire by a slight acclivity before him. Having reformed his ranks, he ascended the top of the hill, and was in full view of the enemy, who immediately opened a warm fire, not only from the work, but on his right flank. Throwing out his two first divisions as skirmishers, he rushed down the slope to the work. The engineer company and rifles had been thrown across an intervening ravine, under the brow of the slope, and from that position swept it in front of his column, and then, inclining towards their left, joined in the attack on the troops outside of the left bank of the fort. In the mean time, General Cadwalader followed the route taken by Riley, and forming his columns as the troops came up, moved on to his (Riley's) support. The first brigade had been ordered to follow the same route; but, while it was still marching in that direction by its right flank up the ravine, and nearly opposite the work, seeing a large body of the enemy on its left flank, I ordered Major Dimick to face the brigade to the left, and, advancing in line, attack this force in flank. This was done in the finest style, and the 1st artillery and 3d infantry, mounting the bank of the ravine, rushing down the next, and up its opposite bank, met the enemy outside of the work just as Riley's brigade poured into it, and the whole giving way. Cavalry, formed in line for the charge, yielding to the bayonets of our foot, the rout was complete, while Riley's brigade cleared the work, and planted their colours on it. The two first pieces captured, which fell into the hands of the 4th artillery, proved to be the pieces lost (but without loss of honour) by a company of that very regiment at Buena Vista. Leaving a force to collect and guard the captured ordnance, the pursuit was continued down the road.

"This, it will be recollected, passed not more than half a mile off the garden and house occupied by a part of General Shields' brigade, placed there to intercept the retreat of the enemy. This skilful and gallant officer, when we marched, had spread his men over the line we had occupied, and directed them to make fires towards daylight, as though preparing their breakfast. The enemy in front had, during the night, placed batteries along the line, and in the morning moved detachments forward to take in flank the attack he saw we were meditating the night before, which he was prepared to meet; supposing, from the indications he found, that we were still in force in the village. When, after daylight, he saw a column moving on Contreros, [the entrenched camp,] and already prepared to turn it, he must have supposed we had been strongly reinforced; for his movements to and fro indicated great perplexity. His doubts were soon resolved, however, by the loss of Contreros, [the camp,] and he immediately commenced a hasty retreat along the top of the hill, inclining towards the San Angel road. Shields' force (five or six hundred men) having, under his skilful direction, thus disposed of one enemy, he turned to the other, who, in their flight, found themselves intercepted at the garden, and, under the sure fire of the South Carolina regiment, broke away over the opposite fields, and, taking shelter in the ditches and ravines, escaped, many of them, to the rocks. Two squadrons of cavalry, either by chance or a wise design, in a narrow part of the road between the

11

wall and dyke, laid down their arms, and so choked the way, that the pursuit was interrupted for upwards of twenty minutes, which sufficed (we having no cavalry) for the safety of many of the fugitives. A large body escaped upwards towards the mountains. I did not pursue them, being entirely out of our direction.

"Accounts from Mexican officers, intercepted since the battle, inform us that there were seven thousand in and about Contreros, [the entrenched camp,] commanded by General Valencia, and upwards of twelve thousand in front of Encelda, [or the hamlet of Contreros,] in reserve, commanded by General Santa Anna. We killed seven hundred, and took fifteen hundred prisoners, among them several generals. We captured twenty-two pieces of brass ordnance, viz: four Spanish sixteen-pounders, four eight-inch howitzers, two five and a half-inch howitzers, six six-pounders, and six smaller pieces, with a large amount of shells and other ammunition. We also took seven hundred pack mules and many horses, and an immense number of small-arms, which we destroyed. After directing the prisoners and property to be collected, I directed the pursuit to be continued, and was forming the column, when General Twiggs arrived. He immediately ordered the most vigorous pursuit, and we moved forwards. As we approached San Angel, the rifles were again thrown forward as skirmishers, and entered the town at the heels of the enemy's lancers, capturing an ammunition wagon. Here General Pillow assumed command, and at Coyoacan the commander-in-chief. 　*　　*　　*　　*　　*　　*　　*

"At this time the tremendous fire from the neighbourhood of the church, showed clearly, not only that there was a strong force stationed there, but that there was also a more considerable work than was at first supposed; but being all surrounded by very high corn, its form could not be discovered. It afterwards proved that the place was regularly fortified. The church buildings formed a large square; the lower front towards us was chiefly a wall scaffolded for infantry. Behind it rose a higher building, also covered with infantry; behind it the church, and the high steeple on its right flank, also filled with men. In front of the first was a curtain, connecting two salient angles which flanked it, and were continued back to the side walls of the church. It was garrisoned by about two thousand men, and mounted seven pieces. What was supposed the one-gun battery, was the right salient angle which enfiladed the road from

Coyoacan; so that when the 1st artillery attempted to turn it, they found themselves in front of this curtain, and exposed to all the musketry of the walls beyond. They, however, stood their ground with great loss, getting such cover as the ground afforded, and firing at the embrasures when opportunity offered. It was now reported that the other brigade (Riley's) was ordered round to the right of the work, and General Pillow's division to its left. I therefore ordered the 2d infantry to be ready, so soon as the fire of these corps began to tell, to advance under the cover of some huts near the right bastion, and, after silencing the fire of its musketry, to assault it. In the mean time, Taylor's battery had continued its fire uninterrupted by the severest shower of grape, canister, musketry, round shot and shell, within short musket range, that was ever witnessed. The conduct of Captain Taylor, Lieutenant French, and the men who remained unhurt, was the admiration of all who witnessed it. The pieces were served as though on drill, while two of the officers, Lieutenants Martin and Boynton, and twenty men wounded, and fifteen horses crippled, laid around, and testified to the danger of their position. Hearing now the fire from the other corps, and finding that of the work to be less steady, I directed Captain Alexander (commanding the 3d infantry) to advance to the position indicated, and commence his work.

"After clearing the ramparts partially of their men, the 3d rushed over the bastion, led by Captain J. M. Smith and Lieutenant Shepherd, and their companies, and a part of the 1st artillery, over the curtain, when the garrison held out a white flag, and urrendered to Captain Smith, who was fortunate enough to be the first in the work. Many had escaped from the back of the church; but one hundred and four officers, among them several generals, and eleven hundred and fifty-five men were counted after the surrender. It is proper here to observe, in order to prevent errors hereafter, that after Captain Alexander's command had received the surrender of the garrison, and had gone up into the gallery of the front house with General Rincon, from which he was displaying the colours of his regiment, a staff officer from another division, who had seen the white flag still flying, rode into the work to receive the surrender which had been made some time before to Captain Alexander. Seven pieces of brass cannon, much ammunition and small-arms, the prisoners before mentioned, and an important position, were the fruits of this victory. I should have mentioned before that Captain Craig had in the morning rejoined the regiment with the three companies left with Captain Magruder; and those companies of riflemen who had been left in the pedregal, [field of rocks and lava,] had also joined the regiment."

General Smith was appointed one of the negotiators for the armistice, and took an active part in the subsequent operations before the capital; the detailed accounts of which have been given elsewhere. He is now with the commander-in-chief, at the capital.

GENERAL SHIELDS.

Page 125.

BRIGADIER-GENERAL SHIELDS.

BRIGADIER-GENERAL JAMES SHIELDS, though appointed to the army from Illinois, is a native of Ireland. He marched with the Central Division, under General Wool, but left on its arrival at Monclova, thus losing an opportunity to participate in the battle of Buena Vista. He was at the siege of Vera Cruz, and in the battle of Sierra Gordo received a musket-ball through the lungs. His recovery from this wound seems almost miraculous.

The services he performed on the 19th and 20th of August, together with his admirable deception of the enemy during their retreat from Contreros, we give in his own words:

"Directing my march upon the village near Contreros, the troops had to pass over ground covered with rocks and crags, and filled with chasms, which rendered the road almost impassable. A deep rugged ravine, along the bed of which rolled a rapid stream, was passed, after dark, with great difficulty and exertion; and to rest the wearied troops after crossing, I directed them to lie upon their arms until midnight. While occupying this position, two strong pickets, thrown out by my orders, discovered, fired upon, and drove back a body of Mexican infantry moving through the fields in a direction from their position towards the city. I have since learned that an attempt had in like manner been made by the enemy to pass the position on the main road occupied by the 1st regiment of artillery, and with a like want of success. About midnight I again resumed the march, and joined Brigadier-General Smith in the village already referred to.

"General Smith, previous to my arrival, had made the most judicious arrangement for turning and surprising the Mexican position about daybreak, and with which I could not wish to interfere. This

11 *   (125)

cast upon my command the necessity of holding the position to be evacuated by General Smith, and which was threatened by the enemy's artillery and infantry on the right, and a large force of his cavalry on the left.   About daybreak the enemy opened a brisk fire of grape and round shot upon the church and village in which my brigade was posted, as also upon a part of our own troops displayed to divert him on his right and front — evidently unaware of the movement in progress to turn his position by the left and rear. This continued until Colonel Riley's brigade opened its fire from the rear, which was delivered with such terrible effect, that the whole Mexican force was thrown into the utmost consternation.

"At this juncture, I ordered the two regiments of my command to throw themselves on the main road, by which the enemy must retire, to intercept and cut off his retreat; and, although officers and men had suffered severely during the march of the night, and from exposure without shelter or cover to the incessant rain until daybreak, this movement was executed in good order, and with rapidity.   The Palmetto regiment, crossing a deep ravine, deployed on both sides of the road, and opened a most destructive fire upon the mingled masses of infantry and cavalry; and the New York regiment, brought into line lower down, and on the roadside, delivered its fire with a like effect.   At this point many of the enemy were killed and wounded; some three hundred and sixty-five captured, of which twenty-five were officers, and amongst the latter was General Nicolas Mendoza.

"In the meanwhile the enemy's cavalry, about three thousand strong, which had been threatening our position during the morning, moved down towards us in good order, and as if to attack.   I immediately recalled the infantry, to place them in position to meet the threatened movement; but soon the cavalry changed its direction and retreated toward the capital.   I now received an order from General Twiggs to advance by the main road towards Mexico; and having posted Captain Marshall's company of South Carolina volunteers and Captain Taylor's New York volunteers, in charge of the prisoners and wounded, I moved off with the remainder of my force, and joined the positions of the 2d and 3d divisions, already *en route* on the main road.   On this march we were joined by the general-in-chief, who assumed command of the whole, and the march continued uninterrupted until we arrived before Churubusco.   Here the enemy was found strongly fortified, and posted with his main force—probably twenty-five thousand.

*   *   *   *   *   *   *   *   *

"Leaving Coyoacan by a left-hand road, and advancing about a mile upon it, I moved thence with my command towards the right, through a heavy corn-field, and gained an open but swampy field, in which is situated the hacienda de los Partales. On the edge of this field, beyond the hacienda, I discovered the road by which the enemy must retire from Churubusco, and found that his reserve of about four thousand infantry already occupied it, just in rear of the town. As my command arrived, I established the right upon a point recommended by Captain Lee, engineer officer, in whose skill and judgment I had the utmost confidence, and commenced a movement to the left to flank the enemy on his right, and throw my troops between him and the city; but finding his right supported by a heavy body of cavalry of some three thousand strong, and seeing, too, that with his infantry he answered to my movements by a corresponding one towards his right flank, gaining ground faster than I could, owing to the heavy mud and swamp through which I had to operate, I withdrew the men to the cover of the hacienda, and determined to attack him upon his front. I selected the Palmetto regiment as the base of my line, and this gallant regiment moved forward firmly and rapidly, under a fire of musketry as terrible, perhaps, as any which soldiers ever faced; the New York, 12th and 15th deployed gallantly on the right, and the 9th on the left, and the whole advanced, opening their fire as they came up, and moving steadily forward. The enemy began to waver, and when my order to charge was given, the men rushed upon and scattered his broken ranks. As we reached the road, the advance of Worth's command appeared, driving the enemy from his stronghold of Churubusco. I took command of the front, and continued in pursuit until passed by Harney with his cavalry, who followed the routed foe into the very gates of the city.

"In this terrible battle, in which a strongly-fortified enemy fought behind his works, under the walls of his capital, our loss is necessarily severe. This loss, I regret to say, has fallen most severely upon my command. In the two regiments of my own brigade, numbering about six hundred in the fight, the loss is reported two hundred and forty in killed and wounded.

"In this last engagement my command captured three hundred and eighty prisoners, including six officers. Of this number forty-two had deserted from the American army during the war, and at their head we found the notorious O'Reilly, who had fought against our troops at Monterey and elsewhere. A particular and detailed report of the loss, as also of the prisoners captured by this command, accompanies this report."

In the recent glorious battles of Mexico, Shields has exhibited the same reckless daring, the same impetuosity and ability which he evinced at Sierra Gordo. He again received a severe, though not dangerous wound.

The personal appearance of the general is thus described by a visitor during his recent tour to the United States, where he still remains.

"In the saloon we saw the gallant General Shields. He is stouter than when we saw him, some two years since, at General Taylor's camp at Camargo. He then, in his undress military uniform, looked like an elegant gentleman. He had not a wrinkle on his brow, and his countenance ever wore a smile. His beard was closely shaven, and his eyes were lighted up with the brilliant fire of hope. And yet, how a short term of service alters a man? Yesterday he looked like the hero of many wars. His brow was seamed with the lines of fatigue and suffering, and his upper lip was garnished with a thick moustache. His complexion was bronzed, his arm, from a late wound, hung in a sling; but his eye was still brilliant with martial fire. There were hundreds who flocked around him and sought to grasp his hand, and all were received by him with the most cordial warmth and friendship. Those around looked upon the gallant hero with feelings of respect and admiration, and there was not one in that broad saloon who went out, without saying in his heart, 'that man is a true soldier.'"

BRIGADIER-GENERAL LANE.

BRIGADIER-GENERAL JOSEPH LANE is a native of North Carolina, but was appointed to the army from Illinois. He entered the army July 1st, 1846, and marched to Mexico as one of General Wool's column. The following is his own account of his operations at Buena Vista :—

"About nine o'clock I was informed by Colonel Churchill that the enemy were advancing toward my position in great force, sheltering themselves in a deep ravine which runs up towards the mountain directly in my front. I immediately put my columns in motion, consisting of those eight battalion companies, and Lieutenant O'Brien's battery, amounting in all to about four hundred men, to meet them. The enemy, when they deployed from the ravine and appeared on the ridge, displayed a force of about four thousand infantry, supported by a large body of lancers. The infantry immediately opened a most destructive fire, which was returned by my small command, both infantry and artillery, in a most gallant manner for some time. I soon perceived that I was too far from the enemy for my muskets to take that deadly effect which I desired, and immediately sent my aid-de-camp to Lieutenant O'Brien, directing him to place his battery in a more advanced position, with the determination of advancing my whole line. By this movement I should not only be near the enemy, but should also bring the company on my extreme left more completely into action, as the brow of the hill impeded their fire. By this time the enemy's fire of musketry, and the raking fire of ball and grape-shot of their battery posted on my left flank had become terrible, and my infantry instead of advancing as was ordered, I regret to say, retired in some disorder from their position, notwithstanding my own and the severe efforts of my officers to prevent them. About the same time, the riflemen and ca-

N   (129)

valry on the mountains retired to the plain below. The Arkansas cavalry, who had been posted by your orders in my rear, at the base of the mountain, to act as circumstances might require, also left their position, the whole making a retreating movement along the plain towards the rear. At the same time one of the Illinois regiments, not under my command, but stationed at some distance in rear of the right of my position, also retired to the rear. These troops, the most of them, were immediately rallied, and fought during the whole day like veterans. A few of them, I regret to say, did not return to the field at all. By this apparent success the enemy were much elated, and poured down along the side of the mountain, on the extreme left of the field, their thousands of infantry and lancers, and formed themselves in good order along the mountain fronting perpendicularly to where our lines had been posted. At this critical juncture, the Mississippi regiment, under the command of Colonel Davis, arrived on the field, and being joined by a part of the 2d Indiana, met the enemy in a most gallant style, and, after a severe and bloody engagement, repulsed them with great loss. In the mean time a large body of lancers, six or eight hundred in number, who had passed down along the left toward our rear, made a most desperate charge upon the Arkansas and Kentucky cavalry, with a view of cutting off and plundering the baggage-train of the army, which was at a rancho near the battle-field.

"This charge was met and resisted most gallantly by those cavalry, aided by about two hundred infantry who had taken refuge there after they had retired from the field. This repulse discouraged the enemy; and the Mississippi regiment and part of the 2d Indiana, being joined by the 3d Indiana regiment, commanded by Colonel James H. Lane, now advanced up towards the foot of the mountain for the purpose of dislodging the enemy's force stationed there. In this enterprise I was aided by Captain ———'s battery of light artillery, and it was crowned with complete success, the enemy retreating in disorder, and with immense loss, back along the side of the mountain to the position which they had occupied in the morning; some flying in terror up the sides of the mountain, and into the ravines, while a few were taken prisoners. Amongst the last desperate attempts of the enemy to regain and hold the left of the field, was a charge made by a large body of lancers upon my command. This charge, for gallantry and determined bravery on both sides, has seldom been equalled. The forces on either side were nearly equal in numbers. Instead of throwing my command into squares to resist the charge, the enemy were received in line of two ranks, my force reserving its fire until the enemy were within about seventy yards, which was delivered with a deadly aim, and which proved most destructive in its effects — the enemy flying in every direction in disorder, and making a precipitate retreat towards their own lines. About sunset the enemy withdrew from the field, and the battle ceased. In a brief report it is impossible to enter into the details of a day like the 23d. The fighting throughout consisted of different engagements in different parts of the field, the whole of them warm and well-contested; many of them bloody and terrible. The men under my command actually discharged eighty, and some ninety, rounds of cartridges at the enemy during the day. The 2d regiment of my command, which opened the battle on the plain in such gallant style, deserves a passing remark. I shall attempt to make no apology for their retreat; for it was their duty to stand or die to the last man until they received orders to retire; but I desire to call your attention to one fact connected with this affair. *They remained in their position, in line, receiving the fire of three or four thousand infantry in front, exposed at the same time on the left flank to a most desperate raking fire from the enemy's battery, posted within point-blank shot, until they had deliberately discharged twenty rounds of cartridges at the enemy.*"

On the 9th of October, 1847, General Lane fought the battle of Huamantla; and on the 18th, he bombarded and captured the town of Atlixco. His despatches contain full details of these two affairs:—

"After my departure from Vera Cruz, and when near the San Juan river, a party of guerillas was observed near the hacienda of Santa Anna. Captain Lewis's company of mounted volunteers was detached in pursuit; a portion of the command, under Lieutenant Lilley, came upon the enemy, and had a smart skirmish with them. Lieutenant Lilley behaved in the most gallant manner, rallying and encouraging his men under a severe fire. Upon leaving Paso de Ovejas, the rear-guard was fired upon by a small guerilla force, and I regret to have to announce the death of Lieutenant Cline, who was shot in the affair. He is reported to have been a most energetic and efficient young officer, belonging to Captain Lewis's company of Louisiana mounted volunteers.

"At various points on the road rumours reached me that a large force was concentrating between Perote and Puebla. These rumours were confirmed on my arrival at the former place, and I also received the additional intelligence that Santa Anna in person commanded them, having about four thousand men and six pieces of artillery. No molestation occurred until my arrival at the hacienda of San Antonio Tamaris, at which place, through the medium of my spies, I learned that the enemy were at the city of Huamantla. My force consisted of Colonel Wynkoop's battalion, (from Perote,) Colonel Gorman's regiment of Indiana volunteers, Captain Heintzelman's battalion of six companies, Major Lally's regiment of four companies of mounted men, under command of Captain Samuel H. Walker, mounted riflemen, and five pieces of artillery under command of Captain George Taylor, 3d artillery, assisted by Lieutenant Field, artillery. On arriving near the city, at about one o'clock P. M., Captain Walker, commanding the advance guard, (of horsemen,) was ordered to move forward ahead of the column, (but within supporting distance,) to the entrance of the city, and if the enemy were in force, to await the arrival of the infantry before entering. When within about three miles, parties of horsemen being seen making their way through the fields towards the city, Captain Walker commanded a gallop. Owing to the thick maguey bushes lining the sides of the road, it was impossible to distinguish his further movements. But a short time had elapsed when firing was heard from the city. The firing continuing, the column was pressed forward as rapidly as possible. At this time a body of about two thousand lancers was seen hurrying over the hills towards the city. I directed Colonel Gorman, with his regiment, to advance towards and enter the west side of the city, while Colonel Wynkoop's battalion, with the artillery, moved towards the east side, Captain Heintzelman's moving on his right, and Major Lally's constituting the reserve.

"Upon arriving at the entrance to the city, Captain Walker discovering the main body of the enemy in the plaza, (about five hundred in number,) ordered a charge. A hand-to-hand conflict took place between the forces; but so resolute was the charge, that the enemy were obliged to give way, being driven from their guns. They were pursued by our dragoons for some distance, but the pursuit was checked by the arrival of their reinforcements. Colonel Gorman's regiment, on arriving at the entrance to the city at about the same time as the reinforcements of the enemy, opened a well-directed fire, which succeeded in routing them. With the left wing of his regiment he proceeded in person towards the upper part of the town, where the enemy still were, and succeeded in dispersing them. Colonel Wynkoop's command, with the batteries, assumed their position; but before they were within range the enemy fled in haste. The same occurred with Captain Heintzelman's command. The enemy entering the town becoming somewhat scattered, Major Lally, with his regiment, proceeded across the fields to cut off his rear and intercept his retreat. This movement not being perceived, I ordered him to advance towards the town; thus depriving him, unintentionally, of an opportunity of doing good service. Captain Walker's force had been engaged some three-quarters of an hour before the infantry arrived to his support. He succeeded in capturing two pieces of artillery from the enemy, but was not able to use them, owing to the want of priming tubes, although every effort was made. On this occasion every officer and soldier behaved with the utmost coolness, and my warmest thanks are due to them.   *   *   *

" The colours of the Indiana regiment were planted on the arsenal the moment the enemy were routed. This victory is saddened by the loss of one of the most chivalric, noble-hearted men that graced the profession of arms—Captain Samuel H. Walker, of the mounted riflemen. Foremost in the advance, he had routed the enemy when he fell mortally wounded. In his death the service has met with a loss which cannot easily be repaired. Our total loss is thirteen killed and eleven wounded. We succeeded in capturing one six-pounder brass gun and one mountain howitzer, both mounted, together with a large quantity of ammunition and wagons, which I was compelled to destroy. The enemy's loss was about one hundred and fifty."

The following is his report of the taking of Atlixco:

"About four o'clock, P. M., when near Santa Isabella, seven leagues from this place, the advance guard of the enemy was discovered. A halt was ordered until the cavalry, which had previously been detached to examine a hacienda, should arrive. The enemy, with his accustomed bravado, came to the foot of the hill in small parties, firing their escopetas and waving their lances. On the arrival of the cavalry a forward movement was made by the column. A large deep ravine appearing on the left of the road, Lieutenant-Colonel Moore, with his Ohio regiment, was ordered to flank it, Major Lally with his battalion leading the advance. Our column had scarcely commenced its movement, when signs of confusion were visible among the enemy, in consequence of which, the cavalry was ordered to charge, follow them up, and engage them until the infantry could arrive. Lieutenant Pratt, with his battery, was ordered to follow in rear of the dragoons at a gallop. Had this movement been performed, the whole force would have been ours. But by an order from Major Lally, Lieutenant Pratt was taken from the place assigned him by me, and in consequence detained until a greater portion of the column had passed; then, owing to the nature of the ground, it was impossible for his battery to proceed with rapidity.

"The cavalry pursued the retreating enemy for about a mile and a half, skirmishing with them. On arriving at a small hill, they made a stand and fought severely until our infantry appeared, when they took flight. Our artillery fired a few shots as soon as it came up, but without effect, as by their rapid retreat they had placed themselves at long range. The dragoons were again ordered to follow and keep them engaged. After a running fight of about four miles, and when within a mile and a half of Atlixco, the whole body of the enemy was discovered on a hill side, covered with chapparal, forming hedges, behind which they had posted themselves. Our cavalry dashed among them, cutting them down in great numbers. So thick was the chapparal that the dragoons were ordered to dismount and fight them on foot. A most bloody conflict ensued, fatal to the enemy. Our infantry for the last six miles had been straining themselves to the utmost to overtake the enemy, pressing forward most arduously, notwithstanding the forced march of sixteen miles since eleven o'clock. Owing to the nature of the road, almost entirely destroyed by gullies, the artillery could only advance at a walk. As soon as the infantry again appeared in sight, the enemy again retreated. So worn out were our horses, (the sun having been broiling hot all day,) that they could pursue the enemy no further. The column was pressed forward as rapidly as possible towards the town; but night had already shut in, giving us, however, the advantage of a fine moonlight. As we approached, several shots were fired at us, and, deeming it unsafe to risk a street fight in an unknown town at night, I ordered the artillery to be posted on a hill near to the town, and overlooking it, and open its fire Now ensued one of the most beautiful sights conceivable. Every gun was served with the utmost rapidity; and the crash of the walls and the roofs of the houses, when struck by our shot and shell, was mingled with the roar of our artillery. The bright light of the moon enabled us to direct our shots to the most thickly populated parts of the town.

"After firing three-quarters of an hour, and the firing from the town having ceased, I ordered Major Lally and Colonel Brough to advance cautiously with their commands into the town. On entering I was waited upon by the ayuntamiento, desiring that their town might be spared. After searching the next morning for arms and ammunition, and disposing of what was found, I commenced my return.

" General Rea had two pieces of artillery; but as soon as he was aware of our approach, he ordered them with haste to Matamoras, a small town eleven leagues beyond. The enemy state their own loss in this action to be two hundred and nineteen killed and three hundred wounded. On our part, we had one man killed and one wounded. Scarcely ever has a more rapid forced march been made than this, and productive of better results. Atlixco has been the head-quarters of guerillas in this section of country, and of late the seat of government of this state. From hence all expeditions have been fitted out against our troops. So much terror has been impressed upon them, at thus having war brought to their own homes, that I am inclined to believe they will give us no more trouble."

The capture of Atlixco has been the last military achievement of General Lane, and he now remains with the army awaiting the course of events.

BRIGADIER-GENERAL CADWALADER.

BRIGADIER-GENERAL GEORGE CADWALADER is a grandson of the illustrious John Cadwalader, of revolutionary memory, and has lately proven himself worthy of his name and family. He acted a conspicuous part in quelling the Philadelphia riots in Kensington and Southwark, in the year 1844, and was appointed to the army in Mexico, March 3d, 1847.

Soon after his arrival at the seat of war, a small party under Colonel McIntosh was attacked by a considerable Mexican force, and experienced some loss. In a few days it was joined by General Cadwalader with eight hundred men and two howitzers, and the whole command advanced toward the National Bridge. On approaching it, the general occupied some neighbouring heights, from which the enemy had previously fired on a party under Captain Bainbridge. Here he was attacked by a large Mexican force, stationed on the ridges and in the chapparal, and a battle ensued which lasted several hours. During this time several brilliant charges were made, the enemy driven from their positions, and the bridge successfully passed. The troops were then attacked by guerilla bands stationed in the thickets along the road, and fired upon during several miles of their march. The total loss of the Mexicans in this affair was nearly one hundred; General Cadwalader's about fifty, of whom fifteen were killed.

In his report of Contreros, General Smith uses the following complimentary language of General Cadwalader, who contributed materially to the fall of that stronghold.

"Brigadier-General Cadwalader [in the morning] brought his corps up from his intricate bivouack in good order, formed the head of his column to support Riley's, and led it forward in the most

(136)

BRIGADIER-GENERAL CADWALADER.
Page 136.

gallant style under the fire directed at the latter. The first brigade was conducted by Major Dimick, who charged in line with it on the enemy's left, driving before him the force formed there outside of the works, and putting to rout a far superior force, displaying the skill of the commander as well as the bravery of the soldier. But the opportunity afforded by his position to Colonel Riley was seized by that gallant veteran with all the skill and energy for which he is distinguished. The charge of his noble brigade down the slope, in full view of friend and foe, unchecked even for a moment, until he had planted all his colours upon their farthest works, was a spectacle that animated the army to the boldest deeds."

During the assault, General Cadwalader was stationed in rear of the fort, to watch the movements of Santa Anna's cavalry; and in the pursuit of the enemy, subsequent to the victory, he exhibited indefatigable courage and perseverance. His operations during the remainder of the day are included with those of the generals already noticed.

The following spirited account of Cadwalader's participation in the storming of Molino del Rey, is from the pen of one in his division :—

"General Worth's division was charged with this duty, as it was not supposed that there would be any thing of a fight, and it would not require more than that division to take the mill. However, General Cadwalader's brigade, of the third division, was brought into the field as a supporting column, though it was not expected that it would be necessary to bring it into the fight. Accordingly, the troops marched from Tacubaya, about three o'clock A. M., on the 8th of September, and daylight saw them drawn up in position in front of what was afterwards ascertained to be an extensive fortification, or rather a series of fortifications, defended by ten thousand of the picked troops of Mexico, with several pieces of artillery.

"General Worth's division, numbering some sixteen or eighteen hundred men, was drawn up in a line, about a cannon's shot distance from the fortification ; and General Cadwalader's brigade was in line some distance in Worth's rear. The action commenced just as day began to dawn, by a few shots from Captain Drum's battery, occupying a position on the right of Worth's division. This did not continue long; for soon the spectator could observe a movement on the part of our troops, and directly an enthusiastic shout arose from

12 *

Worth's ranks, and they rushed on to the charge. But now the Mexicans opened their batteries on our devoted troops, and ten thousand muskets rang their crashing accompaniment. Our men went down by hundreds, and the plain was strewed with their dead and mangled bodies. For a short time nothing could be heard but an incessant roar of artillery and small arms; and when the smoke arose from the scene, the intensely excited spectator might have seen our troops giving way before the dreadful fire of the enemy. It was an awful moment, and calculated to send a thrill of horror through an American heart. The gallant division of General Worth was forced to give way. Could any troops stand such a fire? The 4th, 6th, and 8th infantry, were compelled to retire before those murderous batteries.

"General Cadwalader, seeing the situation of affairs, moved his brigade forward, to retrieve the fortunes of the day. The voltiguers, the advance regiment, was sent off to the left, to protect Duncan's light battery, which was playing on the mill, and to keep in check a large force of the enemy, who then occupied a hill near the scene of action. The duty was performed, and the enemy driven back several times. The 11th regiment was ordered to charge the battery, and the 14th, the remaining regiment of the brigade, was held in reserve. The 11th had to charge over the same ground where fell so many of our gallant troops, and every one looked for its annihilation. Their gallant leader, Lieutenant-Colonel Graham, sat on his horse in the coolest manner, and gave his commands as collectedly as when on a parade. They advance steadily; but now the enemy is vomiting his grape and canister upon them, and they leave a train of dead and dying. Do they falter? No—their gallant commander is waving his sword, and they are now rushing forward in full run. On, on they go! But, see — do they halt? They do, but it is for a moment. Do you hear that shout? Comes it from the Mexican ranks? No—no; that is a true Pennsylvania shout, and tells of danger defied, and glory to be won. There they go, onward, right up to the enemy's guns. Huzza for the Old Keystone! The Mexicans are giving way before our gallant little band, who are now dealing vengeance and death on the murderers of their slaughtered countrymen. Lieutenant Tippin is the first to spring into the fort; he mounts one of the guns, and waves his sword for his men to come on. But just then, an unexpected and terrible fire salutes him from the top of the building, and he is compelled to retire, being grazed by several balls. And see—the enemy are rallying again, and returning to the attack. Their success at the commencement of the action has given them courage. Will the 11th, that gallant band, be crushed now? No! They remain firm and determined. Lieutenant Johnson has just fallen, mortally wounded; he expires while cheering his men on to victory. Captains Irvin and Guthrie are badly wounded, and yet they are both on the field, animating their respective commands, and leading them on to the attack."

General Cadwalader entered the capital with his gallant associates in arms, and is now with General Scott at the National Palace.

o

BRIGADIER-GENERAL PIERCE.

BRIGADIER-GENERAL FRANKLIN PIERCE was appointed to the army March 3d, 1847. He reached the gulf coast soon after the capture of Vera Cruz. His operations from that time until the conclusion of General Scott's armistice with Santa Anna, are thus detailed by himself in a letter to a friend. The letter, not being intended for publication, contains more personal history than it otherwise would.

"Since I left Vera Cruz, to this hour, I have had no means of communicating with the states. Although but a few months in the service, I *know* what is fatigue, anxiety, and exposure. Contrary to my expectations, and contrary to my orders from the department at Washington, I was compelled, for the want of the requisite provisions for transportation, to remain for more than three weeks at Vera Cruz, and more than four in Terra Caliente, (the vomito region, as it is called.) I left the dreaded city on the 10th of July, with two thousand five hundred men of all arms, and a train of wagons, which, when closed up, extended more than two miles. On the 6th of August I reached Puebla, without the loss of a single wagon, with my command in fine condition. My command was attacked six times on the march, but the enemy's force in each instance was easily dispersed, with trifling loss on our side. The National Bridge afforded the enemy great natural advantages, to which they had added breastworks on a high bluff which commanded the bridge perfectly. Across the main bridge they had also thrown a barricade. I soon discovered that there was no way in which his position could be turned, and that my artillery was ineffective from the most commanding point where it could be placed. I determined, of course, to cross under the plunging fire of the enemy's escopetas. My order to advance was admirably executed. At the moment Lieutenant-Colonel Bonham's battalion rushed forward with a shout,

(140)

the enemy poured down a heavy fire, by which several of my men
were severely wounded. Colonel Bonham's horse was shot near
me, and a ball passed through the rim of my hat, in very disagree-
able proximity to my face. Our men leaped the barricade, followed
by Captain Duperu's company of cavalry, and in less than ten minutes the enemy were in flight in every direction, and the American
flag waved upon the high bluff which they had occupied. The
Mexican force, as they said afterwards, consisted of five hundred
men. Had they possessed courage and skill in the use of arms, our
loss must have been very great. You can hardly conceive the
strength of the natural defences of the road over which we passed.
Rumours came to me almost every night that we would be attacked
by large forces the next day, but they made nowhere any thing like
a brave and stern resistance.

"The official reports of the great battle of Mexico will probably
reach you as soon as this letter, and I shall therefore not attempt to
give the minute details. It was fierce and bloody beyond any thing
that has occurred in this war. The battle differed in many respects
from that at Buena Vista. There General Taylor received the
enemy in a strong position selected by himself. Our force on the
20th consisted of less than nine thousand men; the Mexican force,
within supporting distance and engaged, undoubtedly exceeded
thirty thousand. We attacked him in position, upon ground of his
own selection, admirably fortified. You will distinguish, so far as
numbers are concerned, between the battle of the morning and that
of the afternoon, although spoken of in the official reports as one
engagement, under the designation of '*the* battle of Mexico.' We
took, during the day, thirty-five pieces of artillery, an immense
quantity of ammunition, eight hundred mules and horses, and more
than two thousand prisoners, among them eight generals and any
number of colonels.

"The Mexican loss in killed and wounded must have been immense. Our troops buried five hundred Mexicans upon the field
of battle, commenced in the morning at Contreros, and the loss in
the afternoon was much greater. Our loss has been heavy. With
this small army we could not afford to purchase many such victories
at such a price; one of the regiments of my brigade (the 13th) lost
in killed and wounded one-third of its entire force. In killed and
wounded we number not less than one thousand, and among them

I lament to say an unusual proportion of valuable officers. The New England regiment suffered severely, and behaved throughout in the most gallant manner. My horse, at full speed on the evening of the 19th, when leading my brigade through a perfect shower of round shot and shells, fell under me upon a ledge of rocks, by which I sustained a severe injury by the shock and bruises, but especially by a severe sprain in my left knee, which came under him. At first I was not conscious of any serious injury, but soon became exceedingly faint, when Dr. Ritchie, surgeon of the 12th, (a portion of my command,) who was following the advancing columns closely, overtook me, and administered to me as well as he could under the circumstances. In a few moments I was able to walk with difficulty, and pressed forward to Captain McGruder's battery, where I found the horse of poor gallant Lieutenant Johnson, who had just received a mortal wound, of which he died that evening. i was permitted to take him, (my own having been totally disabled,) was helped into the saddle, and continued in it until eleven o'clock that night. It was exceedingly dark, the rain poured in torrents, and, being separated from my servants and baggage, I was without tent or covering; add to this that, during the afternoon of the 19th, we had gained no advantages over the enemy, who remained firmly entrenched with seven thousand men opposed to about four thousand on our side, without the possibility of bringing our artillery to bear, and you will readily conceive that our situation was not the most agreeable. The morning of the 20th was, however, as brilliant as the night of the 19th was dark and gloomy. Soon after daylight the enemy's works were carried with the bayonet, and of their seven thousand men, regular troops, under the command of General Valencia, probably four thousand cannot be found to-day. As we passed this field in pursuit of the fugitives, the scene was awful; the road and adjacent fields everywhere strewed with mangled bodies of the dead and dying. We continued the pursuit until one o'clock, when our front came up with the enemy's strong works at Churubusco and San Antonio, where the great conflict of the afternoon commenced. At San Angel, dispositions having been made to attack in reverse the enemy's works on the San Augustin road, General Scott ordered me to march my brigade, in concert with that of the intrepid General Shields, across the open country between Santa Catarina and the above-named road, in order to cut off the enemy's retreat. We gained the position sought, and, although the enemy's line was perfectly formed, and extended as far as the eye could reach in either direction, they were attacked vigorously and successfully. Arriving at a ditch which it was impossible for my horse to leap, I dismounted and hurried forward, without thinking of my injury, at the head of my brigade, for two or three hundred yards, when, turning suddenly upon my knee, the cartilage of which had been seriously injured, I fainted and fell upon the bank, in the direct range and within perfect reach of the enemy's fire. That I escaped seems to me now providential. The rout and overthrow of the whole Mexican force soon became complete, and we could easily have taken the city; but General Scott was met with a proposition for an armistice, (after demanding the surrender of the city,) with a view to open negotiations for peace.

"In my judgment, the army, full of ardour and confidence, was humanely and wisely restrained. Major-General Quitman, General Persifor F. Smith, and myself, were appointed commissioners to meet the Mexican commissioners to settle the terms of the armistice. I had not taken off my spurs or slept an hour for two nights in consequence of my engagements and the pain of my knee. I obeyed the summons, was helped into my saddle, and rode two and a half miles to Tacubaya, where the commission assembled at the house of Mr. McIntosh, the British consul-general. Our conference commenced late in the afternoon, and at four o'clock the next morning the articles were signed.

"That I was thoroughly exhausted you will readily imagine. I slept an hour or two that morning at General Worth's quarters, and my sprained knee, which was by far my most serious injury, has been daily improving, and to-day I ride without much inconvenience. I have lost several dear friends, although our acquaintance had been of short duration. I visited the hospital yesterday, and saw officers and men with shots in all parts of their persons. Although all who were not really dying seemed cheerful, and many who had lost limbs in high spirits, still I sickened at the sight. My general health has been good. I have been either in my saddle or on my feet every rod since I left Vera Cruz, which can be said by few officers in my command; for almost all were obliged, at some point of the march, in consequence of the change of climate, water, exposure, &c., to avail themselves of the ambulance. Colonel Watson, with his marine corps, accompanied me, and has been uniformly well. He is an excellent agreeable gentleman and admirable officer, and I regret that, having been left with General Quitman's division at San Augustin, he had no opportunity to participate in the battles of the 19th and 20th."

General Pierce was prevented by his wound from participating in the events of September, and he is still an invalid at the Mexican capital.

MAJOR-GENERAL PATTERSON.

Page 145.

MAJOR-GENERAL PATTERSON.

MAJOR-GENERAL ROBERT PATTERSON was born January 12th, 1792, near Strabane, County Tyrone, Ireland. His father, one of the actors in the rebellion of 1798, emigrated to this country on the failure of that ill-starred enterprise, and settled in Delaware county, Pennsylvania. At the age of fourteen, Robert entered the counting-house of Edward Thompson, Esq., who was then the principal American merchant engaged in the East India trade. In October, 1811, he removed with his father's family to Tennessee; but after the declaration of war with Great Britain, he returned to Pennsylvania, obtained a lieutenancy in the army, and after serving for a time on the staff of Brigadier-General Bloomfield, was commissioned captain (April 19th, 1814) in the 32d infantry. When his company was disbanded in consequence of the termination of the war, he embarked in mercantile pursuits, devoting his leisure hours to the study of tactics, and to the discipline and improvement of the volunteers of Philadelphia, with whom he retained his connection till after his appointment as major-general in the United States' army, July 7th, 1846.

The command of the troops called out to repress the disturbances at Harrisburg in the winter of 1838-9, devolved on him as senior major-general; he was again employed to quell the riots in Philadelphia.

During the action at Madeline river, General Patterson brought up a reinforcement of Tennessee volunteers, but declined superseding Colonel Harney, preferring to fight under that gallant officer, rather than by assuming the command to deprive him of the credit of one of the most brilliant affairs of the war. Posting his Tennes-

13   (145)

seeans, he ordered them to lie down, as they were then exposed to a heavy fire from the enemy without the opportunity of returning it effectively. The order was obeyed very reluctantly, and some of the men, thinking that the prudence which protected them should be extended to himself, called out :—" Lie down yourself, general, or they will knock you over presently." " No," said he, " my duty calls me where I am, and yours is to remain where you are, until required to expose yourself. The President can make generals, but he cannot make soldiers."

General Scott, in his general orders subsequent to the battle of Sierra Gordo, says :—

" Major-General Patterson, rendered for the moment supernumerary, with this army, will accompany the returning volunteers of his late gallant division, and render them such assistance on the way as he well knows how to give. * * * * This distinguished general officer will please accept the thanks of the general-in-chief, for the gallant, able, and efficient support uniformly received from the second in rank in this army."

Speaking of this order, a correspondent says :—

" He leaves us with the regrets of all. We saw him at Vera Cruz, and witnessed, during the whole of that harassing siege and severe cannonade, his thorough devotion to his duties. He was so lame as to be compelled to wear crutches, and could not get up the hills into our positions without aid. I have seen him in exposed positions again and again, leaning on his crutches, and examining the enemy's movements, when the shells and round shot were flying around him and passing over him in every direction. At Sierra Gordo, when so ill that it was almost madness to think of leaving his bed, he astonished his command by riding in among them immediately previous to the attack, and was received by a simultaneous shout, from three or four thousand voices, which must have made the enemy shake. At that time he was so weak that he could scarcely manage the animal he rode."

General Patterson was second in command on the Rio Grande, immediately after the capture of Matamoras, and was entrusted with the control of all the forces on the river during General Taylor's march toward Monterey. He assisted at Vera Cruz, but was prevented from taking an active part at Sierra Gordo, in consequence of severe sickness. During Scott's march to the capital, he has been stationed at Vera Cruz, to keep in check the numerous guerilla parties of that region. In connection with his services in this respect a correspondent writes :—

"In the afternoon of the same day, Father Ahrouta (or Jarauta), who commands a guerilla party, and has become notorious by his misdeeds on the road from Jalapa to Vera Cruz, sent in a flag of truce by two of his officers, proposing to surrender as a prisoner of war or join the American army, if General Patterson would guaranty the safety of himself and followers, and their property. To this General Patterson replied that he wanted to have no intercourse with the guerilla priest, but would advise him to return to his prayers, and send his band back to their honest employments, if they had any, as no one would molest them then, while, if they continued to infest the road, and he should catch any of them, he would certainly hang them.

"The name of Pennsylvania operated on the general here like a charm, and in a manner quite gratifying to us. Among the first of his acts on arriving at the bridge, where the 13th regiment and the Baltimore artillery battalion were stationed, was to inquire what amount of provision the garrison had on hand. He was informed, among other things, that Captain Diller had drawn twenty-five hundred rations for Colonel Wynkoop's regiment. 'What is that for ?' said the general, sternly — 'send him to me.' Captain Diller in a few minutes was before the general, who asked him why he had drawn for so many rations. The latter replied, that he had brought but five days' rations with him, as he expected to meet General Patterson's train and obtain more. 'It cannot be done, sir,' said General Patterson, 'you must return them.' 'But, general,' said Captain Diller, 'they are in the wagons, and I have given my receipt for them.' 'I can't help that,' was the stern reply, 'you ought to have brought more with you.' 'But, general,' again said Captain Diller, imploringly, ' remember the Pennsylvania boys have seen hard service and fought nobly, it will not do to let them starve.' ' Ah, yes,' rejoined the general, while his face relaxed into a benevolent smile, and his eye sparkled with proud recollections, 'they were with me at Vera Cruz and Sierra Gordo — say no more, but keep the rations and start back to the Plan with them the first thing in the morning—the Pennsylvania boys shall not starve !'

"On his arrival the next day at the Plan del Rio, General Patterson was received by the regiment with the utmost enthusiasm, and the joy of the men at seeing him seemed to know no bounds. He was much gratified by this demonstration, and appeared as happy to see us as if we had each and all been of his own family and blood. We left him at the Plan that day (the 5th), and started for this place, where, as I have already said, we arrived yesterday, the 6th. He reached here this afternoon, but the rear-guard of his immense train will not be in until long after midnight."*

---

* General Patterson's command on the Rio Grande amounted to nearly eleven thousand men, many of whom having been but recently mustered into service, were destitute both of discipline and subordination. To this difficulty was added the great number of sick, occasioned by the unhealthiness of the climate, and the troops' own carelessness. By judicious management, and an occasional resort to energetic measures, the general succeeded in rendering his command fit for active service.

In December, 1846, orders were issued to the army to prepare for a descent upon Tampico. One part of General Patterson's force was sent to General Taylor, another down the Rio Grande, and the remainder under his own direction, crossed the country from Matamoras, by way of Victoria, a distance of about two hundred miles. Notwithstanding many obstacles to this march, the head of the column entered Victoria simultaneously with that of General Taylor from Monterey. From this place General Patterson was ordered to Tampico, where he met General Scott, and proceeded with him to Vera Cruz.

In October, 1847, the general commenced his march for the capital of Mexico, where he arrived about the latter end of November.

COLONEL HARNEY.

For intrepidity, perseverance, and impetuosity in battle, no man in the American army is superior to Colonel Harney. His dragoon-fight at Vera Cruz, his charge at Sierra Gordo, and his recent heroic actions before the capital, have rarely been surpassed, and have won for him a reputation as brilliant as it is just.

The colonel's personal appearance is thus described by one who visited him during his present journey through the United States:

"Our attention was next arrested by seeing a man of towering height and gigantic frame, with a chest like that of Hercules and an eye like that of Mars. He was, indeed, to use the language of Hamlet, made 'to threaten and command.' With a smile upon his lips and a sparkle of pleasure in his light blue eyes, he stood the 'observed of all observers.' He was the gallant Colonel Harney—one of the most accomplished and heroic soldiers in the army—to whom has been so generally assigned the chief glory of the great victory of Sierra Gordo."

Colonel William S. Harney was born in Louisiana, and received his first appointment as 2d lieutenant 1st infantry February 13th, 1818. He was brevetted colonel December 7th, 1840, and raised to full colonel June 30th, 1846. He served with great credit in the Seminole wars, and when the present war with Mexico opened, joined Wool's Division of the Centre, and was included among the troops despatched for the Gulf coast. His famous dragoon-fight, during the bombardment of Vera Cruz, is thus described by a correspondent:

"Information was received in camp this morning that a body of Mexicans were hanging on our rear, intending to force the lines if possible, and make their way into the city with a number of cattle.

13 *   P   (149)

Colonel Harney, with one hundred and twenty dragoons, was ordered out to search them, and report his observations. He discovered them, about two thousand in number, intrenched at a bridge, and supported by two pieces of artillery, three miles from General Patterson's head-quarters. Colonel Harney started on his return, intending to prepare properly and attack them the next morning. But the gallant old soldier, knowing that delays are dangerous, could not bear the idea of leaving the enemy after having come in sight of them, without having a brush. Accordingly, he returned to the place, took a position where he could watch their movements, and keep his men secure from the enemy's fire. The Mexicans commenced firing at him, and threw a perfect shower of balls all around him, but without injury. Colonel Harney then despatched a messenger to camp for a small reinforcement, and some artillery to break the breastworks. He was reinforced from General Patterson's division, by Lieutenant Judd, with two pieces of artillery, about sixty dragoons, dismounted, and six companies of the 1st and 2d Tennessee volunteers, under the command of Colonel Haskell, accompanied by General Patterson in person, although he did not take the command from Colonel Harney, but merely participated as any other individual who was engaged.

"Colonel Harney then formed the Tennesseeans on the right, his dragoons on the left, and advanced slowly, to draw the fire of the Mexicans, until Lieutenant Judd got his artillery in such a position as he desired. The movement succeeded admirably : Lieutenant Judd got his ground within one hundred and fifty yards of the Mexicans, and commenced firing — they attempted to return it, but as soon as a slight breach was made in the parapet, Colonel Harney ordered a charge, which was answered by a yell from the dragoons and Tennesseeans. Colonel Haskell, Captain Cheatham, and Captain Foster were the first men to leap over the breastwork, and, as a naval officer remarked, who witnessed the whole affair, the balance went over so much 'like a thousand of brick,' that there was no telling who was first or last. As might have been expected, the Mexicans were unable to stand a charge from 'the boys who stood the fire of the Black Fort at Monterey.' A few of the incumbrances were soon thrown out of the way, and Colonel Harney, with his dragoons, leaped the breastwork and gave chase.

"He had not proceeded more than a mile before he found the

enemy formed in line to receive him. He immediately deployed, and from the head of the line ordered a charge. When he approached within about twenty yards of the enemy's line, they gave him a fire from their side-arms, but overshot. Then came the test of strength and skill — the dragoon, with sword in hand, met the confiding lancer, with pointed lance, ready to receive him. The contest was but for a short time. In many instances, lances were twisted from their clenched hold ; the Mexicans were unsaddled, and driven helter-skelter in every direction, and pursued by the dragoons in detachments.

"Colonel Harney and several of his officers met their men in single combat, but none of them received any injury except Lieutenant Neill, adjutant of the regiment, who was wounded severely in two places, from his magnanimity in attempting to capture a Mexican instead of killing him. In full run he overtook the retreating Mexican, and placing his sword in front of him, commanded him to surrender ; whereupon the Mexican drove his lance into his magnanimous adversary. As the lieutenant wheeled his horse to despatch him, another Mexican charged up and struck him with a lance. However, severely wounded as he was, in two places, he conquered one of his foes, and a corporal came up in time to ' settle accounts' with the other.

"The Mexican force was near two thousand ; Colonel Harney's about five hundred."

In the march from Vera Cruz to Sierra Gordo, Colonel Harney performed excellent service as a scout, and advance guard ; and his brilliant storming of the main work at Sierra Gordo elicited the warmest commendation from the commander-in-chief, even on the battle-field. The annexed description of this affair is from the pen of an eye-witness :—

"The storming and capture of the strong works on Sierra Gordo, by the brigade under Colonel Harney, may be looked upon as one of the most brilliant achievements of the Mexican war—the fate of the battle turned upon it, and here the enemy had placed an overwhelming force of his best troops. The hill was steep, and naturally difficult of ascent ; but independent of this, the ground was covered with loose, craggy rocks, an undergrowth of tangled chapparal, besides many small trees, the tops of which were cut off some four or five feet from the ground, and turned down the hill, to impede the

progress of the stormers.   To climb the height at all, even without
arms of any kind, would be an undertaking that few would care
about essaying; what then must it have been to men encumbered
with muskets and cartridge-boxes, and obliged to dispute every step
of the precipitous and rugged ascent? Murderous showers of grape
and canister greeted our men at the onset, and as they toiled unfal-
tering through a tempest of iron hail, a heavy fire of musketry
opened upon them. Not a man quailed—with loud shouts they still
pressed upward and onward. At every step our ranks were thinned ;
but forward went the survivors.   When within good musket range,
but not until then, was the fire of the enemy returned, and then
commenced the dreadful carnage of strife.   The Mexicans held to
their guns with more than their usual bravery, but nothing could
resist the fierce onset of the stormers.   Over the breastworks, with
which the Mexicans had surrounded the crest of the hill, they
charged, and shouting, attacked the enemy in their very stronghold.
The latter now fled, panic-stricken, but still they were pursued ; and
it was not until the affrighted fugitives had reached a point without
the extreme range of their own cannon, which had been turned
upon them at the onset, that they ceased in their flight.   The national colours of our country now supplanted the banner of the
enemy ; the different regimental flags were also planted on the crest ;
and shouts louder than ever from the victors rose upon the air, striking terror into the very hearts of the enemy in the works still un-
taken, for they knew that their strong positions had been turned, and
that they were at the mercy of the men they had scoffed at in the
morning.   Never was victory more complete, although purchased
with the blood of some of our best men.   Lieutenant Ewell, of the
rifles, was among the first within the enemy's breastworks, and it
was here that he received his death wound.   The interior of the
work was covered with the dead of the enemy, among them General
Vasquez, Colonel Palacio, and many of their officers, while the
hill-side down which they fled was strewn as well.   Near two hundred men were left dead, while the wounded would swell the number
to at least five hundred—some even put it down as high as seven
hundred."

In all the subsequent operations of the war Colonel Harney has
been most usefully employed.   We give extracts from his report
of his duties in August :—

"The cavalry force being necessarily weakened by detachments to the different divisions of the army, I found myself on the morning of the 19th instant in the immediate command of nine companies only, consisting of six companies of the 2d dragoons, one company of mounted riflemen, and two companies of mounted volunteers. With this force I was ordered by the general-in-chief to report to Brigadier-General Twiggs, who was at this time covering Major-General Pillow's division in an effort to make a road through the ridge of lava which forms the pass of San Antonio. Owing to the nature of the ground I was compelled to halt within range of the enemy's shells, and to remain in this position for several hours—an idle spectator of the action which ensued. After night I returned with my command to San Augustin, and remained there until the enemy's position at Contreros was carried on the morning of the 20th.

"As soon as the road was ascertained to be opened and practicable for cavalry, I was directed by the general-in-chief to proceed with two squadrons and Captain McKinstry's company of volunteers to the field of battle, and to take charge of the prisoners that had been captured. While in the execution of this order, I received instructions from the general-in-chief to leave one squadron in charge of the prisoners, and to report to him in person with the other three companies. Captain Blake, with his squadron, was directed to perform this duty; while Major Sumner and myself, with Captain Ker's squadron, and Captain McKinstry's company of volunteers, joined the commanding general near the field of Churubusco, just after the engagement at that place had commenced. * * * *

"The three troops of horse brought by me on the field, being ordered away in different directions, Major Sumner and myself soon found ourselves without commands. I then employed myself with my staff in rallying fugitives and encouraging our troops on the left of the main road. Major Sumner, towards the close of the engagement, was placed by the general-in-chief in charge of the last reserve, consisting of the rifle regiment and one company of horse, and ordered to support the left. This force was moving rapidly to take its position in line of battle, when the enemy broke and fled to the city. At this moment, perceiving that the enemy were retreating in disorder on one of the main causeways leading to the city of Mexico, I collected all the cavalry within my reach, consisting of parts of Captain Ker's company 2d dragoons, Captain Kearney's company 1st

dragoons, and Captains McReynolds' and Duperu's companies of
the 3d dragoons, and pursued them vigorously until we were halted
by the discharge of the batteries at their gate.   Many of the enemy
were overtaken in the pursuit, and cut down by our sabres.   I cannot speak in terms too complimentary of the manner in which this
charge was executed.   My only difficulty was in restraining the
impetuosity of my men and officers, who seemed to vie with
each other to be foremost in the pursuit.   Captain Kearney gallantly led his squadron into the very entrenchments of the enemy,
and had the misfortune to lose an arm from a grape-shot fired from
a gun at one of the main gates of the capital.   Captain McReynolds
and Lieutenant Graham were also wounded, and Lieutenant Ewell
had two horses shot under him.   *   *   *   *   *

" In conclusion, I beg leave to state that the dragoons, from the
commencement of the march from Puebla, have been engaged on
the most active and laborious service.   These duties have been the
more arduous in consequence of the small force of cavalry, compared
with the other arms of service.   Small parties being constantly engaged in reconnoitring and on picket guards, the utmost vigilance
and precaution have been required to prevent surprise and disaster.
The gallant Captain Thornton, while reconnoitring the enemy near
San Antonio on the 18th instant, was shot through the body by a
cannon shot, and instantly killed.   His death is much to be regretted.
On the 20th, although I had but four companies of my brigade with
me on the field, the remainder were actively employed in the performance of important and indispensable duties.   Captain Hardee,
while watching the enemy with his company near San Augustin,
was attacked by a band of guerillas ; but the enemy was promptly
and handsomely repulsed, and a number of their horses, with arms
and accoutrements, captured."

After the capture of the Mexican capital, Colonel Harney returned to the United States, where he still remains [January, 1848.]

COLONEL CHILDS.

Page 155.

COLONEL CHILDS.

COLONEL THOMAS CHILDS is a native of Massachusetts. He entered the army as 3d lieutenant, March 11th, 1814; was brevetted colonel, May 9th, 1846; raised to the full rank of major, February 16th, 1847; and soon after raised to his present rank. He greatly distinguished himself at Palo Alto, and on the following day; and at Monterey he led one of the storming parties in General Worth's division. The general mentions him in his official report with high approbation; and he was at the same time recommended by General Taylor to the favourable consideration of the department. He fought side by side at Sierra Gordo with the intrepid Harney, and like him received the highest commendations of the commander-in-chief. After the capture of Jalapa, he was appointed military commander of that place; and, in about a month after, military governor of Puebla. During the absence of the main army from that place, he was attacked, [September 13th, 1847,] by a large Mexican force, and a siege commenced, which lasted nearly a month, conducted part of the time by Santa Anna himself. The colonel gives a minute account of these transactions in his official report, [dated October 13th,] portions of which are subjoined:—

"I have the honour to report that, after twenty-eight days close investment, the enemy yesterday [October 12th] raised the siege and left for Atlixco.

"I will avail myself of this opportunity to submit to the general-in-chief a brief account of the operations of the troops at this point, from the period of my assuming command to the termination of the siege and the arrival of Brigadier-General Lane with reinforcements.

"On entering upon my duties as civil and military governor I found myself in command of Captain Ford's company of cavalry, forty-

(155)

six strong; Captains Kendrick's and Miller's companies of artillery, numbering one hundred; together with six companies of the 1st Pennsylvania volunteers, commanded by Lieutenant-Colonel Black —his total effective strength being two hundred and forty-seven— and hospitals filled with one thousand eight hundred sick.

"With this command, San Jose, the grand depôt in this city, Loreto, and Guadalupe were to be garrisoned, and held against the combined efforts of the military and populace.

"The isolated position selected for the hospitals compelled me to remove them within the protection of San Jose on the first demonstration of hostility. This was not long in exhibiting itself, when I put myself, with such means as I had at my disposal, in the best possible state for defence, confining my efforts to the square immediately around San Jose; and from these points the enemy, during the entire siege, were not able to force in (but for a single moment) a sentinel.

"No open acts of hostility, other than the murdering of straggling soldiers, occurred until the night of the 13th of September, when a fire was opened from some of the streets. On the night of the 14th it recommenced, and from every street, with a violence that knew of no cessation, for twenty-eight days and nights.

"The enemy, with their numerous cavalry, succeeded in cutting off at once every kind of supply, and vainly attempted to change the current of the stream of water, that we might become a more easy prey. The night, however, before the cattle and sheep disappeared from this vicinity, two well-directed parties obtained thirty of the former and four hundred of the latter.

"The various points to be defended for the preservation of San Jose, on which the safety of the other posts depended, demanded the untiring vigilance of every officer and man.

"The enemy augmented in numbers daily, and daily the firing was increased; and finally, on the 22d of September, General Santa Anna arrived with large reinforcements from Mexico, much to the delight of the besiegers, on which occasion a general ringing of bells took place, and was only stopped, as it had been several times before, by a discharge of shells and round-shot from Loreto into the heart of the city.

"On the 25th of September, General Santa Anna demanded my surrender.

"So soon as I had despatched my answer, I supposed not a moment would be lost by the general, who was to attack me at all points with his eight thousand troops. I rode to the different posts, and announced to the troops the demand, the force with which it was backed, and my reply. Their response convinced me that all was safe ; that a hard and bloody battle must be fought ere the great captain of Mexico could overcome my little band.

"The point of attack was San Jose, commanded by Lieutenant-Colonel Black, with Captain Ford's company of cavalry, Captain Miller's company of 4th artillery, and four companies of his own regiment, and one hospital, the guard of which was in command of Captain Rowe, of the 9th regiment of infantry.

"A shower of bullets was constantly poured from the streets, the balconies, the house-tops, and churches, upon their devoted heads. Never did troops endure more fatigue by watching night after night, for more than thirty successive nights, nor exhibit more patience, spirit, and gallantry. Not a post of danger could present itself, but the gallant fellows were ready to fill it ; not a sentinel could be shot, but another was anxious and ready to take his place. Officers and soldiers vied with each other to be honoured martyrs in their country's cause. This is the general character of the troops I had the honour to command, and I was confident the crown of victory would perch upon their standard when the last great effort should be made. Their bold and determined front deprived them of what they anxiously desired.

"On the 30th ultimo, General Santa Anna had established his battery bearing upon San Jose, and opened with much spirit. Having anticipated this movement, I had thrown up a traverse on the plaza, and withdrawn a twelve-pounder from Loreto, by which means I was enabled to answer his shot. Towards night his battery ceased, and on the next morning was withdrawn, together with from three to four thousand of the besieging force, to meet the reinforcements then daily expected at Pinal.

"On the 2d instant, I availed myself of some reduction of the enemy's numbers to make a sortie against certain barricades and buildings, whose fire had become very annoying. One of the expeditions was confided to Captain Small, of the 1st Pennsylvania volunteers. Passing through the walls of an entire square with fifty men, he gained a position opposite the barricade, and drove the

14   Q

enemy with great loss, they leaving seventeen dead on the ground. The barricade, consisting of one hundred and fifty bales of cotton, was consumed. In this affair Captain Small and his command behaved with great gallantry, and for twenty-four hours were unceasing in their labours in accomplishing the object, when I sent Lieutenant Laidley, of the ordnance corps, to blow up a prominent building, which was done by that excellent officer in good style, when the entire party was withdrawn, with few wounded.

"At the same time, Lieutenant Morgan, of the 14th regiment, with a detachment of marines, and Lieutenant Merrifield, of the 15th regiment, with a detachment of rifles, attempted to gain possession of certain buildings from which we were receiving a most galling fire. Lieutenant Merrifield entered the buildings; Lieutenant Morgan was not so fortunate. The enemy being present in great force, I directed him to fall back, with the loss of one man killed. On the 5th instant, Captain Herron was detached with his company to take possession of a building from which the enemy had been enfilading the plaza. This he did in a very handsome manner, and to my entire satisfaction, with only a few men wounded.

"Other minor acts of gallantry and good conduct were exhibited by officers and men at San Jose, and from Guadalupe one or two successful sorties were made upon the enemy when engaged in their daily attacks on San Jose.

"From Lieutenant-Colonel Black, the immediate commander of San Jose, and his officers, I have received the most cordial support. Colonel Black, for more than thirty days, was untiring in his efforts and zeal for the safety of that point. Officers and men were at their posts night and day, without regarding the pelting storm; and I cannot say too much in praise of the gallant colonel, his officers and men, before and during the siege."

Immediately after this gallant defence, General Lane arrived at Puebla; but ascertaining that Santa Anna had retired to Atlixco, he pushed forward for that place, leaving Colonel Childs still in command of the post he had so ably defended.

GENERAL CUSHING.

BRIGADIER-GENERAL CALEB CUSHING is a native of Newburyport, in the commonwealth of Massachusetts. He was educated at Harvard University, where he graduated in the year 1817 with very distinguished honours. He afterwards became a tutor in the University, and was elected a member of the American Academy of Arts and Sciences. During his connection with the University he was one of the ablest of the contributors to the North American Review. Abandoning these purely literary pursuits, he studied law, and practised in his native town till the year 1835, when he was elected a member of Congress from his native district, on the Whig ticket. He continued to be a member of the House of Representatives until the year 1843, when he was sent on the mission to China by President Tyler.

After his return he remained retired from public life until April 14th, 1847, when he was appointed brigadier-general in the army. He joined General Taylor during the summer, but was afterwards ordered to Vera Cruz. A number of important duties detained him at this place until after the capture of the Mexican capital, thus preventing him from participating in the toils and dangers of our army. His prompt discharge of every known duty, and his amiability as an officer and companion, have endeared him to all those with whom the fortune of war has placed him.

COLONEL RILEY.

COLONEL BENNET RILEY is a native of Maryland, and served with distinction in the war of 1812. From the post of ensign of riflemen, to which he was appointed January 19th, 1813, he has risen by regular gradation to his present rank. At Contreros he led the assailing party on both days, and finally carried the work with the bayonet, in a style which has rarely been surpassed. During the whole of those eventful days, his brigade endured hardships, and performed actions, worthy of a place beside the wildest records of chivalry. General Smith thus speaks of it : —

"The opportunity afforded to Colonel Riley by his position was seized by that gallant veteran with all the skill and energy for which he is distinguished. The charge of his noble brigade down the slope, in full view of friend and foe, unchecked even for a moment, until he had planted all his colours upon their farthest works, was a spectacle that animated the army to the boldest deeds."

Similar was the conduct of Colonel Riley in the battle along the aqueducts leading to the capital. He stormed some of the enemy's positions, and on the night of December 13th had arrived before the principal gate. He entered Mexico next morning, in company with the commander-in-chief, and still remains at the head of his troops in the capital.

COLONEL BUTLER.

PIERCE M. BUTLER was colonel of the South Carolina regiment of volunteers, and highly distinguished himself in the battles of the 19th and 20th of August. He had left a sick-bed to share the dangers of battle, and although twice wounded, he continued in the saddle, animating his men, until struck down before Churubusco. When his fall was announced in his native state, it caused sensations of the deepest sorrow; friends who knew his worth mourned for him as for a brother, and strangers, acquainted with him only by reputation, felt that a great and good man had been taken from among them. General Shields thus announces his death to the commander-in-chief: —

"The noble and gallant colonel of the South Carolina regiment, P. M. Butler, had risen from his sick-bed to share the hardships of the field, and the dangers of the combat, with his devoted regiment. He survived the conflict of the morning to lead his command where victory again awaited it. Although wounded himself, and having lost his horse, shot under him, he still continued to press onward near the colours of his regiment, until the fatal ball terminated his life.

"A gallant soldier in his youth, he has won in his death upon the field of battle, fame for himself and his regiment, and added another name to the roll of Carolina's departed heroes."

The New Orleans Delta has the following remarks upon the colonel's death: —

"The death of this gallant South Carolinian, the representative on the bloody field of Churubusco of as noble a race of heroes as any country has produced, will create a profound and extended sorrow in this country. He has been for a long time a conspicuous and prominent citizen of South Carolina, and was noted for his great

14 *   Q 2   (161)

resolution and indomitable courage. He possessed military qualities of the highest order, and gave promise of great success and distinction in a career which, alas! terminated at its very commencement. Colonel-Butler had been very ill for several days previous to the battle, but when he heard that the Palmetto flag was going into the fight, unaccompanied by him to whose special charge it had been committed, he broke loose from his physicians, abandoned his sick couch, and, weak, ghastly, and almost fainting, mounted his charger, and placed himself at the head of his regiment. With such an example, men far less ardent and gallant than the South Carolinians would have been prompted to deeds of superhuman daring. But there was no such incitement necessary to impel the sons of the 'Harry Hotspur of the Union,' as Prentiss once styled the gallant Palmetto State, to the most brilliant and conspicuous display of military qualities. Colonel Butler, though twice badly wounded, and weighed down by faintness and loss of blood, maintained his position until a third wound caused his death."

" We lay before our readers," says the Charleston Mercury, " the following interesting correspondence. Its perusal cannot fail to heighten our admiration of the character, and endear more strongly the memory, of that gallant spirit whose heroic aspirations are now quenched in the grave. Though doomed himself, with his brave command, as was supposed, to inglorious inaction, and gloomy and chafed from the disappointment, Colonel Butler could appreciate the yearnings of a brother soldier for a closer participation in the coming fray—' to be nearer the flashing of the guns'—and lend his friendly aid to secure their gratification. The letter of General Worth is as honourable to himself as to the memory of the gallant Butler. Kindred spirits! they could appreciate each other; and gracefully has the survivor wreathed the laurel and cypress over the grave of his friend. A soldier needs no nobler eulogist.

Letter from Major-General Worth to Hon. A. Butler, [*dated Tacubaya, Mexico, August 26th,* 1847.]

"SIR: I trust a cordial intimacy and friendship of twenty-five years with your late brother, the gallant Colonel Butler, will excuse the trespass of a stranger. Your brother fell most gloriously in the great battle of the 20th, before the gates of Mexico. In that bloody conflict, no man gave higher evidence of valour and patriotism, or exhibited a brighter example. He fell when it was God's will, precisely as he would have desired to die. His body rests here; his memory in the hearts of his countrymen; his spirit, bright and pure as his blade, with his God.

"The enclosed letter, written the day before the battle, I did not receive until the day after, through the hands of Dickinson; and it is not because of the kind things said by a friend's partiality, but because it is probably the last letter he penned, that I send it to you; begging that at some future day it may be returned to me, to be preserved and cherished.

"The gallant Palmettos, who showed themselves worthy of their state and country, lost *nearly* one half. This victory will carry joy and sorrow into half the families of South Carolina. Colonel Dickinson is getting on well, and will, it is hoped, save his leg. An armistice is concluded, and commissioners meet to-morrow to treat of peace. God speed them.

Letter from Colonel Butler to General Worth, [dated San Augustin, August 19th, 1847.]

"DEAR GENERAL: We are here in tribulation; I can but hope, however, it is but temporary. It is ordered that this division remain as protection to the train. There is gloom on us all: while I am one who believes *there will be fighting enough for all.* The moral effect is withering. The regiment, though weak in numbers, is up to the full point, and I trust South Carolina may have a place in the picture.

"We have been watching you and your division for the last two days with fraternal affection; but the entire voice of the army, where I have been, or heard, is unbounded confidence in 'Worth.' 'So mote it be.' But I have strayed from the principal point or purpose of my note, which is to say, our friend, Colonel Dickinson, more impatient, and not so long a soldier as myself, desires a place nearer the flashing of the guns; and with good taste, wishes to get near you. If you can make him useful, he will feel much gratified. I am aware you are surrounded by a talented staff, but a little more of a good thing will render it not the less complete or effectual."

MAJOR VINTON.

THE son of a lady of uncommon powers of mind, joined with great worth and influence of character, the elder of four brothers, now distinguished in the church and the army, Vinton was a boy of unusual promise at school, and was celebrated at West Point, where his instructors, in letters written at the time, pronounced him "unrivalled" in genius, acquirements, and high tone of moral character. He received a commission when scarcely seventeen, was employed for several years on topographical duty on the Atlantic coast and the Canada line, and yet was so good a tactician, that at an early age he was appointed by General Eustis adjutant at the school of practice, and gave entire satisfaction, in that arduous office, to a fastidious commander. While residing at Washington, as aid to General Brown, he was employed by the government in several duties of a special nature, and certain papers which he prepared were so generally admired in Congress, that in a leading speech in favour of the Military Academy, Lieutenant Vinton was referred to as an instance of the kind of men the system of that institution could produce.

By pursuing a course of rigid self-denial and discipline, he was able to perform labours in various departments of art and science, in such a manner as to command the respect of men to whom those pursuits were professional. The works of his pencil are received among artists; his correspondence upon astronomical subjects was valued by men of science; his general scholarship procured him a degree of Master of Arts in a leading university; his edition of the work on military tactics was highly satisfactory to the government and the general-in-chief; and in the second volume of Mr. Sumner's Reports, the lawyer will find an argument prepared by him in a case in which he was personally interested, depending before Judge

(164)

Story, to which that judge paid the best compliment of following, in his decision, the same course of reasoning pursued in the argument.

His letters show him to have been as remarkable for the soundness of his views as for his acquisitions. With reference to several political and theological subjects of those times, they show us how a thoughtful man, removed from the strife of parties and the whirl of events, may take the same views at which the actors come to after the retrospection of years.

But that which most interests us in his character, is the tenderness and depth of his affections. He had married a lady of distinguished merit and beauty, who died early, leaving three children, two daughters and a son, who now survive both their parents. In his relations as a father, a husband, a son, and a brother, he was sensitive to every impression, and gave and received exquisite pleasure in the interchanges of affection and esteem. In one letter we find an earnest plea for the paternal affection, in answer to a suggestion that it might interfere with the love and duty we owe to the Most High. He speaks from the heart, and will not permit the natural affections to be severed from religion, and set over against the love of God.

While in Florida, in the prosecution of the war, his mind came under the influence of religion far more than ever before. His whole soul was warmed into a new life, and for a while, like the bewildered apostles, he seemed to "stand, gazing up into heaven." His journal and letters during this period are of the most intensely interesting character. Nothing, in the famed life of Martyn, more touches the heart, than the humility, self-accusation, and childlike devotedness of this high-minded, heroic man. At a secluded post, in the midst of the interminable pine forests, the solitude and silence of which he describes as awful and almost oppressive, far from his family and friends, his mind and affections ripened into the highest state of Christian experience and discipline. He then turned his thoughts, or rather, they were turned for him, towards the office of the Christian ministry. His letters are full of doubts, hopes, and plannings for taking holy orders. He fears that his health will not enable him to follow a sedentary life; he doubts his fitness; fears that selfish motives, the prospect of being with his family and friends, may combine with others; and examines himself in the most thorough and humble manner. He cannot honour ably quit the army then in the field, and the prospect of retiring from it was somewhat distant. His pecuniary affairs, too, were hardly such as to warrant him in yielding up all income for three or four years ; and the banks in which his property was invested were embarrassed and in danger. Then, too, he doubts if he is not too old to begin the study of a new profession ; but modestly considers his acquirements in the languages, and avers that he aims at no distinction as a scholar or a preacher, but only at that degree of fitness which the rules of the Church require, to enable him to do his work in some humble part of the vineyard. To lose no time, he sends for books, and in his tent and in the forest, he pores over the Greek and Hebrew, the commentators and sermonizers, and devoutly uses the best books of meditation and reflection. He prepared several outlines of sermons, and in his choice of subjects leaned towards those of a pathetic and personal character, that are more likely to bring tears into the eyes than to tax the understanding. As another preparation, he used to read parts of the service aloud, by himself, in the forest. He says, in his journal :—" It requires time and habitude for one to become reconciled to the sound of his own voice. It throws one, at first, into absolute trepidation. In the solitude it is sufficiently appalling. What must it be in an assembly of people, a silent auditory, where a thousand eyes are fixed upon you, a whole congregation of faces bent upon you, ready to criticise and condemn the slightest fault ?" This, from a man who could stand with firm nerves a three-hours' fire from concealed Indians, scale the heights and walls of Monterey, and face the blazing batteries of Vera Cruz !

It was Captain Vinton's fortune to be engaged in one of the few battles of that distasteful war—the action at Lake Munroe. The event, and his own feelings, are faithfully described in his letter of February 12th, 1837 :—

" Early in the morning of the 8th instant, half an hour before daylight, we were aroused by the war-cry of the savages, and a fire was poured into our camp on all sides, except that towards the lake. Our men, though recruits, almost without exception, repaired with alacrity to their posts, and returned upon the enemy full volleys of musketry. The morning was rendered still more obscure by a dense fog, which, with the smoke from the fire-arms, nearly concealed the enemy from our sight. But we had the direction with sufficient precision, and poured in our shot with interest. For three hours this conflict continued, with only one or two slight intermissions, our men gaining confidence and enthusiasm every moment. At length the savages began to slacken their fire, and made off, carrying their dead and wounded, but leaving behind many articles which they would never have relinquished but for discomfiture and necessity. They came down upon us with all their force, thinking, perhaps, to take possession of our camp. Their numbers were large, variously estimated at from three to five hundred, and their fire was sustained with a vigour and pertinacity unprecedented." In this action Captain Mellon was killed, and Lieutenant McLaughlin and thirteen privates wounded. One man was struck down at Captain Vinton's side, so near as to cover him with blood.

The continuance of the war in Florida, and the financial difficulties of the country, as well as his uncertain health, obliged him to abandon his cherished hope of the ministry, and he made up his mind to devote the remainder of his life to the duties of his profession, to general studies, and the education of his children.

Being at Providence during the Dorr insurrection, he entered ardently into the cause of the state, and saw the necessity of military organization and discipline to save the lives and property of the inhabitants from the recklessness of an armed mob. He hastened to Washington, and asked authority to offer his services to the state. This was not given, and he was told that he must act on his own responsibility. As he was not forbidden, he took the responsibility ; and had he been called to account, would have made any sacrifice for the good of his native state. He knew the risk he ran; for it was generally feared that if the Dorr movement prevailed in Providence, it would also prevail in Washington. The people of Rhode Island well remember and appreciate the value of his military counsels in that crisis, of his incessant disciplining of the volunteer companies, and the spirit and intelligence infused into the young citizen soldiers by his course of military lectures.

While stationed at the arsenal at Augusta, Georgia, he received orders to join the army of General Taylor on its march from the Rio Grande toward the city of Monterey. During this march, he performed the duties of a field-officer, often with a separate command, a proof of peculiar confidence in an enemy's country. He was sent to take possession of Mier, which it was thought would be defended, and to act as governor of the place during its occupation. This he did, and remained there until the army passed on,ʾand then rejoined it in season to act a conspicuous part in the battle of Monterey.

On the night before the battle of Monterey, he writes to his daughter, showing a spirit of preparation for the duties and chances of the morrow, which could not but ensure him success in whatever might fall to his lot to attempt.

He was with General Worth's division, and was actively and prominently engaged in the operations of each day. He was with the troops as they passed so long under the fire from the two heights, in the storming of those heights, the capture of the palace, and the penetrating into the town, the digging through walls, and firing from house-tops. He was in five several engagements, in each of which he was exposed to severe fire from the enemy. In the storming of the second hill, he led a battalion on one side of the hill, while Colonel Childs commanded on the other; and after forcing their way up, over rocks and brambles, amid a shower of musket-balls, they drove the enemy from the top, at the point of the bayonet, and forced them to retreat to the stronghold of the Bishop's Palace.

The part performed by him in the capture of the Bishop's Palace was of so distinguished a character, and attracted such admiration at the time, that it deserves a full recital here. We cannot present a juster description of it than is contained in a letter from Captain Blanchard, who served under him at the time.

"I found Captain J. R. Vinton in command of the advance, and he then told me that his plan was to try to draw the enemy from their position, in and near the palace, and when they were fairly out, to rise and charge them vigorously, and, if possible, to get possession of the palace. The advance was covered as much as possible behind the rocks, to protect them from the dreadful shower of grape and musketry which the enemy kept up from their defences. I asked him if we should advance or fire. He told me that I might advance if I did not expose my men too much, and that he wished me to fall back whenever I saw the enemy coming out, until we were upon his line of ambush, and then to close on him and rush on them. It was a well-conceived plan, and the result showed that it was well executed. The enemy were induced to come out and charge, and as they came up the hill, Captain Vinton shouted, 'Now, my men, close and drive them!' With one will they closed to centre, delivered their fire, and with charged bayonets rushed on the Mexicans. They were thunderstruck, and, after a moment's stand, broke and ran. Our men were in the palace and fort before they all escaped, and in ten minutes their own guns were turned upon them. The main body under Colonel Childs came down in solid column, and we were the victors. It was a stirring, thrilling scene, and I cannot do it justice, for it should be seen to be felt. Captain Vinton derived all the credit which his position enabled him to obtain, and I shall always be of opinion that his plan was an admirable one. I hope he will be promoted, not only for his skilful and gallant conduct on that day, but for his general meritorious conduct as an officer."

After some time spent at Monterey and Saltillo, he was ordered with the greater part of the regulars to join General Scott in the attack on Vera Cruz. Here it was that he wrote his last letter, which has already been given to the public. Those who knew him know how truly he speaks of his past life. His country will not forget in what spirit he gave his life to her "in her time of appeal." " I have hitherto lived mostly for others—but my children will reap some of the fruits of my self-denial, by the means I shall leave them of living independently, and securing a good education. I commit them, in full reliance, to the care of their Heavenly Father, and I hope their trust in him will ever be at least as firm as my own. My confidence in the overruling providence of God is unqualified, so that I go to the field of action assured that whatever may befall me will be for the best. I feel proud to serve my country in her time of appeal; and should even the worst, death itself, be my lot, I shall meet it cheerfully."

His habits of order were singularly preserved to the last. On the leaves of a pocket-book he made daily and almost hourly memoranda in pencil, which he afterwards transferred at leisure to his journal. These notes are carried down, in a clear hand, to within less than an hour of his fall, and being found on his person are now in the possession of his friends. The last entry is as follows :—

"*March 22d.*—Ordered to the trenches to command the batteries, early. General Scott sent in a flag for the city to surrender, at 2 P. M.; refused. Seven mortars opened at 4 P. M. Heavy cannonading"—— These were his last words.

15   R

Towards evening of the 22d of March, Major Vinton went out upon an exposed situation, to watch the effect of our shot and the direction of that from the enemy. He remained there for some time, came down, and said to Major Martin Scott, who commanded the covering party, " Tell the officers, major, as you pass the mortars, that our guns are working accurately." He had just returned to his post when a huge shell, striking the top of the parapet, glanced and struck his head, fracturing the skull. He fell instantly dead, lying upon his back, with his arms crossed over his breast; his face, as an officer writes who was present, " retaining its habitual expression, sedate and earnest, but not harsh." The officers and men rushed to him as he fell, and gathered about him. The shell did not burst, fortunately, for it was found to be charged with a pound of powder and three hundred and twenty musket-balls. Upon his body were found letters from his children, stained with his life-blood, which flowed from a wound in his breast. He was buried in the military coat in which he fell. The funeral was attended by the general-in-chief and all the officers who could be spared from duty, and the service of the church was read over him by a brother officer —a friend of many years—amid the roar of cannon, the falling of the enemy's shot, and the whirling of sand in the fierce Norther— snatched from the victory of the morrow, that his spirit might gain a greater victory over death and the grave.

CAPTAIN THORNTON.

Captain Seth B. Thornton was a native of Virginia, and served with credit in the late Seminole war. In June, 1836, he was appointed 2d lieutenant in the army; and in February, 1841, was commissioned captain of the 2d dragoons. He joined the Corps of Observation, at its first organization, and after its arrival at the Rio Grande, was destined to command the first party attacked by the Mexicans, and to begin the war.

In consequence of the rumoured intentions of the enemy, Captain Thornton was despatched on the 24th of April, 1846, to the crossing, above Fort Brown, and Captain Ker below. Accompanying Thornton were Captain Hardee, Lieutenants Mason and Kane, and sixty-one men. After proceeding about twenty-six miles, they encountered a Mexican, who reported that at a short distance, the enemy were stationed to the number of two thousand, under General Torrejon. Partly from the cowardice of their Mexican guide, and partly from ignorance of the country, they were led into a plantation surrounded by a thick chapparal fence, round which was concealed an ambush of more than ten times their number. Thornton, followed by his command, crossed the plantation to the house, where he entered into conversation with one of the residents. While thus engaged, the enemy took possession of the gate, and now for the first time, the party perceived that the chapparal was crowded with infantry, supported by cavalry, who were preparing for a charge. This was met with gallantry and success; but in the struggle Lieutenant Kane was unhorsed, and the captain became separated from his command. The whole Mexican force now poured in a destructive fire upon the few men under Captain Hardee, who, notwithstanding, rallied and endeavoured to retreat by way of the river. This he was unable to accomplish, and after having eleven men killed, including a sergeant and two other officers, he consented to surrender, on condition of his men being treated as prisoners of war, declaring that if this were refused, they would continue the battle at all hazards. This was acceded to, and the captain and twenty-five men were carried into Matamoras.

The bravery of Captain Thornton deserves notice. As we have stated, he met the charge of the cavalry with success, but was unable to break the crowded lines of the infantry by whom they were supported. The chapparal was at this time in one wide blaze of fire, and in rushing toward it, the horse of the captain made a tremendous leap, completely clearing the whole enclosure, and alighted in the midst of the enemy. This feat, however, was not performed with impunity; the animal received a severe wound at the very moment of its accomplishment, and was subsequently obliged to carry his intrepid rider through a host of armed men. The captain escaped unwounded, and though both horse and rider subsequently encountered a severe fall, he succeeded in approaching within about five miles of the American camp. But at this place he was intercepted by an advance-guard of the enemy, and conveyed prisoner to Matamoras.

Lieutenant Mason was killed before the chapparal, and Kane shared the fate of Thornton.

Notwithstanding the disadvantages against which the Americans contended, this affair was a source of unbounded exultation to the enemy. Besides public rejoicing in Matamoras, Arista wrote to General Torrejon in terms of congratulation, which would have been considered extravagant in General Taylor after the battle of Palo Alto.

Captain Thornton was retained by the Mexicans until after the battle of Resaca de la Palma, when an exchange of prisoners restored him to the American army. He was immediately placed under arrest, and a court of inquiry held upon the causes of his capture, which resulted in his honourable acquittal of all blame He accompanied the army to Monterey, and subsequently joined the commander-in-chief in his march toward central Mexico. The hardships of that terrible journey preyed upon his naturally delicate constitution, and rendered him an invalid before the city of the Montezuma's greeted the army's longing sight. Eager, however, for duty, nothing could prevail on him to be inactive, as soon as prospect of battle was presented. During the reconnoissance near San Antonio, on the evening of the 18th August, he accompanied the men, assisting personally in the most fatiguing duties. While thus engaged, a discharge from a battery within the fort struck him dead from his horse, and wounded a guide.

Thornton seemed born to misfortune. He was a passenger in the ill-fated Pulaski, and after doing all he could to rescue others, he attempted to save himself by seizing upon a chicken-coop. He picked several out of the water; but one by one they died and dropped off, and he himself became a half-famished maniac, before he was found. In military affairs he was always unfortunate. He was endowed with a courage which nothing could daunt; but his spirit was much too ardent and impetuous for his physical structure, he being of a small stature and delicate constitution.

GENERAL KEARNY.

BRIGADIER-GENERAL STEPHEN W. KEARNY is a native of New Jersey, and entered the army as first lieutenant of the 13th infantry, March 12th, 1812. He rose by regular gradation to brigadier-general, April 30th, 1846.

Kearny was intended by his parents for one of the learned professions, and being placed at Princeton college, made rapid advances in the various studies pursued there. The outrages perpetrated by Great Britain on our commerce, roused him from a scholar's seclusion, and fired his spirit with ambition for distinction in the coming contest. He marched under Captain [now General] Wool to the Canada border, and fought with the army which so gallantly compensated for the disgrace of Hull's surrender at Detroit. He was with Wool at Queenstown, and in company with Colonel Scott, was taken prisoner by an overwhelming British force on the Canadian side, and sent to Quebec. In a little while he was exchanged, rejoined the army, and served with distinction and usefulness, until the close of the war.

From this time, until the commencement of our struggle with Mexico, he remained in the army, performing various duties, principally among the Indian tribes and the scattered posts owned by government in the western wilderness. He conducted several expeditions to the Rocky Mountains and New Mexico, gaining valuable information of those territories and their inhabitants, and accustoming himself to the labours and privations of a western hunter. At the same time he employed all his leisure hours in gaining a knowledge of military tactics, both from books and by means of personal intercourse with distinguished officers.

On the 30th of June, 1846, by order of government, General

(174)

GENERAL KEARNEY.

Page 174.

DESCRIPTION OF SANTA FE.

Kearny marched from Fort Leavenworth with sixteen hundred regulars and volunteers, on an expedition against Santa Fé, the capital of New Mexico. He took possession of this place in August, having marched in six weeks eight hundred and seventy miles. We annex a rough but lively sketch of the town, from the pen of a volunteer, who wrote since General Kearny's arrival in the United States.

" On the Cimmerone route to Santa Fé, the scene of Indian depredations is chiefly between what is called the ' Pawnee Fork' and Cimmerone river, a distance of, say two hundred miles ; yet the road is by no means safe, even until you arrive within the frontier settlements of New Mexico. We travelled most of the way with three companies of the mounted regiment, and attribute our safety through the Indian country to the fact that the military were with us—as from signs frequently seen, there is no doubt the Indians were constantly around, watching for a favourable opportunity to attack us ; but we were always vigilant, and thus escaped. I am glad the government has sent a force to guard the plains. Every thing will depend upon the material of which the command is composed. Little need be expected if it is made up of officers and men who sought the service because they had nothing to do at home to keep them from starving. God knows there are enough such in the service already. * * * * Every coffee-house in Sante Fé, and their name is legion, was provided with the various implements of gambling, particularly the national game of ' monte.' Intemperance and public disorder — the never-failing attendants of gaming — prevailed in the city.

" By order of the commanding officer, gaming of all kinds was prohibited. Coffee-house keepers were forbidden to sell liquor to soldiers—fandangos were not allowed except on certain conditions and terms. A provost marshal was appointed to enforce these orders. As if by magic the whole condition of things was changed. All this has been brought about by the energetic, and at the same time judicious, exertions of Colonel Easton, who has been industrious and indefatigable in the discharge of his various duties ; at the same time has kept himself aloof from the temptations which so easily beset every American who comes here, whatever be his rank or station. Thoroughly acquainted with the duties of his military profession, he has exhibited in his daily life and manners the example of a well-bred American gentleman—an example seldom seen here, and which has not been lost upon these people. All classes, Mexicans, and others, civil and military, are loud in their praise of him. I only speak the sentiments of every one here, when I say that no officer since General Kearny left, enjoys so universally the good will and esteem of all classes as does Colonel Easton at the present moment. Yet much which I know he contemplated doing towards redeeming this city, is left undone since he was superseded in command ; but during his brief career as commanding officer, he has done enough to secure for him a name which will be long remembered here with much honour. The St. Louis battalion is rapidly improving in drill and discipline — in this last respect it is excellent—while the drill is acknowledged to be superior to any volunteer regiment of last year. * * The battalion is doing well—as an evidence, there are none sick—that is dangerously —in the whole command. They occupy good quarters, barrack-rooms once occupied by the Mexicans, which have since been repaired and altered, so that they are very convenient, with an excellent parade-ground in front. The adjutant, Lieutenant Holmes, is, next to Colonel Easton, the best officer in the battalion. He has been most diligent in his application to his profession, and now acquits himself, in a manner that would honour the post of adjutant in any regular regiment. He is highly esteemed by every officer and soldier of the battalion, and by all who know him, as a good officer and unimpeachable gentleman.

"The Mexicans all seem quiet, and are attending to their regular business; yet many who pretend to know, say that all this quiet is but the calm which precedes the storm—that a general insurrection is brewing, and may at any moment break out. Others, again, who also pretend to understand the Mexicans here, say there is no danger to be apprehended. I am strongly inclined to the opinion that nothing serious is at hand. Among these people, there are many who are always ready for a row, upon the slightest pretence, but I believe the majority are alike indifferent whether the Great Mogul or James K. Polk rules over them, provided they can sell their grapes, peaches, corn and red peppers, and smoke their segars in peace.

"An express, consisting of a captain, lieutenant and fifteen men, started for Washington yesterday. The captain is bearer of despatches from head-quarters here, sent by the commanding officer,

Colonel Newby, of the Illinois foot. * * * * * The Missouri regiment is not in as good a condition as the St. Louis battalion. The appointment of Colonel Price as brigadier-general is by no means popular here. * * * * His command while here was in a constant state of disorganization — no order, no discipline. I could fill a sheet with authentic accounts of the deplorable state, not only of his immediate command, but of the affairs of this post while he was commanding officer, so far as he had the management. One fact will suffice : A private, whom I know, and believe to be a man of truth, told me that at one time there was not an officer or non-commissioned officer of his company on duty ; that they used up their rations, and were obliged to send a private to the colonel to know what to do ; and it was some days, and with great difficulty, before they at last obtained subsistence ! * * * * * Efforts have been made to have Colonel Easton appointed governor of New Mexico. Petitions have been circulated, and signed by almost all the inhabitants and officers of the various regiments, to have the appointment made ; but it is understood that he does not like to be separated from his command ; if it goes south he wishes to go with it. I am inclined to think nothing will be done here until Price arrives, unless an outbreak is attempted. The force now here is more than enough to hold this whole country."

After remaining for some time at Santa Fé, General Kearny marched against the province of California, publishing at the same time a proclamation in which he claimed New Mexico for the United States, and exhorted the inhabitants to submit peaceably to the new government. But on his road he received information that the intended object of his expedition had been already attained by a party under Colonel Fremont. He accordingly sent back the greater part of his force, and with a small troop hurried on to join Colonel Fremont.

New Mexico had been awed but not completely subdued ; and soon after Kearny's departure the inhabitants rose in vindication of their old government. Disturbances were also taking place in California, and several bands of citizens spread themselves over the country and kept up the spirit of opposition. On the 8th of December, 1846, General Kearny encountered one of these under the celebrated Pico, near the Indian town of San Pascual. The following is his own account of this affair :

"Having learned from Captain Gillespie, of the volunteers, that there was an armed party of Californians, with a number of extra horses at San Pascual, three leagues distant, on a road leading to this place, I sent Lieutenant Hammond, 1st dragoons, with a few men to make a reconnoissance of them.

"He returned at two in the morning of the 6th instant, reporting that he had found the party in the place mentioned, and that he had been seen, though not pursued by them. I then determined that I would march for and attack them by break of day. Arrangements were accordingly made for the purpose. My aid-de-camp, Captain Johnson, (dragoons,) was assigned to the command of the advance-guard of twelve dragoons, mounted on the best horses we had ; then followed about fifty dragoons under Captain Moore, mounted, with but few exceptions, on the tired mules they had ridden from Santa Fé (New Mexico, one thousand and fifty miles), then about twenty volunteers of Captain Gibson's company, under his command, and that of Captain Gillespie ; then followed our two mounted howitzers, with dragoons to manage them, and under the charge of Lieutenant Davidson, of the regiment.

"The remainder of the dragoons, volunteers, and citizens, employed by the officers of the staff, &c., were placed under the command of Major Swords (quartermaster), with orders to follow on our trail with the baggage, and to see to its safety.

"As the day (December 6) dawned, we approached the enemy at San Pascual, who were already in the saddle, when Captain Johnson made a furious charge upon them with his advance-guard, and was in a short time after supported by the dragoons ; soon after this the enemy gave way, having kept up from the beginning a continued fire upon us.

"Upon the retreat of the enemy, Captain Moore led off rapidly in pursuit, accompanied by the dragoons mounted on horses, and was followed, though slowly, by the others on their tired mules ; the enemy well-mounted, and among the best horsemen in the world, after retreating about half a mile, and seeing an interval between Captain Moore with his advance, and the dragoons coming to his support, rallied their whole force, charged with their lances, and, on account of their greatly superior numbers, but few of us in front remained untouched ; for five minutes they held the ground from us, when our men coming up, we again drove them, and they fled from the field, not to return to it, which we occupied and encamped upon.

"A most melancholy duty now remains for me : — it is to report the death of my aid-de-camp, Captain Johnson, who was shot dead at the commencement of the action, of Captain Moore, who was lanced just previous to the final retreat of the enemy, and of Lieutenant Hammond, also lanced, and who survived but a few hours. We have also had two sergeants killed, two corporals, and ten privates of the 1st dragoons ; one private of the volunteers, and one man, an *engagé* in the topographical department. Among the wounded are myself, (in two places,) Lieutenant Warner, topographical engineers, (in three places,) Captains Gillespie and Gibson of the volunteers, (the former in three places,) one sergeant, one bugleman, and nine privates of the dragoons ; many of these surviving, although having from two to ten lance wounds, most of them when unhorsed and incapable of resistance.

"Our howitzers were not brought into the action ; but coming to the front at the close of it, before they were turned, so as to admit of being fired upon the retreating enemy, the two mules before one of them got alarmed, and freeing themselves from their drivers, ran off, and among the enemy, and were thus lost to us.

"The enemy proved to be a party of about one hundred and sixty Californians under Andreas Pico, brother of the late governor; the number of their dead and wounded must have been considerable, though I have no means of ascertaining how many, as just previous to their final retreat they carried off all excepting six.

"The great number of our killed and wounded proves that our officers and men have fully sustained the high character and reputation of our troops ; and the victory thus gained over more than double our force may assist in forming the wreath of our national glory.

"I have to return my thanks to many for their gallantry and good conduct on the field, and particularly to Captain Turner, 1st dragoons, (assistant acting adjutant-general,) and to Lieutenant Emory, topographical engineers, who were active in the performance of their duties, and in conveying orders from me to the command.

"On the morning of the 7th, having made ambulances for our wounded, and interred the dead, we proceeded on our march, when the enemy showed himself, occupying the hills in our front, but

s

which they left as we approached ; till reaching San Bernado, a party of them took possession of a hill near to it, and maintained their position until attacked by our advance, who quickly drove them from it, killing and wounding five of their number, with no loss on our part.

" On account of our wounded men, and upon the report of the surgeon that rest was necessary for them, we remained at this place till the morning of the 11th, when Lieutenant Gray, of the navy, in command of a party of sailors and marines, sent out from San Diego by Commodore Stockton, joined us. We proceeded at 10, A. M., the enemy no longer showing himself; and on the 12th (yesterday) we reached this place ; and I have now to offer my thanks to Commodore Stockton, and all of his gallant command, for the very many kind attentions we have received and continue to receive from them."

After this battle, General Kearny continued his march, severely harassed by scouting parties of the enemy, until the 8th of January, 1847, when he came up with their main army at Puebla de los Angelos. Here, in company with Commodore Stockton, he fought a desultory battle, which lasted two days, and terminated in the overthrow of the Mexicans. The American loss was one killed and thirteen wounded ; that of the enemy rather more. Kearny then took possession of the city without further molestation.

The operations attending this battle have unfortunately become a matter of serious misunderstanding between General Kearny, Commodore Stockton, and Colonel Fremont. The commission of the former as governor of California, was given by the President and signed with his signature. To this Stockton objected, on the plea that the province had been captured and placed under military government prior to the date of the general's authority. To this Colonel Fremont agreed, and refused to obey the orders of Kearny. At that time the general's force was so small that he was obliged to yield to circumstances ; but on receiving reinforcements, he entered upon full command, and seizing Colonel Fremont, sent him under arrest to the United States. His trial for disobedience of orders is still going on, and elicits considerable public attention.

COLONEL DONIPHAN.

THE expedition of Colonel Doniphan is one of the most remarkable in all history. Like those of Kearny and Scott, it will form an example to the world of the almost superhuman exertions of which our soldiery, both regular and volunteer, are capable. The Honourable Thomas Benton gave the subjoined vivid description of it in an address to the colonel's command on its return home :—

"Your march and exploits have been among the most wonderful of the age. At the call of your country you marched a thousand miles to the conquest of New Mexico, as part of the force under General Kearny, and achieved that conquest without the loss of a man or the fire of a gun. That work finished, and New Mexico, itself so distant, and so lately the Ultima Thule—the outside boundary of speculation and enterprise — so lately a distant point to be attained, becomes itself a point of departure — a beginning point for new and far more extended expeditions. You look across the long and lofty chain — the Cordilleras of North America — which divide the Atlantic from the Pacific waters ; and you see beyond that ridge a savage tribe which had been long in the habit of depredating upon the province which had just become an American conquest. You, a part only of the subsequent Chihuahua column, under Jackson and Gilpin, march upon them—bring them to terms—and they sign a treaty with Colonel Doniphan, in which they bind themselves to cease their depredations on the Mexicans, and to become the friends of the United States. A novel treaty that ! signed on the western confines of New Mexico, between parties who had hardly ever heard each other's names before, and to give peace and protection to Mexicans who were hostile to both. This was the meeting and this the parting of the Missouri volunteers, with the numerous and savage tribe of the Navaho Indians, living on the waters of the gulf of Cali-

16

fornia, and so long the terror and scourge of Sonora, Sinaloa, and New Mexico.

"This object accomplished, and impatient of inactivity, and without orders, (General Kearny having departed for California,) you cast about to carve out some new work for yourselves. Chihuahua, a rich and populous city of nearly thirty thousand souls, the seat of government of the state of that name, and formerly the residence of the captains general of the Internal Provinces under the vice-regal government of New Spain, was the captivating object which fixed your attention. It was a far distant city—about as far from St. Louis as Moscow is from Paris; and towns, and enemies, and a large river, and defiles, and mountains, and the desert whose ominous name portends death to travellers— *el jornada de los muertos*—the journey of the dead—all lay between you. It was a perilous enterprise, and a discouraging one for a thousand men, badly equipped, to contemplate. No matter. Danger and hardship lent it a charm, and the adventurous march was resolved on, and the execution commenced. First, the ominous desert was passed, its character vindicating its title to its mournful appellation — an arid plain of ninety miles, strewed with the bones of animals that had perished of hunger and thirst—little hillocks of stone, and the solitary cross, erected by pious hands, marking the spot where some Christian had fallen victim of the savage, of the robber, or of the desert itself—no water—no animal life—no sign of habitation. There the Texan prisoners, driven by the cruel Salazar, had met their direst sufferings, unrelieved, as in other parts of the country, by the compassionate ministrations (for where is it that *woman* is not compassionate?) of the pitying women. The desert was passed, and the place for crossing the river approached. A little arm of the river Bracito (in Spanish), made out from its side. There the enemy, in superior numbers, and confident in cavalry and artillery, undertook to bar the way. Vain pretension! Their discovery, attack, and rout, were about simultaneous operations. A few minutes did the work! And in this way our Missouri volunteers of the Chihuahua column, spent their Christmas day of the year 1846.

"The victory of Bracito opened the way to the crossing of the river Del Norte, and to admission into the beautiful little town of the Paso del Norte, where a neat cultivation, a comfortable people, fields, orchards and vineyards, and a hospitable reception, offered the rest and refreshment which toils and dangers and victory had won. You rested there till artillery was brought down from Santa Fé; but the pretty town of the Paso del Norte, with all its enjoyments, and they were many, and the greater for the place in which they were found, was not a *Capua* to the men of Missouri. You moved forward in February, and the battle of the Sacramento, one of the military marvels of the age, cleared the route to Chihuahua, which was entered without further resistance. It had been entered once before by a detachment of American troops; but under circumstances how different! In the year 1807, Lieutenant Pike and his thirty brave men, taken prisoners on the head of the Rio del Norte, had been marched captives into Chihuahua: in the year 1847, Doniphan and his men entered it as conquerors. The paltry triumph of a captain-general over a lieutenant, was effaced in the triumphal entrance of a thousand Missourians into the grand and ancient capital of all the *Internal Provinces!* and old men, still alive, could remark the grandeur of the American spirit under both events—the proud and lofty bearing of the captive thirty—the mildness and moderation of the conquering thousand.

"Chihuahua was taken, and responsible duties, more delicate than those of arms, were to be performed. Many American citizens were there, engaged in trade; much American property was there. All this was to be protected, both lives and property, and by peaceful arrangement; for the command was too small to admit of division, and of leaving a garrison. Conciliation and negotiation were resorted to, and successfully. Every American interest was provided for, and placed under the safeguard, *first*, of good will, and *next*, of guaranties not to be violated with impunity.

"Chihuahua gained, it became, like Santa Fé, not the terminating point of a long expedition, but the beginning point of a new one. General Taylor was somewhere—no one knew exactly where—but some seven or eight hundred miles towards the other side of Mexico. You had heard that he had been defeated — that Buena Vista had not been a *good prospect* to him. Like good Americans, you did not believe a word of it; but, like good soldiers, you thought it best to go and see. A volunteer party of fourteen, headed by Collins, of Boonville, undertook to penetrate to Saltillo, and bring you information of his condition. They set out. Amidst innumerable dangers they accomplish their purpose, and return. You march. A van-

s 2

guard of one hundred men, led by Lieutenant-Colonel Mitchell, led the way. Then came the main body, (if the name is not a burlesque. on such a handful,) commanded by Colonel Doniphan himself.

"The whole table-land of Mexico, in all its breadth, from west to east, was to be traversed. A numerous and hostile population in towns—treacherous Camanches in the mountains—were to be passed. Every thing was to be self-provided—provisions, transportation, fresh horses for remounts, and even the means of victory — and all without a military chest, or even an empty box, in which government gold had ever reposed. All was accomplished. Mexican towns were passed, in order and quiet; plundering Camanches were punished; means were obtained from traders to liquidate indispensable contributions; and the wants that could not be supplied were endured like soldiers of veteran service.

"I say the Camanches were punished. And here presents itself an episode of a novel, extraordinary, and romantic kind—Americans chastising savages for plundering people who they themselves came to conquer, and forcing the restitution of captives and of plundered property. A strange story this to tell in Europe, where backwoods character, western character, is not yet completely known. But to the facts. In the muskeet forest of the Bolson de Mapimi, and in the sierras around the beautiful town and fertile district of Parras, and in all the open country for hundreds of miles round about, the savage Camanches have held dominion ever since the usurper Santa Anna disarmed the people, and sally forth from their fastnesses to slaughter men, plunder cattle, and carry off women and children. An exploit of this kind had just been performed on the line of the Missourians' march, not far from Parras, and an advanced party chanced to be in that town at the time the news of the depredation arrived there. It was only fifteen strong. Moved by gratitude for the kind attentions of the people, especially the women, to the sick of General Wool's command, necessarily left in Parras, and unwilling to be outdone by enemies in generosity, the heroic fifteen, upon the spot, volunteered to go back, hunt out the depredators, and punish them, without regard to numbers. A grateful Mexican became their guide. On their way they fell in with fifteen more of their comrades; and, in a short time, seventeen Camanches killed out of sixty-five, eighteen captives restored to their families, and three hundred and fifty head of cattle recovered for their owners, was the fruit of this sudden and romantic episode.

"Such noble conduct was not without its effect on the minds of the astonished Mexicans. An official document from the prefect of the place to Captain Reid, leader of this detachment, attests the verity of the fact, and the gratitude of the Mexicans; and constitutes a trophy of a new kind in the annals of war. Here it is in the original Spanish, and I will read it off in English.

"It is officially dated from the Prefecture of the Department of Parras, signed by the prefect, Jose Ignacio Arrabe, and addressed to Captain Reid, the 18th of May, and says:

"'At the first notice that the barbarians, after killing many, and taking captives, were returning to their haunts, you generously and bravely offered, with fifteen of your subordinates, to fight them on their crossing by the Paso, executing this enterprise with celerity, address, and bravery, worthy of all eulogy, and worthy of the brilliant issue which all celebrate. You recovered many animals and much plundered property, and eighteen captives were restored to liberty and to social enjoyments, their souls overflowing with a lively sentiment of joy and gratitude, which all the inhabitants of this town equally breathe, in favour of their generous deliverers and their valiant chief. The half of the Indians killed in the combat, and those which fly wounded, do not calm the pain which all feel for the wound which your excellency received defending Christians and civilized beings against the rage and brutality of savages. All desire the speedy re-establishment of your health; and although they know that in your own noble soul will be found the best reward of your conduct, they desire also to address you the expression of their gratitude and high esteem. I am honoured in being the organ of the public sentiment; and pray you to accept it, with the assurance of my most distinguished esteem.

"'God and Liberty!'

"This is a trophy of a new kind in war, won by thirty Missourians, and worthy to be held up to the admiration of Christendom.

"The long march from Chihuahua to Monterey was made more in the character of protection and deliverance than of conquest and invasion. Armed enemies were not met, and peaceful people were not disturbed. You arrived in the month of May in General Taylor's camp, and about in a condition to vindicate, each of you for

16 *

himself, your lawful title to the double *sobriquet* of the general, with the addition to it which the colonel of the expedition has supplied — ragged — as well as rough and ready. No doubt you all showed title, at that time, to that third *sobriquet ;* but to see you now, so gayly attired, so sprucely equipped, one might suppose that you had never, for an instant, been a stranger to the virtues of soap and water, or the magic ministrations of the *blanchisseuse,* and the elegant transformations of the fashionable tailor. Thanks, perhaps, to the difference between pay in the lump at the end of service, and driblets in the course of it.

" You arrived in General Taylor's camp ragged and rough, as we can well conceive, and ready, as I can quickly show. You reported for duty ! you asked for service ! — such as a march upon San Luis de Potosi, Zacatecas, or the ' halls of the Montezumas,' or any thing in that way that the general should have a mind to. If he was going upon any excursion of that kind, all right. No matter about fatigues that were passed, or expirations of service that might accrue ; you came to go, and only asked the privilege.

" That is what I call ready. Unhappily the conqueror of Palo Alto, Resaca de la Palma, Monterey, and Buena Vista, was not in exactly the condition that the lieutenant-general, that might have been, intended him to be. He was not at the head of twenty thousand men ! he was not at the head of any thousands that would enable him to march ! and had to decline the proffered service. Thus the long-marched and well-fought volunteers—the rough, the ready, and the ragged, had to turn their faces towards home, still more than two thousand miles distant. But this being mostly by water, you hardly count it in the recital of your march. But this is an unjust omission, and against the precedents as well as unjust. ' The Ten Thousand' counted the voyage on the Black Sea as well as the march from Babylon ; and twenty centuries admit the validity of the count. The present age, and posterity, will include in ' the going out and coming in' of the Missouri Chihuahua volunteers, the water voyage as well as the land march ; and then the expedition of the One Thousand will exceed that of the Ten by some two thousand miles.

" The last nine hundred miles of your land march, from Chihuahua to Matamoras, you made in forty-five days, bringing seventeen pieces of artillery, eleven of which were taken from the Sacramento and Bracito. Your horses, travelling the whole distance without United States' provender, were astonished to find themselves regaled on their arrival on the Rio Grande frontier, with hay, corn, and oats from the States. You marched further than the farthest, fought as well as the best, left order and quiet in your train, and cost less money than any.

"You arrive here to-day, absent one year, marching and fighting all the time, bringing trophies of cannon and standards from fields whose names were unknown to you before you set out, and only grieving that you could not have gone further. Ten pieces of cannon, rolled out of Chihuahua to arrest your march, now roll through the streets of St. Louis, to grace your triumphal return. Many standards, all pierced with bullets, while waving over the heads of the enemy at the Sacramento, now wave at the head of your column. The black flag, brought to the Bracito, to indicate the refusal of that quarter which its bearers so soon needed and received, now takes its place among your trophies, and hangs drooping in their nobler presence. To crown the whole—to make public and private happiness go together—to spare the cypress where the laurel hangs in clusters—this long and perilous march, with all its accidents of field and camp, presents an incredibly small list of comrades lost. Almost all return! and the joy of families resounds, intermingled with the applauses of the State."

The following is the colonel's account of the great battle of Sacramento :—

"On the evening of the 8th of February, 1847, we left the town of El Paso del Norte, escorting the merchant train or caravan of about three hundred and fifteen wagons for the city of Chihuahua. Our force consisted of nine hundred and twenty-four effective men ; one hundred and seventeen officers and privates of the artillery ; ninety-three of Lieutenant-Colonel Mitchell's escort, and the remainder the first regiment Missouri mounted riflemen. We progressed in the direction of this place until the 25th, when we were informed by our spies that the enemy, to the number of fifteen hundred men, were at Inseneas, the country-seat of Governor Trias, about twenty-five miles in advance.

"When we arrived, on the evening of the 26th, near that point, we found that the force had retreated in the direction of this city. On the evening of the 27th we arrived at Sans, and learned from our spies that the enemy, in great force, had fortified the pass of the Sacramento river, about fifteen miles in advance, and about the same distance from this city. We were also informed that there was no water between the point we were at and that occupied by the enemy; we therefore determined to halt until morning. At sunrise on the 28th, the last day of February, we took up the line of march and formed the whole train, consisting of three hundred and fifteen heavy traders' wagons and our commissary and company wagons, into four columns, thus shortening our line so as to make it more easily protected.

" We placed the artillery and all the command, except two hundred cavalry proper, in the intervals between the columns of wagons. We thus fully concealed our force and its position by masking our force with the cavalry. When we arrived within three miles of the enemy, we made a reconnoissance of his position and the arrangement of his forces. This we could easily do — the road leading through an open prairie valley between the sterile mountains. The Pass of the Sacramento is formed by a point of the mountains on our right, their left extending into the valley or plain so as to narrow the valley to about one and a half miles. On our left was a deep, dry, sandy channel of a creek, and between these points the plain rises to sixty feet abruptly. This rise is in the form of a crescent, the convex part being to the north of our forces.

" On the right, from the point of mountains, a narrow part of the plain extends north one and a half miles farther than on the left. The main road passes down the centre of the valley and across the crescent, near the left or dry branch. The Sacramento rises in the mountains on the right, and the road falls on to it about one mile below the battle-field or entrenchment of the enemy. We ascertained that the enemy had one battery of four guns, two nine and two six-pounders, on the point of the mountain on our right, (their left,) at a good elevation to sweep the plain, and at the point where the mountains extended farthest into the plain.

" On our left (their right) they had another battery on an elevation commanding the road, and three entrenchments of two six-pounders, and on the brow of the crescent near the centre another of two six and two four and six culverins, or rampart pieces, mounted on carriages; and on the crest of the hill or ascent between the batteries, and the right and left, they had twenty-seven redoubts dug and thrown up, extending at short intervals across the whole ground. In these their infantry were placed, and were entirely protected. Their cavalry was drawn up in front of the redoubts in the intervals four deep, and in front of the redoubts two deep, so as to mask them as far as practicable.

" When we had arrived within one and a half miles of the entrenchments along the main road, we advanced the cavalry still farther, and suddenly diverged with the columns to the right, so as to gain the narrow part of the ascent on our right, which the enemy discovering endeavoured to prevent by moving forward with one thousand cavalry and four pieces of cannon in their rear, masked by them. Our movements were so rapid that we gained the elevation with our forces and the advance of our wagons in time to form before they arrived within reach of our guns. The enemy halted, and we advanced the head of our column within twelve hundred yards of them, so as to let our wagons attain the high lands and form as before.

" We now commenced the action by a brisk fire from our battery, and the enemy unmasked and commenced also; our fires proved effective at this distance, killing fifteen men, wounding several more, and disabling one of the enemy's guns. We had two men slightly wounded, and several horses and mules killed. The enemy then slowly retreated behind their works in some confusion, and we resumed our march in the former order, still diverging more to the right to avoid their battery on our left, (their right,) and their strongest redoubts, which were on the left near where the road passes. After marching as far as we safely could, without coming within range of their heavy battery on our right, Captain Weightman, of the artillery, was ordered to charge with the two twelve-pound howitzers, to be supported by the cavalry under Captains Reid, Parsons and Hudson.

" The howitzers charged at speed, and were gallantly sustained by Captain Reid; but, by some misunderstanding, my order was not given to the other two companies. Captain Hudson, anticipating my order, charged in time to give ample support to the howitzers. Captain Parsons, at the same moment, came to me and asked permission for his company to charge the redoubts immediately to the left of Captain Weightman, which he did very gallantly. The remainder of the two battalions of the 1st regiment were dismounted during the cavalry charge, and following rapidly on foot, while Major Clarke advanced as fast as practicable with the remainder of the battery, we charged their redoubts from right to left, with a brisk and deadly fire of riflemen, while Major Clarke opened a rapid and well-directed fire on a column of cavalry attempting to pass to our left so as to attack the wagons and our rear.

" The fire was so well directed as to force them to fall back ; and our riflemen, with the cavalry and howitzers, cleared the parapets after an obstinate resistance. Our forces advanced to the very brink of their redoubts and attacked the enemy with their sabres. When the redoubts were cleared, and the batteries in the centre and on our left were silenced, the main battery on our right still continued to pour in a constant and heavy fire, as it had done during the heat of the engagement; but as the whole fate of the battle depended upon carrying the redoubts and centre battery, this one on the right remained unattacked, and the enemy had rallied there five hundred strong.

"Major Clarke was directed to commence a heavy fire upon it. Lieutenant-Colonels Mitchell and Jackson, commanding the 1st battalion, were ordered to remount and charge the battery on the left, while Major Gilpin passed the 2d battalion on foot up the rough ascent of the mountain on the opposite side. The fire of our battery was so effective as to completely silence theirs, and the rapid advance of our column put them to flight over the mountains in great confusion.

"Thus ended the battle of Sacramento. The force of the enemy was twelve hundred cavalry, from Durango and Chihuahua, with the Vera Cruz dragoons ; twelve hundred infantry from Chihuahua ; three hundred artillerists, and fourteen hundred and twenty rancheros, badly armed with lassoes, lances, and machetoes, or corn knives ; ten pieces of artillery, two nine, two eight, four six, and two fourpounders, and six culverins, or rampart pieces.

" Their forces were commanded by Major-General Hendea, general of Durango, Chihuahua, Sonora, and New Mexico; Brigadier-General Jastimani, Brigadier-General Garcia Conde, formerly Minister of War for the Republic of Mexico, who is a scientific man, and planned this whole field of defence ; General Uguerte and Governor Tria, who acted as brigadier-general on the field, and colonels and other officers without number.

" Our force was nine hundred and twenty-four effective men ; at least one hundred of whom were engaged in holding horses and driving teams.

"The loss of the enemy was his entire artillery, ten wagons, masses of beans and pinola, and other Mexican provisions, about three hundred killed and about the same number wounded, many of whom have since died, and forty prisoners.

"The field was literally covered with the dead and wounded from our artillery and the unerring fire of our riflemen. Night put a stop to the carnage, the battle having commenced about three o'clock. Our loss was one killed, one mortally wounded, and seven so wounded as to recover without any loss of limbs. I cannot speak too highly of the coolness, gallantry and bravery of the officers and men under my command.

"I was ably sustained by field officers Lieutenant-Colonels Mitchell and Jackson of the 1st battalion, and Major Gilpin of the 2d battalion; and Major Clarke and his artillery acted nobly, and did the most effective service in every part of the field. It is abundantly shown, in the charge made by Captain Weightman, with the section of howitzers, that they can be used in any charge of cavalry with great effect. Much has been said, and justly said, of the gallantry of our artillery, unlimbering within two hundred and fifty yards of the enemy at Palo Alto; but how much more daring was the charge of Captain Weightman, when he unlimbered within fifty yards of the redoubts of the enemy.

"On the first day of March we took formal possession of the capital of Chihuahua in the name of our government. We were ordered by General Kearny to report to General Wool at this place; since our arrival, we hear that he is at Saltillo, surrounded by the enemy. Our present purpose is either to force our way to him, or return by Bexar, as our term of service expires on the last day of May next."

We annex a vivid description, by Edwin Bryant, Esq., of the desert through which Doniphan led his troops. A perusal of it will increase our astonishment at his remarkable expedition.

"*Monday, August* 3.—I rose from my bivouack this morning at half-past one o'clock. The moon, appearing like a ball of fire, and shining with a dim and baleful light, seemed struggling downwards through the thick bank of smoky vapour that overhung and curtained the high ridge of mountains to the west of us. This ridge,

T

stretching as far to the north and the south as the eye can reach, forms the western wall (if I may so call it) of the desert valley we had crossed yesterday, and is composed of rugged, barren peaks of dark basaltic rock, sometimes exhibiting misshapen outlines, at others towering upwards, and displaying a variety of architectural forms, representing domes, spires, and turreted fortifications.

"Our encampment was on the slope of the mountain, and the valley lay spread out at our feet, illumined sufficiently by the red glare of the moon, and the more pallid effulgence of the stars, to display imperfectly its broken and frightful barrenness and its solemn desolation. No life, except in the little oasis occupied by our camp and dampened by the sluggish spring, by excavating which with our hands we had obtained impure water sufficient to quench our own and our animals' thirst, existed as far as the eye could penetrate over mountain and plain. There was no voice of animal, no hum of insect, disturbing the tomb-like solemnity. All was silence and dearth. The atmosphere, chill and frosty, seemed to sympathize with this sepulchral stillness. No wailing or whispering sounds sighed through the chasms of the mountains, or over the gulfy and waterless ravines of the valley; no rustling zephyr swept over the scant dead grass, or disturbed the crumbling leaves of the gnarled and stunted cedars, which seemed to draw a precarious existence from the small patch of damp earth surrounding us. Like the other elements sustaining animal and vegetable life, the winds seemed stagnant and paralyzed by the universal dearth around. I contemplated this scene of dismal and oppressive solitude until the moon sunk behind the mountain, and object after object became shrouded in its shadow.

"Rousing Mr. Jacob, who slept soundly, and after him the other members of our small party, (nine in number,) we commenced our preparations for the long and much-dreaded march over the great Salt Desert. Mr. Hudspeth, the gentleman who had kindly conducted us thus far from Fort Bridger as our pilot, was to leave us at this point, for the purpose of exploring a route for the emigrant wagons further south. He was accompanied by three gentlemen, Messrs. Ferguson, Kirkwood, and Minter. Consequently, from this time forward, we are without a guide or any reliable index to our destination, except our course westward until we strike Mary's river and the emigrant trail to California, which runs parallel with it, some two or three hundred miles distant. The march across the Salt Plain, without water or grass, was variously estimated by those with whom I conversed at Fort Bridger at from sixty to eighty miles. Captain Walker, an old and experienced mountaineer, who had crossed it at this point, as the guide of Captain Fremont and his party, estimated the distance at seventy-five miles, and we found the estimate to be correct.

" We gathered the dead limbs of the cedars which had been cut down by Captain Fremont's party when encamped here last autumn, and igniting them they gave us a good light during the preparation and discussion of our frugal breakfast, which consisted to-day of bread and coffee—bacon being interdicted in consequence of its incitement to thirst, a sensation which at this time we desired to avoid, as we felt uncertain how long it might be before we should be able to gratify the unpleasant craving it produces.

" Each individual of the party busied himself around the blazing fires, in making his various little but important arrangements, until the first gray of the dawn manifested itself above the vapoury bank overhanging the eastern ridge of mountains, when, the word to saddle up being given, the mules were brought to the camp-fires, and every arm and muscle of the party was actively employed in the business of saddling and packing ' with care'—with unusual care—as a short detention during the day's march, to readjust the packs, might result in an encampment upon the desert for the coming night, and all its consequent dangers—the death or loss, by staying in search of water and grass, of our mules, (next to death to us,) not taking into account our own suffering from thirst, which, for the next eighteen or twenty hours, we had made up our minds to endure with philosophical fortitude and resignation. A small powder-keg, holding about three or four pints of coffee, which had been emptied of its original contents for the purpose, and filled with that beverage made from the brackish spring near our camp, was the only vessel we possessed in which we could transport water, and its contents composed our entire liquid refreshment for the march. Instructions were given to Miller, who had charge of the important and precious burden, to husband it with miserly care, and to make an equitable division whenever it should be called into use.

" Every thing being ready, Mr. Hudspeth, who accompanied us to the summit of the mountain, led the way. We passed upwards

17

.through the *canada*, (pronounced kanyeada,) or mountain gorge, at the mouth of which we had encamped, and, by a comparatively easy and smooth ascent, reached the summit of the mountain after travelling about six miles. Most of us were shivering with cold, until the sun shone broadly upon us, after emerging by a steep acclivity from the gorge through which we had passed, to the top of the ridge. Here we should have had a view of the mountain at the foot of which our day's journey was to terminate, but for the dense smoke which hung over and filled the plain, shutting from the vision all distant objects.

"Bidding farewell to Mr. Hudspeth and the gentleman with him, (Mr. Ferguson,) we commenced the descent of the mountain. We had scarcely parted from Mr. Hudspeth, when, standing on one of the peaks, he stretched out his long arms, and with a voice and gesture as loud and impressive as he could make them, he called to us and exclaimed, 'Now, boys, put spurs to your mules, and ride like h—!' The hint was timely given and well meant, but scarcely necessary, as we all had a pretty just appreciation of the trials and hardships before us.

"The descent from the mountain on the western side was more difficult than the ascent, but two or three miles by a winding and precipitous path, through some straggling, stunted, and tempest-bound cedars, brought us to the foot and into the valley, where, after some search, we found a blind trail, which we supposed to be that of Captain Fremont, made last year. Our course for the day was nearly due west, and following this trail where it was visible and did not deviate from our course, and putting our mules into a brisk gait, we crossed a valley some eight or ten miles in width, sparely covered with wild sage (artimisia) and grease-wood. These shrubs display themselves and maintain a dying existence, a brownish verdure, on the most arid and sterile plains and mountains of the desert, where no other vegetation shows itself. After crossing the valley, we rose a ridge of low volcanic hills, thickly strewn with sharp fragments of basaltes and a vitreous gravel, resembling junk-bottle glass. We passed over this ridge through a narrow gap, the walls of which are perpendicular, and composed of the same dark material as the debris strewn around. From the western terminus of this ominous-looking passage, we had a view of the vast desert plain before us, which, as far as the eye could penetrate, was of a snowy whiteness, and resembled a scene of wintry frosts and icy desolation. Not a shrub or object of any kind rose above the surface for the eye to rest upon. The hiatus in the animal and vegetable kingdoms was perfect. It was a scene which excited mingled emotions of admiration and apprehension.

" Passing a little further on, we stood on the brow of a steep precipice, the descent from the ridge of hills, immediately below and beyond which a narrow valley or depression in the surface of the plain, about five miles in width, displayed so perfectly the wavy and frothy appearance of highly-agitated water, that Colonel Russell and myself, who were riding together some distance in advance, both simultaneously exclaimed, ' We must have taken a wrong course and struck another arm or bay of the great salt lake.' With deep concern we were looking around, surveying the face of the country to ascertain what remedy there might be for this formidable obstruction to our progress, when the remainder of the party came up. The difficulty was presented to them; but soon, upon a more calm and scrutinizing inspection, we discovered that what represented so perfectly the ' rushing waters,' was moveless and made no sound. The illusion soon became manifest to all of us, and a hearty laugh at those who were the first to be deceived was the consequence, denying to them the merit of being good pilots or pioneers, &c.

" Descending the precipitous elevation upon which we stood, we entered upon the hard, smooth plain we had just been surveying with so much doubt and interest, composed of bluish clay, encrusted in wavy lines with a white saline substance, the first representing the body of the water and the last the crest and froth of the mimic waves and surges. Beyond this we crossed what appeared to have been the beds of several small lakes, the waters of which have evaporated, thickly encrusted with salt, and separated from each other by small mound-shaped elevations of a white sandy or ashy earth, so imponderous that it has been driven by the action of the winds into these heaps, which are constantly changing their positions and their shapes. Our mules waded through these ashy undulations, sometimes sinking to their knees, at others to their bellies, creating a dust that rose above and hung over us like a dense fog.

" From this point, on our right and left, diagonally in our front,

T 2

at an apparent distance of thirty or forty miles, high isolated mountains rise abruptly from the surface of the plain. Those on our left were as white as the snow-like face of the desert, and may be of the same composition, but I am inclined to the belief that they are composed of white clay, or clay and sand intermingled.

"The mirage, a beautiful phenomenon I have frequently mentioned as exhibiting itself upon our journey, here displayed its wonderful illusions, in a perfection and with a magnificence surpassing any presentation of the kind I had previously seen. Lakes dotted with islands and bordered by groves of gently-waving timber, whose tranquil and limpid waves reflected their sloping banks and the shady islets in their bosoms, lay spread out before us, inviting us by their illusory temptations to stray from our path and enjoy their cooling shades and refreshing waters. These fading away as we advanced, beautiful villas, adorned with edifices, decorated with all the ornaments of suburban architecture, and surrounded by gardens, shaded walks, parks, and stately avenues, would succeed them, renewing the alluring invitation to repose, by enticing the vision with more than calypsan enjoyments or elysian pleasures. These melting from our view as those before, in another place a vast city with countless columned edifices of marble whiteness, and studded with domes, spires, and turreted towers, would rise upon the horizon of the plain, astonishing us with its stupendous grandeur and sublime magnificence. But it is in vain to attempt a description of these singular and extraordinary phenomena. Neither prose, nor poetry, nor the pencil of the artist, can adequately portray their beauties. The whole distant view around, at this point, seemed like the creations of a sublime and gorgeous dream or the effect of enchantment. I observed that where these appearances were presented in their most varied forms and with the most vivid distinctness, the surface of the plain was broken, either by chasms hollowed out from the action of the winds, or by undulations formed of the drifting sands.

"About eleven o'clock we struck a vast white plain, uniformly level, and utterly destitute of vegetation, or any sign that shrub or plant had ever existed above its snow-like surface. Pausing a few moments to rest our mules, and moisten our mouths and throats from the scant supply of beverage in our powder-keg, we entered upon this appalling field of sullen and hoary desolation. It was a scene so entirely new to us, so frightfully forbidding and unearthly in its aspects, that all of us, I believe, though impressed with its sublimity, felt a slight shudder of apprehension. Our mules seemed to sympathize with us in the pervading sentiment, and moved forward with reluctance, several of them stubbornly setting their faces for a counter-march.

" For fifteen miles the surface of this plain is so compact that the feet of our animals, as we hurried them along over it, left but little if any impression for the guidance of the future traveller. It is covered with a hard crust of saline and alkaline substances combined, from one-fourth to one-half of an inch in thickness, beneath which is a stratum of damp whitish sand and clay intermingled. Small fragments of white shelly rock, of an inch and a half in thickness, which appear as if they once composed a crust, but had been broken by the action of the atmosphere, or the pressure of water rising from beneath, are strewn over the entire plain and embedded in the salt and sand.

" As we moved onward, a member of our party in the rear called our attention to a gigantic moving object on our left, at an apparent distance of six or eight miles. It is very difficult to determine distances accurately on these plains. Your estimate is based upon the probable dimensions of the object, and unless you know what the object is, and its probable size, you are liable to great deception. The atmosphere seems frequently to act as a magnifier, so much so that I have often seen a raven perched upon a low shrub or an undulation of the plain, answering to the outlines of a man on horseback. But this object was so enormously large, considering its apparent distance, and its movement forward, parallel with ours, so distinct, that it greatly excited our wonder and curiosity. Many and various were the conjectures (serious and facetious) of the party, as to what it might be or portend. Some thought it might be Mr. Hudspeth, who had concluded to follow us; others that it was some cyclopean nondescript animal, lost upon the desert; others that it was the ghost of a mammoth or megatherium wandering on ' this rendezvous of death;' others that it was the d—l mounted on an ibis, &c. It was the general conclusion, however, that no animal composed of flesh and blood, or even a healthy ghost, could here inhabit. A partner of equal size soon joined it, and for an hour or more they

17 *

moved along as before, parallel to us, when they disappeared apparently behind the horizon.

"As we proceeded the plain gradually became softer, and our mules sometimes sunk to their knees in the stiff composition of salt, sand, and clay. The travelling at length became so difficult and fatiguing to our animals that several of the party dismounted, (myself among the number,) and we consequently slackened our hitherto brisk pace into a walk. About two o'clock, P. M. we discovered through the smoky vapour the dim outlines of the mountain in front of us, at the foot of which was to terminate our day's march, if we were so fortunate as to reach it. But still we were a long and weary distance from it, and from the 'grass and water' which we expected there to find. A cloud rose from the south soon afterwards, accompanied by several distant peals of thunder and furious wind, rushing across the plain, and filling the whole atmosphere around us with the fine particles of salt, and drifting it in heaps like the newly-fallen snow. Our eyes became nearly blinded and our throats choked with the saline matter, and the very air we breathed tasted of salt.

"During the subsidence of this tempest there appeared upon the plain one of the most extraordinary phenomena, I dare to assert, ever witnessed. As I have before stated, I had dismounted from my mule, and turning it in with the *caballada*, was walking several rods in front of the party, in order to lead in a direct course to the point of our destination. Diagonally in front, to the right, our course being west, there appeared the figures of a number of men and horses, some fifteen or twenty. Some of these figures were mounted, and others dismounted, and appeared to be marching in front. Their faces and the heads of their horses were turned towards us, and at first they appeared as if they were rushing down upon us. Their apparent distance, judging from the horizon, was from three to five miles. But their size was not correspondent, for they appeared nearly as large as our own bodies, and consequently were of gigantic stature. At first view I supposed them to be a small party of Indians (probably the Utahs) marching from the opposite side of the plain. But this seemed to me scarcely probable, as no hunting or war party would be likely to take this route. I called to some of our party nearest to me to hasten forward, as there were men in front coming toward us. Very soon the fifteen or twenty figures were multiplied into three or four hundred, and appeared to be marching forward with the greatest action and speed. I then conjectured that they might be Captain Fremont and his party, with others from California, returning to the United States by this route, although they seemed to be too numerous even for this. I spoke to Brown, who was nearest to me, and asked him if he noticed the figures of men and horses in front. He answered that he did, and that he had observed the same appearances several times previously, but that they had disappeared, and he believed them to be optical illusions similar to the mirage. It was then, for the first time, so perfect was the deception, that I conjectured the probable fact that these figures were the reflection of our own images by the atmosphere, filled as it was with fine particles of crystallized matter, or by the distant horizon, covered by the same substance. This induced a more minute observation of the phenomenon, in order to detect the deception, if such it were. I noticed a single figure, apparently in front in advance of all the others, and was struck with its likeness to myself. Its motions too I thought were the same as mine. To test the hypothesis above suggested, I wheeled suddenly around, at the same time stretching my arms out to their full length, and turning my face sideways to notice the movements of this figure. It went through precisely the same motions. I then marched deliberately and with long strides several paces, the figure did the same. To test it more thoroughly, I repeated the experiment, and with the same result. The fact then was clear. But it was more fully verified still, for the whole array of this numerous shadowy host in the course of an hour melted entirely away and was no more seen. The phenomenon, however, explained and gave the history of the gigantic spectres which appeared and disappeared so mysteriously at an earlier hour of the day. The figures were our own shadows, produced and reproduced by the mirror-like composition impregnating the atmosphere and covering the plain. I cannot here more particularly explain or refer to the subject. But this spectral population, springing out of the ground as it were, and arraying itself before us as we traversed this dreary and Heaven-condemned waste, although we were entirely convinced of the cause of the apparition, excited those superstitious emotions so natural to all mankind.

"About five o'clock, P. M., we reached and passed, leaving it to our left, a small *butte*, rising solitary from the plain. Around this the ground is uneven, and a few scattering shrubs, leafless and without verdure, raised themselves above the white sand and saline matter, which seemed recently to have drifted, so as nearly to conceal them. Eight miles brought us to the northern end of a short range of mountains, turning the point of which and bending our course to the left, we gradually came upon higher ground, composed of compact volcanic gravel. I was here considerably in the rear, having made a detour towards the base of the *butte*, and thence toward the centre of the short range of mountains to discover, if such existed, a spring of water. I saw no such joyful presentation, nor any of the usual indications; and when I reached and turned the point, the whole party were several miles ahead of me and out of sight. Congratulating myself that I stood once more on terra firma, I urged my tired mule forward with all the life and activity that spur and whip could inspire her with, passing down the range of mountains on my left some four or five miles, and then rising some rocky hills connecting this with a long and high range of mountains on my right. The distance across these hills is about seven or eight miles. When I had reached the most elevated point of this ridge the sun was setting, and I saw my fellow travellers still far in advance of me, entering again upon a plain or valley of salt, some ten or twelve miles in breadth. On the opposite side of this valley rose abruptly and to a high elevation another mountain, at the foot of which we expected to find the spring of fresh water that was to quench our thirst, and revive and sustain the drooping energies of our faithful beasts.

"About midway upwards, in a *canada* of this mountain, I noticed the smoke of a fire, which apparently had just been kindled, as doubtless it had been, by Indians, who were then there, and had discovered our party on the white plain below, it being the custom of these Indians to make signals by fire and smoke whenever they notice strange objects. Proceeding onward, I overtook an old and favourite pack-mule, which was familiarly called ' Old Jenny.' She carried our meat and flour—all that we possessed in fact as a sustenance of life. Her pack had turned, and her burden, instead of being on her back, was suspended under her belly. With the good sense and discretion so characteristic of the Mexican pack-mule, being behind and following the party in advance, she had stopped short in the road until some one should come to re-arrange her cargo and place it on deck instead of under the keel. I dismounted and went through by myself the rather tedious and laborious process of unpacking and repacking. This done, ' Old Jenny' set forward upon a fast gallop to overtake her companions ahead ; and my own mule, as if not to be outdone in the race, followed in the same gait. ' Old Jenny,' however, maintained the honours of the race, keeping considerably ahead. Both of them, by that instinct or faculty which mules undoubtedly possess, had scented the water on the other side of the valley, and their pangs of extreme thirst urged them forward at this extraordinary speed, after the long and laborious march they had made to obtain it.

" As I advanced over the plain, which was covered with a thicker crust of salt than that previously described, breaking under the feet of the animals like a crust of frozen snow, the spreading of the fires in the *canada* of the mountain appeared with great distinctness. The line of lights was regular like camp-fires, and I was more than half inclined to hope that we should meet and be welcomed by an encampment of civilized men, either hunters or a party from the Pacific bound homeward. The moon rose about nine o'clock, displaying and illuminating the unnatural, unearthly dreariness of the scenery.

" ' Old Jenny' for some time had so far beat me in the race as to be out of my sight and I out of the sound of her footsteps. I was entirely alone, and enjoying, as well as a man could with a crust of salt in his nostrils and over his lips, and a husky mouth and throat, the singularity of my situation, when I observed about a quarter of a mile ahead of me a dark stationary object, standing in the midst of the hoary scenery. I supposed it to be ' Old Jenny,' in trouble once more about her pack. But, coming up to a speaking distance, I was challenged in a loud voice with the usual guard salutation, ' Who comes there ?' Having no countersign, I gave the common response in such cases, ' A friend.' This appeared to be satisfactory ; for I heard no report of pistol or rifle, and no arrow took its soundless flight through my body. I rode up to the object, and discovered it to be Buchanan sitting upon his mule, which had become so much exhausted that it occasionally refused to go along, notwithstanding his industrious application of the usual incentives to progress. He said that he had supposed himself to be the ' last man' before ' Old Jenny' passed, who had given him a surprise, and he was quite thunderstruck when an animal, mounted by a man, came charging upon him in his half-crippled condition. After a good laugh and some little delay and difficulty, we got his mule under way again and rode slowly along together.

" We left, to us, in our tired condition, the seemingly interminable plain of salt, and entered upon the sagey slope of the mountain about ten o'clock. Hallooing as loudly as we could raise our voices, we obtained by a response the direction of our party who had preceded us, and, after some difficulty in making our way through the sage, grass, and willows, (the last a certain indication of water in the desert,) we came to where they had discovered a faint stream of water, and made their camp. Men and mules, on their first arrival, as we learned, had madly rushed into the stream and drank together of its muddy waters, made muddy by their own disturbance of its shallow channel and sluggish current.

"Delay of gratification frequently gives a temporary relief to the cravings of hunger. The same remark is applicable to thirst. Some hours previously I had felt the pangs of thirst with an acuteness almost amounting to an agony. Now, when I had reached the spot where I could gratify my desires in this respect, they were greatly diminished. My first care was to unsaddle my mule and lead it to the stream, and my next to take a survey of the position of our encampment. I then procured a cup of muddy water and drank it off with a good relish. The fires before noticed were still blazing brightly above us on the side of the mountain, but those who had lighted them had given no other signal of their proximity. The moon shone brilliantly, and Jacob, Buchanan, McClary, and myself, concluded we would trace the small stream of water until we could find the fountain spring. After considerable search among the reeds, willow, and luxuriant green, we discovered a spring. Buchanan was so eager to obtain a draught of cold pure water, that in dipping his cup for this purpose the yielding weeds under him gave way, and he sunk into the basin, from which he was drawn out after a good 'ducking' by one of those present. The next morning this basin was sounded to the depth of thirty-five feet, and no bottom found. We named this spring 'Buchanan's Well.' We lighted no fires to-night, and prepared no evening meal. Worn down by the hard day's travel, after relieving our thirst, we spread our blankets upon the ground, and, laying our bodies upon them.

slept soundly in the bright moonshine. Several of our party had been on the road upwards of seventeen hours, without water or refreshment of any kind, except a small draught of cold coffee from our powder-keg, made of the salt-sulphur water at our last encampment, and had travelled the distance of seventy-five miles. The Salt Plain has never at this place, so far as I could understand, been crossed but twice previously by civilized men, and in these instances two days were occupied in performing the journey."

"Colonel Doniphan," says a volunteer who accompanied him in the march, "is in age about forty, and in stature, six feet two inches, of large frame, and with a very intelligent face. His great charm lies in his easy and kind manner. On the march he could not be distinguished from the other soldiers, either by dress or from his conversation. He ranked high as a lawyer in Missouri."

U

LIEUTENANT-COLONEL FREMONT.

~~~~~~~~~~~~~~~~~~~~~~

LIEUTENANT-COLONEL JOHN C. FREMONT is a native of South Carolina. He served as first assistant to the celebrated Nicollet, and was appointed to the United States' army as second lieutenant topographical engineers, July 7th, 1838, and in that capacity has several times conducted expeditions across the Rocky Mountains to the Pacific. By the instrumentality of his father-in-law, Hon. Thomas H. Benton, he has lately [May 27th, 1846] been appointed to his present station.

In May, 1845, Fremont received orders from the War Department at Washington, to pursue his explorations in the regions beyond the Rocky Mountains. His force amounted to sixty-two men. One of the objects contemplated, was the discovery of a new and shorter route from the western base of the Rocky Mountains to the mouth of the Columbia river. To accomplish this it was necessary to journey, for a part of the distance, through the unsettled portions of California, and a small tract of the inhabited region. He approached these settlements in the winter of 1845-6, and halting his command on the frontier, one hundred miles from Monterey, he proceeded alone to that city, to explain the object of his coming, and obtain permission to enter the valley of the San Joaquin. This was granted, but scarcely had he reached the desired spot, than he received authentic information, that the Mexican general, Castro, was preparing to attack him with a large force of artillery, cavalry and infantry, supposing that, under cover of a scientific mission, Fremont was exciting the American settlers to revolt. The captain did not retreat; but taking a position on a mountain overlooking Monterey at a distance of about thirty miles, he entrenched it, raised the

COLONEL FREMONT.

Page 201.

flag of the United States, and with his men awaited the approach
of the enemy.

From the 7th to the 10th of March, Lieutenant-Colonel Fremont and his little band maintained this position. General Castro
did not approach within attacking distance, and Captain Fremont,
adhering to his plan of avoiding all collisions, and determined neither
to compromit his government, nor the American settlers, ready to
join him at all hazards if he had been attacked, abandoned his position, and commenced his march for Oregon, intending by that route
to return to the United States. Deeming all danger from the Mexicans to be passed, he yielded to the wishes of some of his men who
desired to remain in the country, discharged them from his service,
and refused to receive others in their stead, so cautious was he to
avoid doing any thing which would compromit the American settlers, or give even a colour of offence to the Mexican authorities.
He pursued his march slowly and leisurely, as the state of his men
and horses required, until the middle of May, and had reached the
northern shore of the greater Tlamath lake, within the limits of the
Oregon Territory, when he found his further progress in that direction obstructed by impassable snowy mountains and hostile Indians,
who had been excited against him by General Castro, had killed and
wounded four of his men, and left him no repose either in camp or
on his march. At the same time, information reached him that
General Castro, in addition to his Indian allies, was advancing in
person against him, with artillery and cavalry, at the head of four
or five hundred men ; that they were passing around the head of
the Bay of San Francisco to a rendezvous on the north side of it,
and that the American settlers in the valley of the Sacramento were
comprehended in the scheme of destruction meditated against his
own party. Under these circumstances, he determined to turn upon
his Mexican pursuers, and seek safety both for his own party, and
the American settlers, not merely in the defeat of Castro, but in the
total overthrow of the Mexican authority in California, and the establishment of an independent government in that extensive department. It was on the 6th of June, and before the commencement
of the war between the United States and Mexico could have been
known, that this resolution was taken ; and, by the 5th of July, it
was carried into effect by a series of rapid attacks by a small body
of adventurous men, under the conduct of an intrepid leader, quick

to perceive and able to direct the proper measures for accomplishing such a daring enterprise. On the 11th of June, a convoy of two hundred horses for Castro's camp, with an officer and fourteen men, were surprised and captured by twelve of Lieutenant-Colonel Fremont's party. On the 15th, at daybreak, the military post of Sonoma was surprised and taken, with nine brass cannon, two hundred and fifty stands of muskets, and several officers, and some men and munitions of war. Leaving a small garrison in Sonoma, Lieutenant-Colonel Fremont went to the Sacramento to arouse the American settlers: but scarcely had he arrived there, when an express reached him from the garrison of Sonoma, with information that Castro's whole force was crossing the bay to attack that place. This intelligence was received in the afternoon of the 23d of June, while he was on the American fork of the Sacramento, eighty miles from the little garrison at Sonoma ; and, at two o'clock on the morning of the 25th, he arrived at that place with ninety riflemen from the American settlers in that valley. The enemy had not yet appeared. Scouts were sent out to reconnoitre, and a party of twenty fell in with a squadron of seventy dragoons, (all of Castro's force which had crossed the bay,) attacked and defeated it, killing and wounding five, without harm to themselves ; the Mexican commander, De la Torre, barely escaping with the loss of his transport boats, and nine pieces of brass artillery, spiked.

The country north of the Bay of San Francisco being cleared of the enemy, Lieutenant-Colonel Fremont returned to Sonoma on the evening of the 4th of July, and, on the morning of the 5th, called the people together, explained to them the condition of things in the province, and recommended an immediate declaration of independence. The declaration was made, and he was selected to take the chief direction of affairs. The attack on Castro was the next object. He was at Santa Clara, an intrenched post on the upper or south side of the Bay of San Francisco, with four hundred men and two pieces of field-artillery. A circuit of more than one hundred miles must be traversed to reach him. On the 6th of July the pursuit was commenced, by a body of one hundred and sixty mounted riflemen, commanded by Colonel Fremont in person, who, in three days, arrived at the American settlements on the Rio de los Americanos. Here he learnt that Castro had abandoned Santa Clara, and was retreating south, towards Ciudad de los Angelos, the seat of the governor-general of the Californias, and distant four hundred miles. It was instantly resolved to pursue him to that place. At the moment of departure, the gratifying intelligence was received that war with Mexico had commenced; that Monterey had been taken by our naval forces, and the flag of the United States there raised on the 7th of July; and that the fleet would co-operate with the army against Castro and his forces. The flag of independence was hauled down, and that of the United States hoisted amidst the hearty greetings, and to the great joy of the American settlers and forces under the command of Lieutenant-Colonel Fremont.

The combined pursuit was rapidly continued; and on the 12th of August, Commodore Stockton and Lieutenant-Colonel Fremont, with a detachment of marines from the squadron, and some riflemen, entered the City of the Angels without resistance; the governor-general, Pico, the commandant-general, Castro, and all of the Mexican authorities, having fled and dispersed. Commodore Stockton took possession of the whole country as a conquest of the United States, and appointed Lieutenant-Colonel Fremont governor, under the law of nations; to assume the functions of that office when he should return to the squad on.

Unfortunately, Colonel Fremont became involved in the dispute between Commodore Stockton and General Kearny, concerning the supreme command of the conquered territories. As he had served under the Commodore previous to this affair, he still continued to do so, in violation of the commission from the President held by General Kearny. For awhile the latter submitted; but on the arrival of reinforcements he assumed the chief command, arrested Fremont, and sent him as a prisoner to Washington. On his arrival he addressed the following letter [dated September 17th, 1847] to the adjutant-general:—

" *To the Adjutant-General:*—Sir: According to the orders of Brigadier-General Kearny, I have the honour to report myself to you in person, in a state of arrest, and to make the following requests:

" 1. A copy of the charges filed against me by the said general.

" 2. A copy of the orders under which the said general brought back from California to the United States myself and the topographical party of which I formerly had the command.

" 3. A copy of the communication from Senator Benton, asking for my arrest and trial on the charges made in the newspapers against me, and which application from him I adopt and make my own.

"4. That charges and specifications, in addition to those filed by General Kearny, be made out in form against me, on all the newspaper publications which have come, or shall come to the knowledge of the office, and on all other information, oral or written.

"5. That I may have a trial as soon as the witnesses now in the United States can be got to Washington; for, although the testimony of the voice of California, through some of its most respectable inhabitants, is essential to me, and also that of Commodore Stockton, who has not yet arrived from that province, yet I will not wish the delay of waiting for these far-distant witnesses, and will go into trial on the testimony now in the United States—part of which is in the state of Missouri, and may require thirty days to get it to Washington. I therefore ask for a trial at the end of that time.

"These requests I have the honour to make, and hope they will be found to be just, and will be granted. I wish a full trial, and a speedy one. The charges against me by Brigadier-General Kearny, and the subsidiary accusations made against me in newspapers, when I was not in this country, impeach me in all the departments of my conduct (military, civil, political, and moral) while in California, and, if true, would subject me to be cashiered and shot under the rules and articles of war, and to infamy in the public opinion. It is my intention to meet these charges and accusations in all their extent; and for that purpose to ask a trial upon every point of allegation or insinuation against me, waiving all objections to forms and technicalities, and allowing the widest range to all possible testimony. These charges and accusations are so general and extensive as to cover the whole field of my operations in California, both civil and military, from the beginning to the end of hostilities, and as my operations, and those of which I was the subject or object, extend to almost every act and event which occurred in the country during the eventful period of those hostilities, the testimony on my trial will be the history of the conquest of California, and the exposition of the policy which has been heretofore pursued there, and the elucidation of that which should be followed hereafter. It will be the means of giving valuable information to the government, which it might not otherwise be able to obtain, and thus enlighten it both with respect to the past and the future. Being a military subordinate, I can make no report, not even of my own operations; but my trial may become a report, and bring to the knowledge of the government what it ought to know, not only with respect to the conduct of its officers, but also in regard to the policy observed, or necessary to be observed, with regard to the three-fold population (Spanish-Americans, Anglo-Americans, and aboriginal Americans) which that remote province contains. Viewed under these aspects of public interest, my own personal concern in the trial — already sufficiently grave — acquires an additional and public importance; and for these high objects, as well as to vindicate my own character from accusations both capital and infamous, it is my intention to require and to promote the most searching examination into every thing that has been done in that quarter.

"The public mind has become impressed with the belief that great misconduct has prevailed in California ; and, in fact, it would be something rare in the history of remote conquests and governments, where every petty commander might feel himself invested with proconsular authority, and protected by distance from the supervision of his government, if nothing wrong or culpable has been done by the public agents of the United States in that remote province. The public believe it; and the charges filed against me by Brigadier-General Kearny — the subsidiary publications made against me whilst I was not in this country—my arrest on the frontier, and the premonitory rumours of that event—the manner of my being brought home for trial, not in irons, as some newspapers suppose, but in chains stronger than iron, and with circumstances of ostentatious and galling degradation — have all combined to present me as the great malefactor, and the sole one.

"Heretofore I have said nothing, and could have said nothing, in my own defence. I was ignorant of all that was going on against me ; ignorant of the charges sent from California ; ignorant of the intended arrest, and of the subsidiary publications to prejudice the public mind. What was published in the United States in my favour, by my friends, was done upon their own view of things here, and of which I knew nothing. It was only on my arrival at the frontiers of the United States that I became acquainted with these things, which concerned me so nearly. Brought home by General Kearny, and marched in his rear, I did not know of his design to

18 *

arrest me until the moment of its execution at Fort Leavenworth. He then informed me that, among the charges which he had preferred, were mutiny, disobedience of orders, assumption of powers, &c.; and referred me to your office for particulars. Accordingly, I now apply for them, and ask for a full and speedy trial, not only on the charges filed by the said general, but on all accusations contained in the publications against me.

"The private calamity [the severe illness of his mother] which has this evening obtained for me permission from the department to visit South Carolina, does not create any reason for postponement or delay of the trial, or in any way interfere with the necessary preliminaries.

"Hoping, then, sir, that you will obtain and communicate to me an early decision of the proper authorities on these requests, I remain, &c."

In conformity with the desire of Colonel Fremont, his trial commenced soon after his arrival at the capital, and is still [January, 1848] progressing.

The following account of the Colonel's celebrated ride in California, will exhibit his capability of enduring fatigue and hardships:—

"It was at daybreak on the morning of the 22d of March, that the party set out from la Ciudad de los Angelos (the City of the Angels,) in the southern part of California, to proceed in the shortest time to Monterey, on the Pacific Ocean, distant full four hundred miles. The way is over a mountainous country, much of it uninhabited, with no other road than a trace, and many defiles to pass, particularly the maritime defile of El Rincon, or Punto Gordo, fifteen miles in extent, made by the jutting of a precipitous mountain into the sea, which can only be passed when the tide is out and the sea calm, and even then in many places through the waves. The towns of Santa Barbara and San Luis Obispo, and occasional ranchos, are the principal inhabited places on the route. Each of the party had three horses, nine in all, to take their turns under the saddle. The six loose horses ran ahead, without bridle or halter, and required some attention to keep to the track.

"When wanted for a change, say at distances of twenty miles, they were caught by the *lasso*, thrown either by Don Jesus Pico, or the servant Jacob, who, though born and raised in Washington, in his long expeditions with Colonel Fremont had become as expert as a Mexican with the lasso, as sure as a mountaineer with the rifle, equal to either on horse or foot, and always a lad of courage and fidelity. None of the horses were shod, that being a practice unknown to the Californians. The most usual gait was a sweeping gallop. The first day they ran one hundred and twenty-five miles, passing the San Fernando mountain, the defile of the Rincon, several other mountains, and slept at the hospitable rancho of Don Tomas Robberis, beyond the town of Santa Barbara. The only fatigue complained of in this day's ride was in Jacob's right arm, made tired by throwing the lasso and using it as a whip to keep the loose horses to the track.

" The next day they made another one hundred and twenty-five miles, passing the formidable mountain of Santa Barbara, and counting upon it the skeletons of some fifty horses, part of near double that number which perished in the crossing of that terrible mountain by the California battalion on Christmas day, 1846, amidst a raging tempest, and a deluge of rain and cold more killing than that of the Sierra Nevada—the day of severest suffering, say Fremont and his men, that they have ever passed. At sunset, the party stopped to sup with the friendly Captain Dana, and at nine San Luis Obispo was reached, the home of Don Jesus, where an affecting reception awaited Lieutenant-Colonel Fremont, in consequence of an incident which occurred there, that history will one day record ;* and he was detained till eleven o'clock in the morning, re-

* This affecting incident is thus related by Lieutenant Talbott, who accompanied Colonel Fremont. Pico had headed an insurrection, and being captured was condemned to death :—

"There was no time to lose; the hour of twelve, next day, was fixed for the execution. It was eleven o'clock, and I chanced to be in the Colonel's room, when a lady with a group of children, followed by many other ladies, burst into the room, throwing themselves upon their knees, and crying for mercy for the father and husband. It was the wife and children and friends of Pico. Never did I hear such accents of grief. Never did I witness such an agonizing scene. I turned my eye, for I could not look at it, and soon heard from Colonel Fremont (whose heart was never formed to resist such a scene,) the heavenly word of pardon.

"Then the tumult of feeling took a different turn. Joy and gratitude broke out, filled the room with benedictions, and spread to those without. To finish the scene, the condemned man was brought in, and then I saw the whole impulsiveness and fire of the Spanish character, when excited

ceiving the visits of the inhabitants, (mothers and children included,) taking a breakfast of honour, and waiting for a relief of fresh horses to be brought in from the surrounding country.

"Here the nine horses from Los Angelos were left, and eight others taken in their place, and a Spanish boy added to the party to assist in managing the loose horses. Proceeding at the usual gait till eight at night, and having made some seventy miles, Don Jesus, who had spent the night before with his family and friends, and probably with but little sleep, became fatigued, and proposed a halt for a few hours. It was in the valley of the Salinas, (Salt river, called *Buena Ventura* in the old maps,) and the haunt of marauding Indians. For safety during their repose, the party turned off the trace, issued through a *canada* into a thick wood, and lay down, the horses being put to grass at a short distance, with the Spanish boy in the saddle to watch. Sleep, when commenced, was too sweet to be easily given up, and it was half way between midnight and day when the sleepers were aroused by an *estampedo* among the horses and the calls of the boy.

"The cause of the alarm was soon found ; not Indians, but white bears—this valley being their great resort—encountered some hundred of them before, killing thirteen upon the ground. The character of these bears is well known, and the bravest hunters do not like to meet them without the advantage of numbers. On discovering the enemy Colonel Fremont felt for his pistols, but Don Jesus desired him to lay still, saying that 'people could scare bears,' and immediately he hallooed at them in Spanish, and they went off.

---

by some powerful emotion. He had been calm, composed, quiet, and almost silent, under his trial and condemnation, but at the word pardon, a storm of impetuous feeling burst forth, and throwing himself at the feet of Colonel Fremont, he swore to him eternal fidelity, and demanded the privilege of going with him and dying for him.

"But it was not all over yet with Colonel Fremont. His own men required the death of Pico—he had done so much harm, and in fact was the head of the insurrection in that district, and had broken his parole The Colonel went among them, and calmed the ferment in his own camp. He quieted his own men ; but others, who were not there, have since cried out for the execution of Pico, and made his pardon an accusation against Colonel Fremont. The pacified state of the country will answer the accusation, and show that it was a case in which policy and humanity went together."

Sleep went off also ; and the recovery of the horses frightened by the bears, building a rousing fire, making breakfast from the hospitable supplies of San Luis Obispo, occupied the party till daybreak, when the journey was resumed. Eighty miles and the afternoon brought the party to Monterey.

" The next day, in the afternoon, the party set out on their return ; and the two horses ridden by Colonel Fremont from San Luis Obispo being a present to him from Don Jesus, he (Don Jesus) desired to make an experiment of what one of them could do. They were brothers, one a grass younger than the other, both of the same colour, (cinnamon,) and hence called *el canalo* or *los canalos*, (the cinnamon, or the cinnamons.) The elder brother was taken for the trial ; and the journey commenced upon him at leaving Monterey ; the afternoon well advanced. Thirty miles under the saddle done that evening, and the party stopped for the night. In the morning, the elder canalo was again under the saddle for Colonel Fremont, and for ninety miles he carried him without a change and without apparent fatigue. It was still thirty miles to San Luis Obispo, where the night was to be passed ; and Don Jesus insisted that canalo could easily do it, and so said the horse by his looks and action. But Colonel Fremont would not put him to the trial ; and shifting the saddle to the younger brother, the elder was turned loose to run the remaining thirty miles without a rider.

" He did so, immediately taking the lead and keeping it all the way, and entering San Luis in a sweeping gallop, nostrils distended, snuffing the air, neighing with exultation of his return to his native pastures, his younger brother all the while running at the head of the horses under the saddle, bearing on his bit, and held in by his rider. The whole eight horses made their one hundred and twenty miles each that day, (after thirty the evening before) the elder cinnamon making ninety of his under the saddle that day, besides thirty under the saddle the evening before ; nor was there the least doubt that he would have done the whole distance in the same time if he had continued under the saddle.

" After a hospitable detention of another half day at San Luis Obispo, the party set out for Los Angelos on the same nine horses which they had ridden from that place, and made the ride back in about the same time they had made it up, namely, at the rate of one hundred and twenty-five miles a day.

" On this ride the grass on the road was the food for the horses. At Monterey they had barley; but those horses, meaning those trained and domesticated, as the canalos were, eat almost anything in the way of vegetable food, or even drink, that their master uses, by whom they are petted and caressed, and rarely sold.' Bread, fruits, sugar, coffee, and even wine, (like the Persian horse,) they take from the hand of their master, and obey with like docility his slightest intimation. A tap of the whip on the saddle springs them into action; and the check of a thread rein (on the Spanish bit) would stop them; and stopped short at speed they do not jostle the rider or throw him forward. They leap at any thing—man, beast, or weapon, on which their master directs them. But this description, so far as conduct or behaviour is concerned, of course only applies to the trained and domesticated horse."

ADJUTANT-GENERAL JONES.

BRIGADIER-GENERAL JONES.

BREVET BRIGADIER-GENERAL ROGER JONES, Adjutant-General of the United States' army, is a native of Westmoreland county, Virginia, and brother to the distinguished Commodore Jones. After receiving a good education, he entered the army [January 26th, 1809] while quite young, as a lieutenant of marines, in which capacity he was actively employed until July 6th, 1812, when he was appointed a captain of artillery.

At the opening of the campaign of 1813, Captain Jones joined the regiment of Colonel [General] Macomb, at Greenbush, where was established a camp of instruction. Soon after, the whole army, under Major-General Dearborn, marched to Sackett's Harbour and prepared for a descent upon Upper Canada. Immediately after the capture of York, and in full view of Fort Niagara, Captain Jones received from Brigadier-General Chandler the appointment of major of brigade, a station for which his high reputation as a disciplinarian and an active, zealous officer, eminently qualified him.

In his new capacity, Captain Jones was actively and efficiently engaged in the taking of Fort George, May 27th, 1813; and eight days afterward [June 5th] he was with Brigadier-General Chandler at the battle of Stony Creek, where, after displaying great bravery, he received a severe wound from a bayonet. On the 13th of August he was transferred to the staff as assistant adjutant-general, with the brevet rank of major.

In the memorable campaign of 1814 on the Niagara frontier, Major Jones bore a distinguished part. At its commencement ne was attached to the staff of Major-General Brown, commanding the left division of the army. He assisted in the crossing of the Niagara, and taking of Fort Erie, [July 3d, 1814,] and was in the battle of Chippewa, July 5th, 1814. In his official report of this event, General Brown says : —

"Colonel Gardner, Major Jones," &c., "have been as active, ,and as much devoted to the cause as any officers of the army. Their conduct merits my warmest acknowledgments; of Gardner and Jones I shall have occasion again to speak to you."

For his "distinguished services in the battle of Chippewa," Major Jones received from President Madison the brevet rank of major in the corps of artillery to which he belonged.

In the great battle of Niagara, [July 25th, 1814,] Major Jones again acted well and honourably his part, and received high commendation from Major-General Brown. He participated in the battle of Fort Erie [August 15th, 1814] under General Gaines, when that post was assaulted by the British under Lieutenant-General Drummond. In his official report of the battle, General Gaines says : —

"To Major Jones, assistant adjutant-general, Major Hall," &c., "much credit is due for their constant vigilance and strict attention to every duty previous to the action, and the steady courage, zeal, and activity, which they manifested during the action."

Major Jones was engaged in the subsequent defence of Fort Erie, and sortie from the works, where "one thousand regulars," says General Brown, "and an equal number of militia, in one hour of close action, blasted the hopes of the enemy, destroyed the fruits of fifty days' labour, and diminished his effective force one thousand men at least." For his conduct in the affair the major received from President Madison the further promotion of brevet lieutenant-colonel. During the whole siege, he performed the duties of adjutant-general (chief of staff) during the sickness of Colonel Gardner. When General Izard's command arrived, he was transferred to the left division of the army, and continued to exercise the duties of his office until the close of the campaign of 1814, when the Americans retired into winter quarters at Sackett's Harbour.

In June, 1815, at the solicitation of General Brown, Lieutenant-Colonel Jones joined the staff of that officer as aid-de-camp and adjutant-general. When he left the general's military family, he received from him an elegant sword as a testimonial of his friendship and gratitude ; and a short time previous to the close of the war, Generals Brown, Porter, and Scott each addressed letters to the

Secretary of War, [Mr. Monroe,] warmly recommending Brevet Lieutenant-Colonel Jones for the full lieutenant-colonelcy of the 24th infantry.

On the 15th of February, 1834, the legislature of Virginia voted swords to Colonel Jones and his brother of the navy, as proofs of esteem for their distinguished services. Owing to accidental causes, this testimonial was not presented to the colonel until February 22d, 1841.

Brevet Lieutenant-Colonel Jones remained with his company from December, 1815, until August, 1818, and the admirable condition to which he brought it is still remembered in the service. It excelled in all that constitutes a model corps. August 10th, 1818, he was appointed adjutant-general of the Northern Division, with the brevet rank of colonel. He remained in this capacity until 1821, when, notwithstanding the reduction of the army, he was retained with his full lineal rank, and assigned to the 3d regiment of artillery. While yet a captain in the line, he was appointed [March 7th, 1825] adjutant-general of the United States' army, with the rank of colonel. On the 17th of February, 1827, he was promoted as major of the 2d artillery in the regular line. In 1829 he received the brevet of colonel, [ranking from September 17th, 1824,] and on June 17th, 1832, he was raised to brevet brigadier-general, which rank he now holds in the military service.

In October, 1844, Brigadier-General Jones, Lieutenant-Colonel Mason, and Governor Butler, Cherokee Agent, were constituted by the President a commission to the Cherokees, in order to invest and report upon the causes and extent of the discontents and difficulties among them. The report which, as president of the commission, General Jones drew up, was able and conclusive, eventuating in the formal pacification of the Indians.

General Jones has now been adjutant-general of the army for more than twenty years. A glance at the army regulations will show, that his office is one of the principal military bureaus of the war department. Its civil and ministerial relations to the head of the department are numerous, weighty, and often confidential; whilst in all organizations of the general staff of the army, it occupies a position, as regards matters purely military, of the first importance. As the chief of staff to the commander of the army, the adjutant-general is charged with all orders, military correspondence,

19

&c. And it should be remembered that the amount of business connected with his office, which had been more than quadrupled since the war of 1812, has been vastly augmented during our dispute with Mexico.

How General Jones has sustained the heavy pressure of official business, how faithfully and intelligently he has performed his duty to the army and the country, is well known. No officer stands higher in the estimation of those who are best able to form a correct judgment of his character and services. The successive chief magistrates of the nation, the various secretaries of war and generals-in-chief, and the records of Congress during the last twenty years, have all testified to his official worth and the value of his labours.

During the Florida war and other Indian outbreaks, together with the troubles on our northern and north-eastern borders, the labours of General Jones have been great; but the country is especially indebted to him, for his able, zealous, and unremitting services, during the war with Mexico. The increase of the regular army to more than double its previous number; the raising, organizing, and sending to the field fifty thousand volunteers; the legislation necessary to meet the change from peace to war, and to place the enlarged military establishment upon the proper basis; the voluminous and highly important orders and correspondence indispensable to such a state of affairs, has each received due attention at his hands. And no small share of the efficiency of our armies in Mexico results from the skilful administration of Adjutant-General Jones.

LIEUT. CHRISTOPHER CARSON.

Page 219.

LIEUTENANT CHRISTOPHER CARSON.

THE famous Christopher Carson was born in Kentucky, in 1810, but in the following year his father removed, and settled in Missouri. In this wilderness young Carson remained until he arrived at the age of fifteen, when he joined a trading party destined for Santa Fé. After roaming over the vast plains beyond the Missouri, he reached New Mexico after various adventures, and was employed as teamster in the copper mines of Chihuahua.

When seventeen years old, he made his first expedition as a trapper. The party proceeded to the Rio Colorado (California), met with numerous hardships and adventures, and had several battles with the Indians. It returned, however, safely to Taos, New Mexico; and soon after "Kit" joined another party, to visit the headwaters of the Arkansas. After this he passed eight years as a trapper among the Rocky Mountains and in Oregon. Here he became noted as a successful hunter, an unfailing shot, an unerring guide, and a brave, sagacious, and steady warrior. At one time, with a party of twelve, he tracked a band of nearly sixty Crows, who had stolen some of their horses; cut loose the animals, which were tied within ten feet of a strong log fort belonging to the Indians, attacked them and made good his retreat with the horses—a friendly Indian bringing away a Crow scalp as a trophy. In a combat with the Blackfeet Indians, Carson received a rifle-ball in his left shoulder, breaking it; but excepting this he has escaped the manifold dangers to which he has been exposed without serious injury.

Colonel Fremont owed his good fortune in procuring Carson's services, to an accidental meeting on a steamboat above St. Louis—neither having ever before heard of the other. It was at the commencement of Fremont's first expedition. Carson continued with

(219)

it until, in its return, it had recrossed the mountains. His courage, fidelity, and excellent character, so far conciliated the good will of the commander, that in his second expedition he gladly availed himself again of Kit's services, on meeting with him, as he chanced to do, on the confines of New Mexico. Kit again left the party after its arrival this side of the mountains—not, however, until Fremont had obtained a promise from him to join the third expedition in case one should be organized. Some incidents will be interesting, connected with this latter expedition, which was interrupted in its purely scientific character, by the hostility of the Mexican chief (Castro), compelling Fremont to change his peaceful employment.

In the interim between Fremont's second and third expeditions, Carson had settled himself near Taos, and had begun to farm, preparing to lead a quiet life, when he received a note from Fremont, written at Bent's Fort, reminding him of his promise, and telling him he would there wait for him. In four days from receiving the note, Carson had joined the party, having sold house and farm for less than half the sum he had just expended upon it, and put his family under the protection of his friend, the late Governor Bent, until he should return from a certainly long and dangerous journey. This protection, unfortunately, was taken from them in the late massacre at Taos, when Carson's brother-in-law was also one of the victims to the fury of the Mexicans against all connected with the Americans. Mrs. Carson saved her life by flight, leaving them to rob the house of every thing.

The route of the third expedition led the party to the southern and western side of the great Salt Lake — a region entirely unexplored, and filled, according to the superstitions and tales current among the Indians and trappers of the mountains, with all imaginable horrors. A vast desert, void of vegetation and fresh water, abounding in quicksands and in brackish pools and rivers, with only subterranean outlets. The southern border of the lake was found to be skirted with a salt plain of about sixty miles in width. Over this, as elsewhere, Carson, in his capacity of scout, was always with the advance party, to search for water and convenient places for camp—the usual signal of the prairies, a fire, serving, by its column of smoke, to point out where the advance were halting.

When Fremont's party, in May, 1846 (not knowing of the existence of the war with Mexico), retired from California, they proceeded north as far as the Tlamath lake, in Oregon, proposing to explore a new route into the Willhameth valley.

A courier having reached Colonel Fremont there, to say that Mr. Gillespie and five men were endeavouring to overtake him, he took ten men and returned sixty miles with the courier; making all haste in order to reach them before night, and prevent any attack which the Indians might be tempted to make on a small party. The events of that night and the days following illustrate so fully the nightly danger of an Indian country, and the treacherous nature of savages, that they will be given in Carson's own words:

"This was the only night in all our travels, except the one night on the island in the Salt Lake, that we failed to keep guard; and as the men were so tired, and we expected no attack now that we had sixteen in the party, the colonel didn't like to ask it of them, but sat up late himself. Owens and I were sleeping together, and we were waked at the same time by the licks of the axe that killed our men. At first, I didn't know it was that; but I called to Basil, who was that side—'What's the matter there?—what's that fuss about?'— he never answered, for he was dead then, poor fellow, and he never knew what killed him—his head had been cut in, in his sleep; the other groaned a little as he died. The Delawares (we had four with us) were sleeping at that fire, and they sprang up as the Tlamaths charged them. One of them caught up a gun, which was unloaded; but, although he could do no execution, he kept them at bay, fighting like a soldier, and didn't give up until he was shot full of arrows—three entering his heart; he died bravely. As soon as I had called out, I saw it was Indians in the camp, and I and Owens together cried out 'Indians.' There were no orders given; things went on too fast, and the colonel had men with him that didn't need to be told their duty. The colonel and I, Maxwell, Owens, Godey, and Stepp, jumped together, we six, and ran to the assistance of our Delawares. I don't know who fired and who didn't; but I think it was Stepp's shot that killed the Tlamath chief; for it was at the crack of Stepp's gun that he fell. He had an English half axe slung to his wrist by a cord, and there were forty arrows left in his quiver—the most beautiful and warlike arrows I ever saw. He must have been the bravest man among them, from the way he was armed, and judging by his cap. When

19 *   w

the Tlamaths saw him fall, they ran; but we lay, every man with his rifle cocked, until daylight, expecting another attack.

"In the morning we found by the tracks that from fifteen to twenty of the Tlamaths had attacked us. They had killed three of our men, and wounded one of the Delawares, who scalped the chief, whom we left where he fell. Our dead men we carried on mules; but, after going about ten miles, we found it impossible to get them any farther through the thick timber, and, finding a secret place, we buried them under logs and chunks, having no way to dig a grave. It was only a few days before this fight that some of these same Indians had come into our camp; and, although we had only meat for two days, and felt sure that we should have to eat mules for ten or fifteen days to come, the colonel divided with them, and even had a mule unpacked to give them some tobacco and knives."

The party then retraced its way into California, and two days after this rencontre they met a large village of Tlamaths—more than a hundred warriors. Carson was ahead with ten men, but one of them having been discovered, he could not follow his orders, which were to send back word and let Fremont come up with the rest in case they found Indians. But as they had been seen, it only remained to charge the village, which they did, killing many, and putting the rest to flight. The women and children, Carson says, we didn't interfere with; but burnt the village, together with their canoes and fishing-nets. In a subsequent encounter the same day, Carson's life was imminently exposed. As they gallopped up, he was rather in advance, when he observed an Indian fixing his arrow to let fly at him. Carson levelled his rifle, but it snapped, and in an instant the arrow would have pierced him, had not Fremont, seeing the danger, dashed his horse on the Indian and knocked him down.

The hostile and insulting course of Castro drew Fremont into retaliatory measures; and, aided by the American settlers, he pursued the Mexicans for some time; but being unable to make them stand and fight, they always flying before him, the flag of independence was raised at Sonoma, on the 5th of July, 1846. Learning soon after of the existence of the war, the American flag was promptly substituted, and the party proceeded to Monterey, where they found the fleet under Commodore Sloat already in possession.

Castro, with his forces, had retreated before Fremont, and, to prevent their escape into Sonora, Colonel Fremont with a hundred and sixty men, was offered the sloop of war Cyane to carry them down to San Diego and facilitate the pursuit, as he hoped by that means to intercept Castro at Pueblo de los Angelos. Then Carson, for the first time, saw the blue ocean, and the great vessels that, like white-winged birds, spread their sails above its waters. The vast prairies, whose immense green surface has been aptly likened to the sea, together with all objects ever seen upon it, were familiar to him; but it proved no preparation for actual salt water, and the pride and strength of the backwoodsmen were soon humbled by the customary tribute to Neptune. The forces were landed, and raised the flag at San Diego, and then they proceeded jointly to the capital, Ciudad de los Angelos, where, although from the detention at sea, Castro had escaped, American authority was also established.

From this point, on the 1st of September, 1846, Carson, with fifteen men, was despatched by Fremont with an account of the progress and state of affairs in that distant conquest. Carson was to have made the journey from Puebla to Washington city and back in one hundred and forty days. He pushed ahead accordingly, not stopping even for game, but subsisting on his mules, of which they made food as the animals broke down in the rapidity of the journey. He had crossed the wilderness, as he expected, in thirty days, when, meeting with General Kearny's company, within a few days of Santa Fé, he was turned back by that officer, to whose orders he believed himself subject, and with infinite reluctance resigned his despatches to another, and returned to guide Kearny's command into California.

General Kearny entered California without molestation until the fight of San Pascual; an official account of which has been published. In the charge made upon the Mexicans, Carson, as usual, was among the foremost, when, as he approached within bullet-range of the enemy, who were drawn up in order of battle, his horse stumbled and fell, pitching him over his head, and breaking his rifle in twain. Seizing a knife, he advanced on foot, until he found a killed dragoon, whose rifle he took, and was pressing on, when he met the mounted men returning from the charge, the Mexicans having gallopped off. At the instance of Carson, the American party then took possession of a small rocky hill, near the scene of the bat tle, as the strongest position in reach. Not being in a situation to go forward, they encamped here; and the enemy collecting in force, they remained in a state of siege. There was little of grass or water on the hill, and soon both animals and men began to suffer. The way was so thickly beset with the enemy, that the commander doubted the propriety of attempting to cut a passage through, when, after a four days' siege, Carson and Passed Midshipman Beale, of the navy (who had been sent to meet Kearny, with some thirty men, as a complimentary escort to San Diego), volunteered to go to Commodore Stockton, at that place, and bring a reinforcement.

Leaving the frontier settlements of California on the 25th of February, Carson arrived in St. Louis about the middle of May — making the journey, notwithstanding the inclemency of the season, and an unavoidable detention of ten days at Santa Fé, in a shorter time than it was ever before accomplished.

Carson subsequently visited Washington, where he received from President Polk a commission of lieutenant in Fremont's rifle regiment, in reward for his numerous services.

THE END.